Approaches to Teaching the Works of Jorge Luis Borges

Approaches to Teaching the Works of Jorge Luis Borges

Edited by

José Eduardo González

The Modern Language Association of America
New York 2025

85 Broad Street, New York, New York 10004
www.mla.org

To order MLA publications, visit www.mla.org/books. For wholesale and international orders, see www.mla.org/bookstore-orders.

The MLA office is located on the island known as Mannahatta (Manhattan) in Lenapehoking, the homeland of the Lenape people. The MLA pays respect to the original stewards of this land and to the diverse and vibrant Native communities that continue to thrive in New York City.

Approaches to Teaching World Literature 180
ISSN 1059-1133

Library of Congress Cataloging-in-Publication Data

Names: González, José Eduardo, editor.
Title: Approaches to teaching the works of Jorge Luis Borges / edited by José Eduardo González.
Description: New York : The Modern Language Association of America, 2025.
Series: Approaches to teaching world literature, 1059-1133 ; 180 |
Includes bibliographical references.
Identifiers: LCCN 2024025830 (print) | LCCN 2024025831 (ebook) |
ISBN 9781603296830 (hardcover) | ISBN 9781603296847 (paperback) |
ISBN 9781603296854 (EPUB)
Subjects: LCSH: Borges, Jorge Luis, 1899-1986—Study and teaching. | Borges, Jorge Luis, 1899-1986—Criticism and interpretation. | LCGFT: Literary criticism. | Essays.
Classification: LCC PQ7797.B635 Z5314 2025 (print) | LCC PQ7797.B635 (ebook) |
DDC 868/.6209—dc23/eng/20240920
LC record available at https://lccn.loc.gov/2024025830
LC ebook record available at https://lccn.loc.gov/2024025831

CONTENTS

ABBREVIATIONS FOR COMMONLY CITED EDITIONS

CF *Collected Fictions*. Translated by Andrew Hurley, Viking, 1998.

OC *Obras completas: Edición crítica*. Edited by Rolando Costa Picazo and Irma Zangara, Emecé, 2009. 3 vols.

SNF *Selected Non-fictions*. Edited by Eliot Weinberger, translated by Esther Allen et al., Viking, 1999.

Part One

MATERIALS

Biographical and Literary Overview

Jorge Luis Borges was born on 24 August 1899 in the city of Buenos Aires, Argentina. During his childhood, Georgie, as he was called at home, and his family resided in Palermo, a working-class neighborhood on the outskirts of the city, a place that would later be mentioned frequently in some of his writings. At some point, the area had been home to *compadritos*, hoodlums who were known for knife fights and whose legends captured young Georgie's imagination. He was taken with the bravery of outlaws, and his fascination later in life with the stories of gauchos stemmed from his interest in the courage of knife fighters (Williamson, *Borges* 43–44). His father, Jorge Guillermo Borges, was a lawyer who supplemented his income by teaching psychology, and his anarchism strongly influenced his son. Whether it was because of his father's distrust of the state or his parents' concern for his weak health, Borges was educated at home by his paternal grandmother and an English tutor until he was about ten or eleven years old. He spent most of those formative years reading from his father's personal library of over a thousand volumes, mostly in English and French. "If I were asked to name the chief event in my life," Borges would say, remembering his childhood, "I should say [it was] my father's library" ("Autobiographical Essay" 140). There he spent hours discovering books of adventure, traveling in his mind to faraway lands (India, China, Arabia) that would later inspire many of his fictional tales. As a result, however, he had no childhood friends and was isolated from the outside world (Woodall 12–13; Williamson, *Borges* 41).

Borges was proud of his ancestry on both sides of his family. On his mother's side, one of his ancestors, Isidoro Suárez, fought in the wars of independence as part of Simón Bolívar's army in the 1800s and later opposed the dictatorship of Juan Manuel de Rosas in Argentina. On his father's side, his grandmother, Fanny Haslam, had emigrated from England and in the early 1870s married his grandfather, Colonel Francisco Borges, another warrior from Borges's point of view, who fought in the frontier wars against the indigenous people. From the tales about the frontier days that his grandmother told him, Borges found inspiration for "Historia del guerrero y de la cautiva" ("Story of the Warrior and the Captive Maiden"; *OC* 1: 1009–11; *CF* 208–11), one of his best-known stories (Borges, "Autobiographical Essay" 137). He used both English and Spanish at home, but it was in the former that he did his most important childhood readings, including *Huckleberry Finn* and *Treasure Island* as well as Richard Francis Burton's translation of the *Thousand and One Nights*. He claimed to have read *Don Quixote* in English first and that all other versions in Spanish that he read afterward sounded to him like translations. Only after he started going to school did Spanish become his preferred language. Borges's mother, Leonor Acevedo, helped increase her son's awareness of the criollo side of the family. She would reminisce about old Buenos Aires and transmit to Borges her love for a city that would figure prominently in his early poetry and prose (Williamson, *Borges* 36). Leonor was a force to be reckoned with in the Borges household, and this became evident in the later years of Borges's life, and more so after blindness set in. She lived with Borges until her death in 1975 at the age of ninety-nine.

European Years

Borges's father's eyesight was already failing by the age of forty, and looking for a cure for the condition forced the family to move to Europe, specifically to Geneva, where he could be treated by a famous eye doctor. That young Georgie might have been the target of bullying at school was an added motive for the journey. His parents had planned to tour the Continent while Borges and his sister, Nora, stayed in Geneva with their maternal grandmother, but shortly after they arrived, the First World War broke out. Their original plan to stay in Europe for one year became a four-year exile. Knowing little French when he started school, Borges felt cut off from his environment. His grades were unremarkable, but he made a few friends, and one of his most treasured memories from this period was when his classmates interceded for him with the headmaster, asking the headmaster to take into consideration that Georgie's first language was not French and to let him pass to the next grade (Williamson, *Borges* 55–57). As in Buenos Aires, he was more interested in the books he was discovering at home than he was in the world outside his library. He discovered authors who would greatly influence his later work as a writer. He read Thomas Carlyle, Arthur Schopenhauer, and G. K. Chesterton, among others. But it was the poetry of Walt Whitman and German expressionism that had an overwhelming impact on him. His growing awareness of the war and the concurrent revolutionary events in Russia led Borges to look toward Russia as part of a generational desire to find an alternative to Western social systems. Influenced by socialism and expressionism, Borges's desire to break from the isolationism that his family favored began to grow around 1917, which would be important when the family moved to Spain in 1919, once the war was over, and he became interested in participating in avant-garde literary movements (Williamson, *Borges* 60–63). Around this time, in Geneva, his father arranged for him to have his first sexual experience, and as a result of this encounter Borges would develop a lifelong ambivalence toward women. In Spain, Borges joined a group of poets who called themselves "ultraists," members of an avant-garde movement born under the tutelage of the Spanish writer Rafael Casinos-Asséns that sought to go beyond established notions of poetry. Soon Borges became a regular member of Casinos-Asséns's weekly *tertulias*, or informal literary gatherings. It was in Madrid where Borges thought of writing a series of Bolshevik poems. He later destroyed them, but a few still exist (Williamson, *Borges* 68–79; Woodall 33–43).

Return to Buenos Aires

When he returned to Argentina, Borges founded a branch of the ultraist movement, and the new ideas of this avant-garde group challenged the local literary establishment, which was still heavily influenced by the nineteenth-century *modernismo* aesthetic of Rubén Darío, a sort of Latin American version of French symbolism. During the same time, however, Borges's allegiance to the ultraists' extreme individualism began to disappear as his interest in philosophy and the influence of Macedonio Fernández's ideas led him to begin writing essays that questioned the traditional notion of the self. While at first Borges felt that Buenos Aires was provincial, with time he fell in love with the city again, and this would become evident in his early books of poetry and essays. But he was less interested in the urban downtown than in the suburbs, the outlying neighborhoods, the *orillas* of the city. He wanted to help create the mythology that he thought this great city needed and thus slowly moved from an avant-garde poetics to *criollismo*, his version of nationalism (Williamson, *Borges* 93–102, 139–41). The end of the 1920s was emotionally and financially difficult for Borges and his family. Norah Lange, a fellow poet who had joined the ultraist movement in 1926 and with whom Borges had fallen in love, rejected him for Oliverio Girondo. Hipólito Irigoyen, an enormously popular politician whose campaign Borges supported but whose politics represented a challenge to the hegemony of the local elites, would become president in 1928 only to be overthrown in 1930 for being unable to handle the Great Depression. High inflation would also affect Borges's family situation, eroding his father's pension, and in the next few years would force Borges to begin contributing to the household income.

First Fictions

The 1930s was a period of important meetings and associations. Victoria Ocampo, a cultural promoter and a friend of Borges's, launched *Sur*, a quarterly literary journal, in 1931. While his idiosyncratic contributions were not paid, this was the place where Borges would grow as a writer (Woodall 83–86). The cosmopolitan character of the journal had a great influence on him. His provincial *criollismo* and *ultraísmo* from the 1920s were left behind as he embarked on the creation of a new type of fiction. In 1932 Borges met Adolfo Bioy Casares, and the two would strike up a lifelong friendship that resulted in their frequent collaboration. Sometimes using pseudonyms, they wrote short fiction and edited works on topics of interest to both of them, such as fantastic literature and detective fiction (Woodall 88–89). Borges's most important work during the early part of the 1930s came from his editorial job at the popular newspaper *Crítica*. The newspaper had begun to publish a Saturday colour supplement, *Revista Multicolor de los Sábados* (*Saturday Multicolor Magazine*), and Borges was put in charge of it. It was there that Borges, using the name of his great-great-grandfather Francisco Bustos, published his first original work of fiction, "Hombres de las orillas" ("Men from the Suburbs"), later retitled "Hombre de la esquina rosada" ("Man on Pink Corner"). Perhaps the most important detail of this story was the twist at the end, a technique that would become a trademark of his mature fiction. Around the same time, he was also writing his versions of other stories derived from his eclectic readings, tales of violence and crime combining fiction with real historical figures (Woodall 92–94). They were collected in his book *Historia universal de la infamia* (*A Universal History of Iniquity*), the preface to which listed all his influences and sources. In a preface added in 1954, he called the collection "el irresponsable juego de un tímido que no se animó a escribir cuentos y que se distrajo en falsear y tergiversar . . . ajenas historias" 'the irresponsible sport of a shy sort of man who could not bring himself to write short stories, and so amused himself by changing and distorting . . . the stories of other men' (*OC* 1: 593; *CF* 4). He also took up other jobs that paid more. He wrote book reviews and articles on important contemporary figures for the illustrated magazine *El Hogar* (*Home*), and in 1937, through his connection with Bioy Casares, he got a job at the Miguel Cané Library (Woodall 101–04). But the most difficult year was yet to come: early in 1938 his father died, making him the head of the household and adding greater responsibilities, and then, on Christmas Eve of that year, Borges suffered an accident. There are different versions of the account, but it seems that Borges was running upstairs toward the apartment of a girl he was going to introduce to his mother when he hit his head against a newly painted casement window that had been left open. Bits of glass got lodged in his head, and he had to be operated on (possibly to remove them) because he had developed septicemia and was losing the power of speech. He convalesced for weeks, and during that time he was afraid that the accident might have affected his intellectual faculties (Williamson, *Borges* 238). According to Borges himself, after he recovered, he decided to write something he had never written before, original works of fiction, instead of poetry. Thus, if he failed, it would be less dreadful for him. The two stories that followed, "Pierre Menard, autor del *Quijote*" ("Pierre Menard, Author of the *Quixote*"; *OC* 1: 842–47; *CF* 88–95) and "Tlön, Uqbar, Orbis Tertius" (*OC* 1: 831–41; *CF* 68–81), would be among the most original written in the twentieth century.

Ficciones *and Resistance to Nazi Ideology*

Borges was still unsure about committing himself to becoming a fiction writer. Like his earlier tales of iniquity, both "Pierre Menard, autor del *Quijote*" and "Tlön, Uqbar, Orbis Tertius" have an essay-like structure. They read like scholarly investigations into a topic and include very little action. First published in *Sur* in 1939, "Pierre Menard" is the story of the obscure post-symbolist French poet told by a snobbish literary critic who describes the late writer's attempt at rewriting Miguel de Cervantes's *Don Quixote*. However, Menard's intention is not to create a new version of the text for modern audiences but to reproduce the exact same text, down to its commas and periods. With this story, Borges was challenging his readers to question the traditional notion of literature as originating from an author whose historical existence has shaped the meaning of the written text. A year later, when "Tlön, Uqbar, Orbis Tertius" appeared, the magazine's readers might have found the story puzzling because, again, there is very little action. A large portion of the text is devoted to describing philosophical ideas that exist in an imaginary world whose order and logic becomes so attractive that, toward the end of the story, people prefer it to reality. At the time, the fictional text seemed distant from everyday concerns, and Borges's compatriots very likely missed the relevance of the message, the warning, that the story was seeking to transmit. The fictional universe described in the story, its illogical but alluring and well-organized systems of thought, was a critique of the Nazi ideology that was spreading throughout the world. Borges had become preoccupied with the advance of totalitarianism and antisemitism in Europe and had expressed his views in some of his essays for *El Hogar.* He published "Pierre Menard" and "Tlön, Uqbar, Orbis Tertius" alongside another six stories, most of which also appeared first in *Sur,* as a small collection titled *El jardín de senderos que se bifurcan* (*The Garden of Forking Paths*). The local audience, accustomed to realist and nationalist fiction, completely ignored a text full of foreign locations, metaphysical questions, and labyrinths. Borges submitted the book for the Premio Nacional de Literatura (National Award for Literature), but out of six jury members only one voted to give it second place (Williamson, *Borges* 260; Woodall 123). The jury could not see any connection between the obscure and erudite fantastic tales and the contemporary political situation in Argentina, which was rapidly deteriorating. Democratic processes had been failing in the country since the 1930s, and the intentions of the army were already evident early in the 1940s. A bloodless coup d'état took place in 1943. All political parties were abolished, and the freedom of the press restricted. Juan Domingo Perón would soon emerge as a populist leader. Already worried about the impact of totalitarian ideas in Europe, Borges could not avoid thinking that local politicians would follow in the footsteps of European politicians (Williamson, *Borges* 269–70). In the early 1940s he continued writing the fantastic stories that would make him famous. In 1943 he published in *Sur* a story titled "El milagro secreto" ("The Secret Miracle"; *OC* 1: 900–04; *CF* 157–62), about a Jewish playwright in Prague, Jaromir Hladík, who is going to be executed by the Nazis, who have invaded his country. Hladík's greatest regret as an intellectual is leaving his final play unfinished, and in a dream he asks God to allow him to complete it. As Hladík is facing the firing squad, God grants him his secret wish, stopping time so that Hladík can finish writing his work in his mind. Hladík is the only person who can notice that time has stopped—he is both the author and the only audience his play will ever have. Once his play is complete, time resumes, and he is killed by the firing squad's bullets. His mind, his thoughts, become a place of freedom that no totalitarian state can touch. *Ficciones* (*Fictions*), which included new stories in addition to the ones previously collected in *El jardín*, was published three years later. The book was better received, and Borges's fame began to rise during the next decade. The mass demonstrations in favor of Perón in 1945 appalled Borges, who thought his compatriots were turning into Nazis without being aware of it

(Williamson, *Borges* 285–86). When Perón became president the following year, Borges's life became more difficult.

Rising Fame and Peronism

A couple of months after Perón became president, Borges was removed from his position as librarian at the municipal library and assigned the post of inspector of poultry and chickens. According to Borges, the change was retaliation for his having taken the side of the Allies during the war, thus effectively forcing him to retire ("Autobiographical Essay" 172). Receiving little income from his publications, Borges obtained a job teaching and lecturing on literature in different cities in Argentina and Uruguay, frequently traveling between the two countries. In 1947 he wrote a text that circulated clandestinely among intellectuals who opposed Perón. Titled "La fiesta del monstruo" ("The Monster's Celebration"), it tells the story of a young Jewish man who is killed by supporters of the party in power (Saítta 50). In 1949 he published *El Aleph* (*The Aleph*), which, like *Ficciones*, included fantastic stories he had previously published in *Sur*. The main story in the collection, "El Aleph" ("The Aleph"; *OC* 1: 1061–70; *CF* 274–86), is about a mediocre poet who discovers a place in his cellar where one can see an aleph, a point in space that contains all other points in the universe. The story is dedicated to Estela Canto, a woman whom Borges had been in love with since 1944. While they enjoyed each other's company and Borges asked her to marry him, she was not physically attracted to him. Borges did not publish any fiction again for many years, but his fame began to grow, and by 1951, his texts were being translated into French. Though his friends tried to get him to admit how some of Perón's reforms had benefited the working class, Borges's anti-Peronism bordered on paranoia. Because of the mass support that Peronism enjoyed, Borges would often take antidemocratic positions, arguing, for example, that thousands of individuals proclaiming something did not make it right (Woodall 174–75). After Perón was ousted in 1955, Borges was appointed director of the National Library as reparation for the indignities he had endured. Borges had been blind since the mid-1950s, and he commented on the unusualness of a blind writer becoming a librarian in his "Poema de los dones" ("Poem of the Gifts"). With splendid irony, God, Borges wrote, "me dio a la vez los libros y la noche" 'granted me the books and blindness at one touch' (*OC* 2: 300; *Selected Poems* [Coleman] 129). While his reputation was growing at home, with at least five scholarly studies written about him in the late 1950s, his international fame came only after he received the Formentor Prize with Samuel Beckett in 1961 (Williamson, *Borges* 245–46). *Ficciones* was translated into English the next year, and Borges, an expert traveling lecturer by then, was invited to visit the United States. In 1962, after a semester at the University of Texas, Austin, as a visiting professor, Borges gave lectures at Harvard, Yale, and Columbia and visited New Mexico, California, Connecticut, and Massachusetts. His mother, Leonor, accompanied him and helped him move around. The next year they toured Europe, but it was clear that Borges was going to need a younger companion on these trips. In the next few years other friends accompanied him until in 1967 he married Elsa Astete Millán. It is believed that the marriage was arranged by his mother so that someone could help him during his travels, but they were very different from each other, and the union did not last long (Williamson, *Borges* 371–72). They separated in 1970.

A New Love

During this period Borges began to work with the translator Norman Thomas di Giovanni in Buenos Aires, with the intention of creating new translations of his work for the American market. Di Giovanni encouraged Borges to write fiction again (Williamson, *Borges* 381). Borges would produce two new collections of stories in the years to come, *El informe de Brodie* (*Brodie's Report*) and *El libro de arena* (*The Book of Sand*), which are simpler in style than his previous collections but whose plots sometimes resemble the topics he employed in his fiction from the 1940s. In the early 1970s, Borges fell in love once again, this time with one of his students, María Kodama, who was forty years his junior. He declared his love for her during a trip to Iceland in 1971, and it is believed that she was the inspiration for his short story "Ulrica" ("Ulrikke"; Williamson, *Borges* 395, 398). While his family and friends were not always supportive of their relationship, Kodama was a constant presence in Borges's life as he continued to travel around the world, receiving awards and honorary doctorates. In 1986 Borges married Kodama a few months before he passed away in Geneva, the city that changed his childhood and made him happy.

Texts and Editions

There are many editions of Borges's *Obras completas* (*Complete Works*), all of them, unfortunately, incomplete. In 1996 Emecé published an edition in four volumes: volume 1 includes works published from 1923 to 1949; volume 2, from 1952 to 1972; volume 3, from 1975 to 1985; and volume 4, from 1975 to 1988. Most versions of his *Obras completas* include his four main collections of short stories: *Ficciones*, *El Aleph*, *El informe de Brodie*, and *El libro de arena*. They tend to differ in terms of the collections of prose and poetry included, especially the prose and poetry written in his later years. A critical edition in three volumes, *Obras completas: Edición crítica*, edited by Rolando Costa Picazo and Irma Zangara, was published by Emecé in 2009. It contains notes identifying people and places mentioned in the texts, written with a general audience in mind. This is the edition used throughout this volume. Any version of Borges's *Obras completas* is more suitable for research or graduate seminars than for use in the undergraduate classroom. Luckily, there is no shortage of paperback editions of Borges's individual short story collections, which are perfect for introducing Borges to students in the United States. Among the books not included in either edition of *Obras completas* are some of Borges's early books: *Inquisiciones* (*Inquisitions*), *El tamaño de mi esperanza* (*The Size of My Hope*), and *El idioma de los argentinos* (*The Language of the Argentines*). This is because the author disavowed them and they were not republished while he was alive. New editions of these texts were issued in 1994 by Seix Barral. Several collections of texts that Borges wrote for magazines, journals, or newspapers have been published. *Textos cautivos: Ensayos y reseñas en "El Hogar,"* edited by Emir Rodríguez and Enrique Sacerio-Garí, was published in 1986. This collection includes Borges's contributions between 1936 and 1939 to the magazine *El Hogar*. Similar volumes have followed: *Borges en* Sur, *1931–1980*, edited by Sara Luisa del Carril and Mercedes Rubio de Zocchi, was published by Emecé in 1999. It contains texts that Borges published in the magazine *Sur* but that had not been collected in book form and do not appear in either edition of Emecé's *Obras completas*. Borges contributed essays, short notes, film reviews, book reviews, and translations to different sections of *Sur*. Between 1997 and 2003, three large volumes of previously uncollected texts, edited by del Carril and Rubio de Zocchi, were published under the umbrella title of *Textos recobrados*. The first volume includes writings from 1919 to 1929; the second, from 1931 to 1955; and the third, from 1956 to 1986. One collection of texts that we cannot recommend is *Borges en "Revista Multicolor de los Sábados,"* edited by Zangara and published by Atlántida in 1995. The book's objective appears to have been to collect texts written by Borges for *Crítica*'s colour supplement, where his first fiction was published. However, the editor attributes many of the texts and translations that either were unsigned or appeared under other names to Borges, arguing that he might have been involved in their creation without providing sufficient evidence to support this claim in many cases (Louis, "Instrucciones").

In addition to his single-author works, Borges published books in collaboration with other writers. With Bioy Casares, he wrote several texts under joint pseudonyms. As H. Bustos Domecq, they produced the collections *Seis problemas para don Isidro Parodi* (*Six Problems for Don Isidro Parodi*) and *Dos fantasías memorables* (*Two Memorable Fantasies*), and as B. Suárez Lynch, the novella *Un modelo para la muerte* (*A Model for Death*). These were followed much later by other collections like *Crónicas de Bustos Domecq* (*Chronicles of Bustos Domecq*) and *Nuevos cuentos de Bustos Domecq* (*New Stories by Bustos Domecq*). Both authors also collaborated in the creation of film scripts. Emecé's 1991 volume *Obras completas en colaboración* (*Complete Works in Collaboration*) includes these texts as well as other collaborations (Borges et al.): *Leopoldo Lugones* (*Leopoldo Lugones*), with Betina Edelberg; *El Martín Fierro* (*The Martin Fierro*) and *El libro de los seres imaginarios* (*Book of Imaginary Beings*), with Margarita Guerrero; *Qué es el budismo* (*What Is Buddhism*), with Alicia Jurado; *Breve antología anglosajona* (*Brief Anglo-Saxon Anthology*), with Kodama; *Introducción a la literatura inglesa* (*Introduction to English Literature*) and

Literatura germánicas medievales (*Medieval Germanic Literatures*), with María Esther Vázquez. Not included are three other books: *Antiguas literaturas germánicas* (*Ancient Germanic Literatures*), with Delia Ingenieros; *La hermana de Eloísa* (*Eloisa's Sister*), with Luisa Mercedes Levinson; and the other book he wrote with Kodama, *Atlas*.

Translations

Borges is unique among Latin American writers in the US market in terms of the incredible number of translations and editions of his works in English. The most recent versions were three volumes of fiction, essays, and poetry published by Viking between 1998 and 1999. *Collected Fictions*, translated by Andrew Hurley, includes Borges's short stories from *A Universal History of Iniquity*, *Fictions*, *The Aleph*, *Brodie's Report*, and *The Book of Sand* as well as fictions from *The Maker*, *Museum*, *In Praise of Darkness*, and *Shakespeare's Memory*. *Selected Non-fictions* includes versions of some of Borges's most famous nonfictional texts, edited and translated by Eliot Weinberger in collaboration with Esther Allen and Suzanne Jill Levine. Finally, *Selected Poems*, edited by Alexander Coleman, is a bilingual anthology of Borges's poems translated by a group of thirteen translators. Unless otherwise indicated, this volume uses the translations of Borges's stories, essays, and poems from the three abovementioned Viking editions.

Borges is an important figure for translation studies, and, as is evident in a few of the essays included in this volume, comparing translations of his short stories can be an effective teaching strategy. Prior to the Viking volumes, Borges's fantastic fiction was the object of several translations. The first translation, published shortly after Borges won the Formentor Prize, was *Labyrinths: Selected Stories and Other Writings*. *Labyrinths* includes a selection of stories from both *Ficciones* and *El Aleph* and a few essays and notes from *Otras inquisiciones* (*Other Inquisitions*) and *El hacedor*. Most of the texts were translated by James E. Irby, one of the first Borges scholars in the United States, and the rest were translated by a group that included Donald A. Yates, John M. Fein, Julian Palley, and Harriet de Onís. The same year, *Ficciones* was translated, under the same title, by Anthony Kerrigan, Anthony Bonner, Alastair Reid, Helen Temple, and Ruthven Todd. In 1964 *El hacedor* was translated by Mildred Boyer and Harold Borland as *Dreamtigers*. Beween 1969 and 1984, di Giovanni retranslated several of Borges's stories as *"The Aleph" and Other Stories, 1933–1969* and translated for the first time some of his other prose books, including *Doctor Brodie's Report*, *A Universal History of Infamy*, *The Book of Sand*, and *Evaristo Carriego: A Book about Old-Time Buenos Aires*. Di Giovanni's translations are, however, out of print and no longer available for purchase.

In addition to di Giovanni's *Evaristo Carriego*, there are other volumes where readers can find essays and nonfiction not included in Weinberger's *Selected*

Non-fictions. Borges's best-known book of essays, *Other Inquisitions*, was translated by Ruth L. C. Simms. Edgardo Cozarinsky collected Borges's film reviews in *Borges y el cine*, which was later translated by Gloria Waldman and Ronald Christ as *Borges in/and/on Film*. *On Argentina*, edited by Suzanne Jill Levine and Alfred Mac Adam, reprints material from the *Selected Non-fictions* collection, but it also includes a few essays that were previously unavailable. In addition to Coleman's *Selected Poems*, collections of Borges's poetry include *Selected Poems, 1923–1967* and *In Praise of Darkness*, both translated by di Giovanni. Two other books worth mentioning are *Poems of the Night*, edited by Efraín Kristal, and *The Sonnets*, edited by Stephen Kessler. While these books reprint many of the translations found in Coleman's *Selected Poems*, they also include new ones. Several of the books that Borges wrote in collaboration with other authors are also available in translation. Written with Bioy Casares, *Six Problems for Don Isidro Parodi* and *Chronicles of Bustos Domecq* were both translated by di Giovanni. *The Book of Imaginary Beings*, written in collaboration with Guerrero, was not only translated by di Giovanni but also enlarged in collaboration with Borges. *Atlas*, written with Kodama, was translated by Kerrigan.

The Instructor's Library

The following sections offer an overview of important secondary texts relating to Borges's life and works as well as critical studies about major topics in his writings.

Background Studies and Introductions

Instructors interested in the history of Argentina during Borges's time will find an excellent overview in Luis Alberto Romero's *A History of Argentina in the Twentieth Century*. Chapter 2, "The Radical Governments, 1916–1930," is particularly helpful for understanding the emergence of the new reading public that Borges encountered upon his return to Argentina and the political climate that led to Irigoyen's victory in 1930. Chapter 4, "The Perón Government, 1943–1955," is a good introduction to the emergence of Peronism. *The Argentina Reader*, edited by Gabriela Nouzeilles and Graciela Montaldo, is a selection of primary sources and critical studies, such as James Scobie's description of the living conditions at the turn of the century in "The Paris of South America" and Daniel James's "Peron and the People," which could be paired with Borges's stories or assigned as an introduction to the history and culture of Argentina. Beatriz Sarlo's book *Una modernidad periférica: Buenos Aires, 1920 y 1930* (*A Peripheral Modernity: Buenos Aires, 1920 and 1930*) offers a study of the intellectual climate in early-twentieth-century Argentina, with special attention to Borges's place in it. Those interested in the subculture of the *suburbios* can find information about the tango in Russell Salmon's classic article "The Tango: Its Origins and Meaning" or in more recent books on the subject, such as *Tango: Sex and Rhythm of the City*, by Mike Gonzalez and Marianella Yanes.

The young Borges was also attracted to the avant-garde. Adam Shellhorse presents a balanced view of the place of *ultraísmo* within the Latin American avant-garde movements in his essay "The Avant-Garde: From *Creacionismo* to *Ultraísmo*, Brazilian *Modernismo*, *Antropofagia*, and Surrealism," which appears in *The Cambridge Companion to Latin American Poetry*, edited by Stephen M. Hart. An older but still relevant study of this poetic movement and politics in Borges is Jorge Ruffinelli's "Borges y el ultraísmo: Un caso de estética y política" ("Borges and Ultraism: A Case of Aesthetics and Politics"). Gauchos and gauchoesque poetry are a recurrent motif in Borges's stories and his reflections on Argentine character and culture. Chapter 1 of Richard Slatta's *Gauchos and the Vanishing Frontier*, titled "Who Was the Gaucho?," is a good introduction to the topic, and Alfonso García Morales's article "Jorge Luis Borges, autor del *Martín Fierro*" ("Jorge Luis Borges, Author of *Martín Fierro*") studies Borges's constantly changing views on the author of the classic epic poem. Instructors looking for a philosophical background relevant to some stories can find an overview of the topic in Clive Griffin's "Philosophy and Fiction," in *The Cambridge Companion to Jorge Luis Borges*, edited by Edwin Williamson. Borges's interest in idealism, which plays an important role in stories like "Tlön, Uqbar, Orbis Tertius," is studied in Marina Martín's "Borges via the Dialectics of Berkeley and Hume." A few scholars have written on the influence of Schopenhauer's philosophy on Borges. Charles Li presents a succinct description of this influence in "Schopenhauer's Fictions." Religion is a key element in many of Borges's works. Max Ubelaker Andrade's contribution to this volume focuses on the topic of Islam and provides useful secondary sources on the topic. An early overview of Borges's interest in Judaism is Edna Aizenberg's *The Aleph Weaver: Biblical, Kabbalistic and Judaic Elements in Borges*. Evelyn Fishburn's "Borges and Buddhism," in *Jorge Luis Borges in Context*, edited by Robin Fiddian, discusses Borges's writings on Buddhism and how the religion influenced some of his stories.

There are several introductions to Borges's work that provide an overview of the writer's life in relation to his writings. Some recent ones include *A Companion to Jorge Luis Borges*, by Steven Boldy, and two books titled *Jorge Luis Borges*, one by Tim McNeese and one by Jason Wilson. Rex Butler's *Borges' Short Stories* provides a good introduction to Borges's narrative strategies. Two excellent introductions to the themes and structures of Borges's fiction are *Borges:* Ficciones, by Donald Shaw, and *Jorge Luis Borges*, by Jaime Alazraki (in Spanish). *Jorge Luis Borges in Context*, edited by Fiddian, and *The Cambridge Companion to Jorge Luis Borges*, edited by Williamson, include essays that serve as helpful introductions to a variety of topics.

For a more comprehensive look at Borges's life, the two major biographies are those written by Williamson and by James Woodall, each of which is titled *Borges: A Life*. While both books benefit from access to more sources and better information about Borges's life compared with *Jorge Luis Borges: A Literary Biography*, by Emir Rodríguez Monegal, the latter is still an important critical interpretation of how Borges's main topics and views are connected to his personal and intellectual journey. Rodríguez Monegal's book is heavily based on Borges's "Autobiographical Essay," another excellent reading for introducing students to Borges's life. Finally, there are two books that attempt to present a compendium of all the erudite philosophical, literary, and cultural allusions in Borges's work: *The Literary Universe of Jorge Luis Borges*, by Daniel Balderston, and *A Dictionary of Borges*, by Fishburn and Psiche Hughes. While students can now easily find plenty of information on the Internet, these volumes remain extremely valuable resources on real or imagined characters and places as well as references to concepts and titles.

Studies on Borges

The first critical approaches to Borges mostly focused on understanding the structure of his stories and discovering their sources. Alazraki's studies are a good example of these tendencies. In *La prosa narrativa de Jorge Luis Borges* (*The Narrative Prose of Jorge Luis Borges*), Alazraki tracks recurrent topics and stylistic features in Borges's prose. Among other early approaches, some of the most influential were *La expresión de la irrealidad en la obra de Jorge Luis Borges* (*Representation of Irreality in the Work of Jorge Luis Borges*), by Ana María Barrenechea; *The Narrow Act: Borges' Art of Allusion*, by Ronald Christ; *Paper Tigers: The Ideal Fictions of Jorge Luis Borges*, by John Sturrock; and Irby's unpublished dissertation, *The Structure of the Stories of Jorge Luis Borges*. Among the books focusing on literary form, one of the most useful to teachers seeking a general understanding of the Borgesian universe is Gene Bell-Villada's *Borges and His Fiction: A Guide to His Mind and Art*. In *El precursor velado: R. L. Stevenson en la obra de Borges* (*A Veiled Precursor: R. L. Stevenson in Borges's Work*), Balderston traces the influence of Stevenson in Borges's construction of his narrative art. Somewhat less approachable in style, Sylvia Molloy's *Signs of Borges* is essential to understanding Borges's techniques for constantly destabilizing the meaning of his texts and readers' relationship to them.

For a long time, perhaps because of their metaphysical topics, Borges's writings, especially his fictional texts, were seen as disconnected from the immediate environment in which they were created. In the early 1990s, however, scholars began to focus on interpreting the social and political background against which these texts were written. Sarlo published an important book, *Jorge Luis Borges: A Writer on the Edge*, unveiling, for example, the antitotalitarian ideas in stories such as "Tlön, Uqbar, Orbis Tertius," the ideological implications of *El informe de Brodie*, and Borges's use of the term *orillas* (meaning "edge," "shore," "margin," or "limit") to interpret Argentine culture and literature. Other studies analyzing the connection between Borges's writings and his politics include *Borges and the Politics of Form*, by José Eduardo

González, which focuses on Borges's aesthetic choices. More recently, new research has studied Borges's distrust of governments from new perspectives. Luis Othoniel Rosa, in *Comienzos para una estética anarquista: Borges con Macedonio* (*Beginnings of an Anarchist Aesthetic: Borges with Macedonio*), and Alejandra Salinas, in *Liberty, Individuality, and Democracy in Jorge Luis Borges*, focus on anarchism and individualism from two completely different perspectives. Important studies analyzing Borges's fight against Nazism and totalitarianism include Annick Louis's book *Borges ante el fascismo* (*Borges Facing Fascism*), which describes the importance of Borges's militant attitude against fascism for contextualizing the work he created in the 1930s and 1940s (12). Another useful contribution in contextualizing Borges's work is Balderston's *Out of Context: Historical Reference and the Representation of Reality in Borges*, which provides historical details that are needed in order to understand how closely some of Borges's stories were tied to the periods described in their plots.

As postmodernist approaches began to dominate literary studies in the 1990s, Borges came to be seen as a precursor of postmodernism. Carlos Alonso explains many of the connections to poststructuralist theories in "Borges y la teoría" ("Borges and Theory"). The readings of Borges that marked that period of literary criticism undoubtedly had a strong influence on how Borges has since been interpreted, leading to many creative and inspiring analyses. A great example of this is Kate Jenckes's *Reading Borges after Benjamin: Allegory, Afterlife, and the Writing of History*. Jenckes utilizes the German critic Walter Benjamin's insights into allegory as a form of writing history in order to interpret Borges's work, especially the early poetry and prose. Fiddian benefits from the history of the relationship between the discourse of postcoloniality and Latin American culture in *Postcolonial Borges: Argument and Artistry*. Philosophical approaches to Borges's fiction have always been part of Borges scholarship. Examples of sophisticated studies include Silvia Dapía's *Jorge Luis Borges, Post-analytic Philosophy, and Representation*, which finds in Borges's texts questions that antedate ideas later posed by postanalytic philosophers. David E. Johnson, in *Kant's Dog: On Borges, Philosophy and the Time of Translation*, focuses on the problem of temporality and the centrality of Borges's ideas about translations to understanding it. In fact, beyond the philosophical approach, Borges's translations and his theories about this practice of interpretation have received attention from several scholars. Kristal's *Invisible Work: Borges and Translation* studies the link between Borges's views on translation and his creative work. The second part of Emron Esplin's *Borges's Poe: The Influence and Reinvention of Edgar Allan Poe in Spanish America* (65–100) reads Borges's translations of Poe as a challenge to *modernista* poetics. Esplin's contribution to this volume contains additional references and suggestions regarding translation. Studying Borges's use of religion has been a common practice in Borges scholarship since its inception. Some important studies in this area are Alazraki's *Borges and the Kabbalah*, which focuses on the influence of Jewish mysticism in Borges's work, and Ubelaker Andrade's *Borges beyond the Visible*, which investigates how Borges creatively borrows from Islam's prohibitions on visual representation. In *Borges, Buddhism and World Literature*, Dominique Jullien studies Borges's fascination with "stories of renunciation" (xi–xxv), including the most famous one, that of Buddha, and the implications of Borges's interpretation of Buddhism for his aesthetics. Sexuality has also been a topic of interest to many Borges scholars, especially as it relates to the author's creative output, and the first book to address it, from a psychoanalytic perspective, was Julio Woscobinik's *The Secret of Borges*. However, the most authoritative study on the topic is without doubt Ariel de la Fuente's *Borges, Desire, and Sex*.

A new direction in Borgesian studies is related to the availability of manuscripts that have facilitated insights into the author's creative process. Balderston's *How Borges Wrote* develops a close reading of several of Borges's manuscripts, paying attention to drafts, marginal notes, and textual modifications, with the intention of discovering the details of Borges's writing style that facilitate new interpretations of his work. Balderston's book includes facsimiles and transcriptions of pages from the manuscripts discussed, making it an accessible and invaluable resource for teaching and studying Borges's writing process. In collaboration with María Celeste Martín, Balderston has continued making these resources available with the recent publication of facsimiles in three different volumes, each one including transcriptions and commentaries: *Poemas y prosas breves* (*Poems and Short Prose*), *Ensayos* (*Essays*), and *Cuentos* (*Stories*), which includes popular stories such as "La casa de Asterión" ("The House of Asterion"), "La lotería en Babilonia" ("The Lottery in Babylon"), and "Emma Zunz." This emphasis on the materiality of the text, the physical form of Borges's work, is one of the inspirations behind Nora Benedict's recent study *Borges and the Literary Marketplace*, which uses Borges as a case study to look at how editorial practices influenced reading in Latin America.

Internet, Audiovisual, and Digital Humanities Resources

The most complete online source of information on Borges is the Borges Center website (www.borges.pitt.edu), sponsored by the Department of Hispanic Languages and Literatures and the Dietrich School of Arts and Sciences of the University of Pittsburgh. It contains a "Finder's Guide," the most comprehensive index of names, places, and ideas related to the Borgesian universe. It contains a large collection of literary criticism focused on Borges, with links to PDF copies of essays, and an interactive time line with biographical and bibliographic information. Instructors wishing to bring Borges's voice to the classroom have plenty of options to choose from. In Spanish, for example, recordings of the seven lectures that Borges gave in Buenos Aires in 1977, which became the basis of his book *Seven Nights*, can be found on *YouTube* ("Jorge Luis

Borges: Siete Noches"). In English, the Norton lectures that Borges gave at Harvard University in 1967–68 are available on Harvard Library's website ("Borges"). Several other interviews and documentaries are available, many of which are listed in the "Other Resources" section of the Borges Center website. In its digital archive, *Project Gutenberg* has a copy of the eleventh edition of the *Encyclopædia Britannica*, which was Borges's main source of reference for many of his stories. The best way to access it is through the well-organized *Wikisource* index ("1911 *Encyclopædia Britannica*").

In addition to the resources mentioned in Pablo Brescia's essay in this volume, some of the movies based on scripts Borges wrote by himself or in collaboration with Bioy Casares are available on *YouTube*. These include *Invasión* (*Invasion*) and *Les autres* (*The Others*), directed by Hugo Santiago, and *Los orilleros* (*The Hoodlums*), directed by Ricardo Luna. Borges also participated in creating the screenplay for *Días de odio* (*Days of Hate*), based on "Emma Zunz" and directed by Leopoldo Torre Nilson. Other adaptations of his short stories include *Hombre de la esquina rosada* (*Man on Pink Corner*), directed by René Mugica; *The Immortal*, directed by Ewan Jones Morris; and *Cacique Bandeira* (*Boss Bandeira*), based on "El muerto" ("The Dead Man") and directed by Héctor Olivera. *Los cuentos de Borges* (*Borges's Short Stories*), a 1993 Spanish television series, is available on DVD and includes cinematic versions of "El Sur" ("The South"), "La muerte y la brújula" ("Death and the Compass"), "La intrusa" ("The Interloper"), "La historia de Rosendo Juárez" ("The Story from Rosendo Juárez"), and "El evangelio según Marcos" ("The Gospel according to Mark").

There are a few online tools and resources that make it easy for students and instructors learning about humanities computing for the first time to study Borges's texts quantitatively. *Voyant Tools* (voyant-tools.org) is a web-based application that offers a set of options for analyzing a document's elements or tokens, providing tables with frequencies as well as visualizations of the main linguistic characteristics of the text. While it is possible to generate concordances with *Voyant*, a far better and more versatile tool is *AntConc* (www.laurenceanthony.net/software/antconc), a freeware program that is available for Windows, MacOS, and Linux. *AntConc*'s easy-to-use interface allows users to look up keywords in context, create word lists, and compare different documents to each other. While *AntConc* is slightly more sophisticated than *Voyant*, Heather Froehlich's tutorial, "Corpus Analysis with AntConc," provides a quick and excellent introduction to the program and teaches users how to create clusters of words that frequently appear together; "collocates," or groups of words that are statistically likely to appear together; and simple visualizations of concordances. These tools could be very useful for students wishing to explore how Borges frequently connects similar ideas across texts. There are several digital humanities projects on the web that can serve as teaching tools and as inspiration for students wishing to create their own projects. Nora Benedict's *Mapping Borges in the Argentine Publishing Industry* (norabenedict.github.io/borges/index.html) is an interactive map visualizing the Buenos Aires publishing and literary world (publishers, printers, booksellers) during the first half of the twentieth century and Borges's connections to it. Jonathan Basile's *Library of Babel* (libraryofbabel.info) is a web-based version of Borges's idea of a place that would contain every book that has ever been (and could ever be) written by using all possible combinations of written characters. Rhizome, a group that creates born-digital art and culture and is affiliated with the New Museum in New York City, has designed *Borges: The Complete Works* (borgeslibrary.com), a giant word-search game using all the writings from Borges, both in Spanish and in English. Finally, Ricardo Vazquez and Christopher D. Warnes have created the digital project *"El jardín de senderos que se bifurcan": Testigos de una escritura* (borges.pitt.edu/v-machine/samples/huellas_project.html), which employs Balderston's genetic criticism approach to create an online application that allows users to study and compare different manuscripts of Borges's story "El jardín de senderos que se bifurcan" ("The Garden of Forking Paths"; *OC* 1: 867–74; *CF* 119–28).

Part Two

APPROACHES

Introduction: The Challenges and Rewards of Teaching Borges Today

José Eduardo González

The challenge of teaching Borges today is to navigate the difficulty of his prose while making it relevant to contemporary readers. MLA survey participants who shared their experiences teaching Borges almost unanimously point to his erudition—the myriad of references and allusions to books, thinkers, religious concepts, historical events, and so on—as the greatest hurdle that their students encounter. At the same time, these references are often what students find most interesting about Borges's work. Should students spend their time locating these references, or is their time better spent trying to understand the story? The answer in both cases is no, because the experience of reading and enjoying a typical Borgesian text requires that students submerge themselves in the complex web of intertextualities that shape his writings. Thus, to navigate the difficulty of Borges's texts while making them relevant to today's readers, we need to show how his daring, unconventional work, some of which was written and published a hundred years ago, connects with our current social, cultural, and political reality.

Borges's erudition may seem unapproachable for readers who lack familiarity with ancient history, mythology, or intellectual history. Some of the responses to our survey mentioned strategies to help students overcome the feeling of being overwhelmed by his erudition. These strategies, also found in many of the essays in this collection, include introducing important themes with the most straightforward texts first, alerting students to important concepts before starting an assignment, reading slowly, spending ample time on each story or poem, previewing the vocabulary students will encounter, or tracking down references using the "Finder's Guide" on the Borges Center website.

Borges's interest in abstract theories, temporal concepts, and metaphysics can give the impression that the author is not interested in personal experiences. However, focusing on how his experiences and inner conflicts are transmuted and represented in his literary texts can help students visualize an author with a deep sense of history, molded by private situations that we all can relate to. Without a doubt, one of the most problematic areas of teaching Borges today has to do with his erratic political comments and antidemocratic positions. His support of the military juntas that governed Argentina in the 1970s and his positive assessment of Augusto Pinochet's dictatorship in Chile have received well-deserved criticism. It is important to make students aware of his lesser-known comments and actions when the truth about the atrocities of the so-called Dirty War became known. He denounced the "disappearances" and welcomed the return to democracy in 1983. But, most importantly, the study of the anti-fascist, anti-totalitarian themes that run through his work should generate reflective moments for our students that bring contemporary political practices and situations into focus. The ethical stance of the most metaphysical of fiction writers shows how the political dimension of his work should be especially effective in motivating students.

Borges's self-declared agnosticism, combined with his fascination with different religious ideas and practices, which play a central role in many of his poems and stories, can be confusing to students. However, this writing practice can be presented as an example of Borges's interest in the innate human desire to find meaning and our endless attempts to construct systems of thoughts to explain the universe. Borges holds a radical skeptic view about the possibility of human beings understanding the universe. For him, the human mind is always seeking to impose an artificial order on what would otherwise be a chaotic reality. With the help of an insufficient tool—language—human beings create coherent mental constructs whose internal consistency only betrays their falsehood. Borges's position in many of his texts, that all human knowledge is fictitious but that people are irresistibly attracted to fictional designs over truth, remains the aspect of his writings that makes his fiction relevant today. An effective teaching approach to Borges, then, would be to focus on the central role that theories of social constructionism play in today's view of the world and in contemporary debates about human relationships. Some of the most original and innovative contemporary readings of Borges focus on looking for those ideas in his work that defy normative thinking and conventional assumptions. The study of Borges should encourage our students to challenge their preconceived notions by taking risks that enable them to critically analyze traditional beliefs.

According to data available through the *Open Syllabus* project, a website that provides access to millions of English-language syllabi from over a hundred countries, Borges is the most widely taught Spanish-language writer in the world. Miguel de Cervantes is a distant second.[1] A more interesting result, however, is the type of courses that include Borges's books or stories. *Labyrinths: Selected Stories and Other Writings*, the popular English-language anthology of his work, is used not only in courses on Spanish and English literature and philosophy, as expected, but also, surprisingly, in architecture, theology, history, film, and library science courses. Also surprisingly, the book is taught in quite a few courses on basic computer skills. Considering the diversity of academic courses that utilize Borges's writings, this book aspires to provide a range of teaching and interpretative resources for different instructional levels. While the strategies included in these essays can easily be modified depending on the target student group, a level-based arrangement is followed: The first essays in part 2 focus on the introduction of some of Borges's main themes. This section is followed by essays that focus on strategies for teaching Borges in more complex settings, in new contexts, or in conversation with nonliterary fields. Part 2 ends with essays whose teaching approaches employ slightly more scholarly oriented methodologies.

Part 2 consists of four sections that emphasize different pedagogical scenarios. The essays in the first section, "Instructional Contexts," present practical and historical information useful for many teaching purposes and situations. The essays by Luciano Martínez, Stephen Buttes, and Rhona Trauvitch discuss how to design and develop courses that account for, among other things, Borges's place in world literature while helping students learn to read and write critically about his works. Carol Mastrangelo Bové and Max Ubelaker Andrade each provide readers with the necessary context to use Borges's texts in order to discuss complex questions about religion, ethnicity, and gender. In these two essays the authors show how to use Borges to challenge the conventional expectations of students.

The second section, "Classroom Creativity," contains essays that outline a variety of interpretative frameworks that could be used with students of any level. Using humor (Christian Reed), film (Pablo Brescia), and translation (Emron Esplin), these essays propose new ways to engage students and help them study Borges in connection to fields outside literary criticism. These essays offer alternative paths to connecting Borges with students' interests—whether this means creating games based on Borges's stories, comparing different translations of the same text, or reading Christopher Nolan's films as Borgesian tales.

The third section, "Pedagogical Strategies and Innovations," includes a group of essays that combine theoretical and critical insights with teaching strategies to implement in the classroom. Kate Jenckes helps her students explore philosophical themes such as the autonomy and sovereignty of the subject and uses *Google Doodles* and music, among other strategies. In creative writing workshops, Audrey Harris Fernández compares Borges and Sandra Cisneros and their approaches to mentorship, to the metonymic use of body parts, and to urban encounters and dis-encounters. Kimberly A. Nance shows how to use game theory concepts, such as a player's desire not only to discover and explore but also to return and replay, in order to understand Borges's literary games. Jeffrey P. Thompson and Manuel Chinchilla make connections between Borges's short stories, the novel, and the podcast in order to highlight issues of racial and ethnic identity, masculinity, and prejudice. Stephanie Contreras and Aldo Mendoza employ a wide variety of strategies to help students understand the plot, historical context, paratextual content, and narratological techniques of one of Borges's most famous stories, "The House of Asterion."

The final section, "Scholarly Perspectives," includes a group of essays that focus on the sources of Borges's work and on the historical, literary, and material history of these texts. Daniel Balderston utilizes Borges manuscripts to teach students about the author's compositional practice, paying attention to the text as process. Nora Benedict is interested not only in Borges's writing practices but also in the material evidence of the production and manufacture of Borges's works. Adelaida López-Mejía focuses on identifying the historical sources of Borges's stories and on demonstrating how he often distorts them for aesthetic purposes. While the essays in this section appear to be aimed at more advanced students, their insights are meant to be relevant to the teaching of Borges at all levels, both in literature courses and in other disciplines.

NOTE

1. *Open Syllabus*'s ranking of authors is inaccurate because it does not take into account partial spellings and misspellings of an author's name. Instead, I used the author search box available on *Open Syllabus Analytics* (analytics.opensyllabus.org) and aggregated the results. As of 14 March 2024, Borges was mentioned 4,218 times; Cervantes, 1,780; and Federico García Lorca, 1,764.

Teaching Borges Effectively: A Pedagogy of Literary Reading

Luciano Martínez

Even as a college professor, Jorge Luis Borges was unorthodox and avant-garde. He rejected historical approaches to the study of literature, those that delved into literary criticism and the compilation of critical bibliographies or that emphasized literary movements.[1] In consonance with his vision of the reader as writer, Borges advocated for a teaching of literature centered on the aesthetic pleasure that emanates from the act of reading, "la emoción singular llamada belleza, ese misterio hermoso" 'that singular emotion called beauty, that lovely mystery' when art happens (*Biblioteca personal* iv; *SNF* 513). As he explained in an interview, "I judge literature in a hedonistic manner. That is, I judge literature according to the pleasure or emotion it inspires in me. I've been a professor of literature for many years, and I'm not unaware that the pleasure caused by literature is one thing and the historical study of that literature is another" (*Seven Conversations* [1982] 83). For twelve years (1956–68), Borges taught English literature at the University of Buenos Aires, where he abided by a teaching philosophy that sought to inspire students to approach literature as art and, as such, to read in personally meaningful ways, to uncover beauty not as a property of the text but rather as a subjective response.[2]

In this Borgesian vein, the central concern of this essay is to elaborate a sound teaching approach to Borges that retains a sense of transcendence and beauty so that students can be moved, changed, and inspired to read critically, write persuasively, and speak with confidence about Borges. Certainly, teaching Borges seems a daunting and overwhelming task. How does one approach works constructed as intricate mosaics of quotations from world literature, absorbed and transformed in irreverent ways? How does one address Borges's constant retooling and reorganization of Argentine literary traditions? How does one teach short stories that embrace metafiction and anticipate the principal topics of postmodern critical theory? How does one elicit connections between Borges's texts and their multiple philosophical and religious references?

These are valid questions that immediately confront us with the problem of what to include in a course and of the limits of interpretation. A prerequisite for teaching a class on Borges is to try not to cover too many texts. A crowded syllabus will detract from substantive class discussions and in-depth analysis. Borges's texts yield multiple readings, but presenting too many interpretations can be discouraging and intimidating to students, particularly at the beginning of the semester. Avoiding the propensity to describe every intertextual and cultural reference is crucial, particularly if a reference is not central to explaining how a particular text achieves its effects. With careful course design, engaging activities, and meaningful assessment, not only is it possible to teach Borges effectively, it can also be an enjoyable and long-lasting, transformative experience for students. Challenges aside, the preeminence of the short narrative form, Borges's metaphysical concerns (the questioning of identity, time, truth, and human knowledge), and the connections of his works with mathematics and natural sciences present remarkable opportunities to reinvigorate the humanities curriculum and attract a diverse group of students.

Broadly defined, effective teaching refers to "teaching that is oriented to and focused on students and their learning" (Devlin and Samarawickrema 112). Effective teaching occurs when learning goals are aligned with instructional activities and assessments that afford students opportunities to demonstrate and practice the skills articulated in those goals ("Teaching Principles"). In this regard, setting a few achievable and measurable goals for a Borges course can help ease instructor anxiety by narrowing the amount of works and topics that will be included and limiting expectations about students' close reading skills. For instance, the following could be three basic learning goals for a Borges course: identify and analyze Borges's major themes, analyze Borges's works through class discussion and writing, and generate and articulate personal responses to Borges's short stories. This set of goals implies a student-centered approach to literature instruction, where interpreting Borges emerges as a dialogic practice. Coverage will be narrow because the goal is not to present exemplary and exhaustive interpretations but rather to help students progressively develop critical interpretative skills.

What follows is a discussion of how to effectively teach a special topics course devoted to the works of Borges, either in Spanish or in translation, for third-year and fourth-year college students. Nonetheless, these instructional suggestions can easily be adapted to any survey course that includes Borges. I also hope it will be informative in a wider sense, showing how to develop a literature class that accounts for a pedagogy of literary reading, which requires time, dedication, and concentration. For clarity, the essay is organized in three sections: course design and development, class implementation, and assessment.

Less Is More: Course Design and Development

Finding the right approach to presenting Borges's texts involves recognizing the parameters of the class (e.g., course position within the curriculum, students' linguistic backgrounds and literary preparation, class size), the scope and sequence of the material that will be covered, and a set of learning goals that can realistically be accomplished. I have taught courses on Borges for many years, and I have experimented with two different approaches: a diachronic approach and a synchronic, thematic approach.

A diachronic approach, starting with Borges's first three collections of poems, or *poemarios*, lends itself easily to a capstone seminar for fourth-year students. Reading Borges chronologically allows students to discover how his literary project changed over time by identifying recurrent symbols and themes and analyzing how he consciously crafted his literary language and style. The historical background and ideological context surrounding Borges's literary production (e.g., his return to Argentina in 1921, where he wrote *Fervor de Buenos Aires* [*Fervor of Buenos Aires*] in the midst of a city completely changed by modernization and immigration, or "Poema conjetural" ["Conjectural Poem"] and the coup d'état of 1943) can easily be presented using a diachronic method.[3]

Creating a debate between Harold Bloom's and Beatriz Sarlo's critical views on Borges is an interesting way to organize a diachronic syllabus. In *The Western Canon*, Bloom offers a list of indispensable authors in Western culture, and there he places Borges, affirming that he is the most universal Latin American writer (471). Sarlo acknowledges that viewing Borges as a writer liberated from national confines is a gesture of aesthetic justice. Borges, in Sarlo's view, rightfully gained the liberty to explore diverse cultural traditions available to Latin American writers without being confined solely to themes and subjects rooted in their own countries of origin. However, according to Sarlo, "this process of triumphant universalization" disregards the ties that unite him to Argentinean and Latin American cultural traditions (*Jorge Luis Borges* [1993] 2). The goal of the course, then, is to read Borges from this double perspective: as a universal writer who transcends national borders and as a writer who seeks to reinvent the history and the traditions of his own country. Thus, a class could be structured around the dichotomy of "Argentine Borges" versus "Universal Borges." Beginning with Borges's first three poetry collections, *Fervor de Buenos Aires* (*OC* 1: 15–54), *Luna de enfrente* (*Moon across the Way*; *OC* 1: 115–34), and *Cuaderno San Martín* (*San Martín Copybook*; *OC* 1: 167–89)[4] as part of the "Argentine Borges" section, the curriculum could then progress to *Historia universal de la infamia* (*A Universal History of Iniquity*) as part of the "Universal Borges" section. Selections from *Ficciones* (*Fictions*) could also be categorized accordingly, using some stories that align with the Argentine paradigm ("El fin" ["The End"] and "El Sur" ["The South"], for instance) and others that fit within the universal perspective (such as "La biblioteca de Babel" ["The Library of Babel"] and "La lotería en Babilonia" ["The Lottery in Babylon"]).[5]

One of the challenges of this approach is that it requires a great deal of student engagement in order for students to draw evidence from multiple texts and make connections among ideas that appear scattered across multiple books, some of them read at the beginning of the semester, and others near the end. For this reason, it is important that the instructor focus on helping students draw meaningful connections among texts and that class time is set aside to summarize major ideas.

In contrast, a thematic or synchronic approach permits more focused class discussions because it allows close scrutiny of a single topic. Students can read before class with a better understanding of what will be the focus of the class, which is conducive to richer class discussions. The challenge in crafting such a course lies in establishing the organization of thematic clusters. These clusters may center on Borges's key themes and symbols, probe the intertextual links between Borges's works and global literature, or explore topics customized to suit curricular frameworks and student preferences (such as Borges's intersections with mathematics, physics, philosophy, etc.).

The following provide some examples of easily organizable thematic clusters: labyrinths, crime fiction, justice and revenge, infamy, memory and time, identity and doubles, reading and writing, gauchos and *compadritos* (the tough guys of the slums), the fantastic, the violence of history, and female characters.

If the course will be taught in English, it can be organized around problems of literary theory, philosophy, and cultural studies, and Borges's stories can serve as a launching pad for interdisciplinary explorations. In my teaching experience, this has proven popular among English majors and students from engineering, the natural sciences, and the social sciences, who find that the class offers something different than a traditional literature course. Possible topics include the following: the theory of intertextuality, the limits of the referential illusion, the relationship between knowledge and language, the dilemmas of representation, chaos and order, and history and narration. This type of course works better in English because it requires supplemental readings on these theoretical problems.

Reading Didactics and Class Implementation

A well-crafted syllabus paves the way for a teaching and learning process that is clear and methodical, setting aside unrealistic expectations and striking a good balance between breadth and depth—that is to say, achieving an adequate balance between the number of Borges's texts that will be covered and the degree to which students will analyze and discuss those texts. The success of a Borges course also rests on designing lesson plans that guide students as they learn how to read Borges's challenging fictional and nonfictional texts. A Borges class becomes convoluted when the instructor tries to do everything at once: introduce cultural-historical context, explain references and other elements of the text, and present a wide range of possible interpretations. Students' reading skills also need to be considered. Students are not tabulae rasae, and it is essential to have a good understanding of their literary backgrounds and language skills.[6]

Teaching Borges effectively, I believe, requires knowledge of a didactics of literary reading. An awareness of the reading phases can help an instructor organize a class efficiently and assist students as they interpret Borges's texts through close reading, or, to be more precise, "slow reading," which "teaches us to bring our full attention to what is before us on the page, to explore its ways of *making meaning* as well as what we may ultimately see as its messages" (Brooks 22). I cannot underscore enough how important it is for instructors to prepare students to develop this habit of close, or slow, reading, which accustoms them to engage with Borges's works through a patient, detailed, and slow process of deep reading and rereading.[7] How students read Borges matters much more than how many texts they read.

Reading is an interactive process between the reader and the text that occurs in different phases or stages known as pre-reading, while-reading, and post-reading.[8] The pre-reading phase introduces students to a particular Borges text, providing context, previewing the text, and encouraging students to make predictions and activate their world knowledge. A preview of vocabulary or providing lexical clues on how Borges uses adjectives and nouns, for example, can serve to facilitate the while-reading phase. These activities can be presented as a preview for the upcoming class, or they can be integrated into a reading guide.

While-reading refers to the act of reading in itself. Instructors can support students in the while-reading phrase by preparing a reading guide or an annotated text to help them confront difficult passages or problematic vocabulary. The post-reading phase generally takes place in class, where students share and validate their personal interpretations and establish connections with other texts. At this stage, reading becomes a "collective interpretative enterprise" (Brooks 22), and the instructor supplements students' interpretations with new ideas and suggestions. Writing assignments are also part of this stage, where students integrate their acquired knowledge. From my own teaching experience, using these reading phases to design lesson plans can help accomplish more in each class. Designing lesson plans with these phrases in mind enables a more productive use of class time and promotes lively discussions where the instructor's role is to help students develop good interpretations, not to give a lecture. Let me illustrate this point with an example: "Tema del traidor y el héroe" ("The Theme of the Traitor and the Hero"; *OC* 1: 889–91; *CF* 143–46) is undoubtedly one of Borges's "most complex fictions in technical and conceptual terms" (Fiddian, "Borges" 744), and without careful planning, teaching this short story can take an inordinate amount of class time. A pre-reading activity encourages students to activate prior knowledge of the topic by asking them to consider the links between history and fiction, provide examples of fictional representations that displaced real historical accounts, make predictions about the story based on the title, or find out information about the two Shakespeare plays quoted in the story. Students can also be asked to read the poem "Nineteen Hundred and Nineteen," by William Butler Yeats, quoted by Borges in the epigraph, and to investigate its relationship to the first year of the Anglo-Irish War (1919–21). When students finally start reading the short story, they will be able to better understand how the story achieves its intertextual effects in relation to history repeating itself, history copying fiction, or both. Given the complexity of the story—its tiered structure, the role of the author-narrator, and the characters who also act as readers—a reading guide is a must. The layers of historical correspondence between Ireland, Poland, the Republic of Venice, Greece, and ultimately South America and the Battle of Junín must be included in this reading guide.[9] By doing these pre-reading and while-reading activities, students will come to class prepared to discuss the short story at a deeper and more meaningful level. Otherwise, the instructor will have to spend the entire class presenting all these components, and students will not have enough time to integrate all this information with their initial at-home reading. In sum, the end goal of these reading activities is to enable deeper class discussions and to facilitate the exchange of interpretations. Particularly at the beginning of the semester, it is important to guide students so that they can read at home purposely, without getting stuck trying to fully understand the meaning of the text.

When teaching a Borges course in Spanish—at any reading stage—I encourage students to pay close attention to the linguistic, syntactic, and semantic aspects of Borges's writing. For example, I ask them to analyze the oxymorons that appear in the titles of the stories in *Historia universal de la infamia* ("atroz redentor" 'cruel redeemer,' "impostor inverosímil" 'improbable impostor' [*OC* 1: 597, 603; *CF* 6, 13]) or the meaning of "catálogo falaz" 'deceitful catalog' and "cipreses infaustos" 'dreary cypresses' in "Pierre Menard, autor del *Quijote*" ("Pierre Menard, Author of the *Quixote*"; *OC* 1: 842; *CF* 88). I also read out loud passages from Borges's texts, underscoring pauses and intonation, and ask students to pay attention to how Borges creates long enumerations and masterfully uses subordinate clauses. Students whose first language is not Spanish savor Borges's use of the Spanish language. Incorporating this language learning component is pedagogically valuable for two reasons. First, it is important to focus not only on what the text says but also on how it says it. Second, it helps students acquire metalinguistic awareness about their own use of the language, which will increase their academic writing proficiency. Comparing different English translations of Borges's texts with their Spanish originals is another activity that students greatly enjoy. A comparison of the four English translations of "La muerte y la brújula" ("The Death and the Compass") is a particularly engaging exercise for students.[10]

During the first week of class, I choose to focus not on fiction but rather on the analysis of two influential essays by Borges: "Sobre los clásicos" ("On the Classics"; *OC* 2: 134–35) and "La muralla y los libros" ("The Wall and the Books"; *OC* 2: 13–14; *SNF* 344–46). My goal is to offer students some insights on Borges's ideas about canon formation, the preeminence of the reader, and the aesthetic phenomenon as a deeply personal experience. After they read "La muralla y los libros," I ask students to elaborate their own personal list of things that "quieren decirnos algo, o algo dijeron que no hubiéramos debido perder, o están por decir algo" 'want to tell us something, or have told us something that we shouldn't have lost, or are about to tell us something' (*OC* 2: 14; *SNF* 346). This activity challenges students' preconceived ideas about Borges as an overly intellectual and inaccessible writer. We then move on to "El escritor argentino y la tradición" ("The Argentine Writer and Tradition"; *OC* 1: 438–44; *SNF* 420–27) to discuss how Borges envisions a literary tradition that is not bound by local color and regional customs and can borrow from dominant cultural centers with creative irreverence. I actualize these ideas by asking students to debate why readers from economically developed countries expect cultural productions from economically underdeveloped countries to reflect their "native," "original roots" and be "picturesque" and "autochthonous." Although students struggle with Borges's discussion of *gauchesca* literature, an artistic recreation of the gaucho speech and culture, "El escritor argentino y la tradición" is always very well received, particularly by bicultural and biracial students who struggle with duality and who empathize with Borges's refusal to be devalued as not being Argentine enough. The stories about slavery, racism, and xenophobia contained in *Historia universal de la infamia* are the perfect segue to surprise students and capture their attention.[11]

Borgesian Assessments

The greatest challenge in literature courses is, perhaps, aligning instruction and assessment—that is to say, finding the right tasks and assignments so that students can show what they have learned and how they have achieved the learning goals. I would like to propose three interactive and integrative assessment activities that allow students to reflect on their progress in interpretative literary analysis and become more self-aware of the quality of their work.

Jamboard, a free digital whiteboard developed by Google, can be a practical and interactive way for students to summarize key ideas throughout the semester because it allows real-time coauthoring. I provide a topic (e.g., labyrinths, female characters, stages of Borges's literary production, a provocative quotation from a literary critic, etc.), and students start writing succinct comments about it either individually or in groups.[12] Afterward, students read the entire *Jamboard* and share with the class additional observations. Students generally use the written notes to gain footing on the discussion, which is very useful during the first half of the semester.

Another assignment, which I call "The Death of the Author," is a proven pedagogical method to help students demonstrate to their peers what they know about Borges. The assignment also helps familiarize students with the idea of offering criticism of one another's papers in a truly Borgesian fashion. This activity requires some planning and logistics, and it is essential to have first taught "Pierre Menard, autor del *Quijote*." First, one student writes a short paper about a specific text that is clearly focused on a particular aspect (plot, character, point of view, theme, structure, etc.) of the work at hand. Second, before class I post the paper online without the author's name for the entire class to read. Finally, another student presents their own reading of the paper, evaluates its main argument and how it is articulated, and then offers constructive criticism and suggestions. The entire class also provides additional feedback.[13] Students put a lot of effort into writing this paper because they know their classmates will read and discuss it.[14] They experience how the text's meaning frees itself from its authorial intention and how their classmates' interpretations create a slightly different text. In other words, students learn firsthand about the effacement of the empirical author fostered by Borges and about the emergence of a "model author" created by each reader based on their own interpretative work (Eco 64).

The final assessment described in this essay is a scaffolded final paper. In a Borges course, as the semester progresses, students witness the evolution of their critical analysis skills, noting significant improvements in the quality of their later papers compared to their initial attempts. They often perceive their early work as naive and unsophisticated and feel frustrated with themselves and their grades. This is a usual phenomenon in Borges courses as students learn to read in a more rigorous, creative, and disciplined way. To remedy this situation, instructors can implement a structured approach where students write a single paper in four stages, refining it throughout the semester.[15] Initially, I ask students to write four short papers, analyzing in each one what they consider to be a major literary theme, or keyword, in Borges's short stories.[16] The final revised paper integrates these themes, featuring a brief introduction that ties the four themes together, and reflects on Borges's literary project. Additionally, students explain why these themes offer insights into his literary world. This final stage allows students to polish their writing (whether in Spanish or English) and make any necessary adjustments to the different sections. As a professor, I provide useful suggestions at each stage to help them with their revisions for the final submission. The scaffolding method, as Annie Dell'Aria observes, "increase[s] the incidence of pleasurable and rewarding research papers and decrease[s] the dreaded end-of-term chores," which, I might add, are particularly cumbersome when students must write in a second language.

Reflecting on his experience as a professor of English literature at the University of Buenos Aires, Borges said:

> I have preferred to teach my students, not English literature—which I know nothing about—but my love for certain authors, or, even better, certain pages, or even better than that, certain lines. And this is enough, I think. One falls in love with a line, then with a page, then with an author. Well, why not? It is a beautiful process. I have tried to lead my students toward it. (*Professor Borges* 259)

At first glance, teaching Borges effectively might seem an intimidating task, but it is achievable, and it can be a rewarding and memorable teaching and learning experience. The act of reading and writing about Borges makes students better readers of literature in general and gives them the opportunity to find common ground with their diverse group of peers as they walk together through Borges's labyrinths. As teachers, we must allow ourselves to learn how to innovate and hone our approach to teaching literature. Ultimately, we must think creatively about how to engage our students in this beautiful process of sharing our "fervor," our love for Borges, undeniably one of the most fascinating and influential writers in world literature.

NOTES

1. See "Borges y la Universidad" for a summary of Borges's controversial comments on the teaching of literature at the University of Buenos Aires and the formal reprimand he received from the university authorities.

2. "What Borges tries to do as a professor," as Martín Arias explains, "more than prepare his students for exams, is excite them and entice them to read the works, to discover the writers" (254). In the 1985 prologue to *Biblioteca personal* (*A Personal Library*), Borges reflects once again on his teaching career, highlighting how much he differed from formally trained literature teachers: "Los profesores, que son quienes dispensan la fama, se interesan menos en la belleza que en los vaivenes y en las fechas de la literatura y en el prolijo análisis de libros que se han escrito para ese análisis, no para el goce del lector" 'The professors, who are the ones who dispense fame, are interested less in beauty than in literature's dates and changes, and in the prolix analysis of books that have been written for that analysis, not for the joy of the reader' (*Biblioteca personal* iii; *SNF* 513).

3. Assigning selected chapters from Edwin Williamson's *Borges: A Life* as outside reading has proven a useful and economical way to give students a well-rounded historical and cultural context.

4. Translated selections from these books of poems appear in *Selected Poems*, edited by Alexander Coleman.

5. Needless to say, this is not a perfect critical arrangement: Borges's preoccupations with his homeland constantly reemerge, and there is always an element within the most seemingly non-Argentine text that hampers the possibility of reading Borges as a writer without nationality. Students feel empowered when they start identifying these "inconsistencies" and understand how Borges blends Latin American localism and universalism.

6. A student who is studying linguistics, for example, could read "Tlön, Uqbar, Orbis Tertius" in a creative and interesting way, while a political science student could reflect on totalitarian political systems in "La lotería en Babilonia."

7. David Mikics, in *Slow Reading in a Hurried Age*, offers valuable new ideas on how to practice slow reading in the digital age, which can be pedagogically useful with students that are primed to practice skimming and rapid informational reading (17).

8. For an explanation on pre-, while-, and post-reading stages—known in Spanish as "prelectura," "lectura," and "postlectura"—see Ibrakhimovna; Marín 20–23; and Toprak and Almacioğlu.

9. See Fiddian, "Borges," for an in-depth analysis of these layers of historical parallelisms and the story's *mise en abyme* structure.

10. I am referring to the translations of "La muerte y la brújula" by Anthony Kerrigan (Borges, *Ficciones* 129–41), Donald A. Yates (Borges, *Labyrinths* 76–87), Norman Thomas

di Giovanni and Borges (Borges, *"The Aleph"* 41–53), and Andrew Hurley (*CF* 147–56). Certain noun phrases ("temeraria perspicacia," "rigurosamente extraño," "periódica serie," and "interminable odor") present translation challenges. The four translations present compelling lexical and semantic differences in the last two paragraphs of the story, and students enjoy discussing the different solutions. This is also a good opportunity to introduce students to Borges's avant-garde ideas on translation.

11. "El atroz redentor Lazarus Morell" ("The Cruel Redeemer Lazarus Morell"; *OC* 1: 597–602; *CF* 6–12), "El impostor inverosímil Tom Castro" ("The Improbable Impostor Tom Castro"; *OC* 1: 603–06; *CF* 13–18), and "El asesino desinteresado Bill Harrigan" ("The Disinterested Killer Bill Harrigan"; *OC* 1: 616–18; *CF* 31–34) in particular have tremendous cultural relevance these days and never fail to engage students and create lively class discussions.

12. At the end of one semester, I created a *Jamboard* titled "Ahora Borges es tuyo. ¿Cómo es 'tu Borges'?" ("Now Borges is yours. How is 'your Borges'?"). Students wrote insightful reflections about Borges's literary project and how their perceptions of him changed throughout the course.

13. I have often witnessed how the student who wrote the paper detaches from it and becomes one of its fiercest critics.

14. Regarding this pedagogical exercise, in an anonymous course evaluation, one student expressed the following: "We also got to have our mid-semester papers read and discussed in class by our peers (anonymously: we'd send them to him [the instructor] and he'd forward them, with no name, to the class). I absolutely loved the method and enjoyed getting feedback not only from him but also from my classmates. It is a shame that a lot of time none of us know what our classmates are writing about, or how they are going about it, so it was nice to have that option and see how they reacted to the texts we each produced."

15. As Annie Dell'Aria notes, "The basic means of scaffolding projects is to break down a large assignment into smaller steps, building one upon another. The assignments are spread throughout the term, encouraging students to manage their time effectively and to refine their thinking on a topic, and allowing you to flag any potential issues."

16. Students could also think about these literary themes as four keywords that, according to their own interpretations, could serve to define Borges's literary project. This scaffolding project is particularly useful when the class syllabus is organized by topics.

Against the Tropological: Teaching Borges in and with Literary History

Stephen Buttes

In the opening lines of his important and essential essay "Borges y la teoría" ("Borges and Theory"), Carlos Alonso argues that while Jorge Luis Borges "escribió muchos cuentos a lo largo de su carrera literaria . . . en realidad, escribió principalmente variaciones de dos narrativas fundamentales" 'wrote many stories throughout his career . . . in reality, he essentially used variations of two basic narrative structures' (437; my trans.). The first of these two structures is one in which two diametrically opposed beings, concepts, categories, or discourses are swapped, as exemplified in "The Circular Ruins." The second is one that explores the process and effects of gaining (or failing to gain) a total and absolute knowledge, as exemplified in "The Aleph." Alonso asserts that the variations on these narrative structures are "múltiple[s] aunque no infinit[as]" 'multiple but not infinite' (437; my trans.), and this point enables him to correct the kinds of misreadings of so-called Borgesian tropes that have been essential both to the creation of poststructuralist thought and to the poststructuralist reading of Borges's fictions. While poststructuralist criticism stakes its approach to Borges on an open-ended linguistic and literary system that makes any and all meanings undecidable, Alonso argues that Borges actually proceeds from the premise of a closed and historically specific linguistic and literary system, which is what makes his narrative procedures both possible and intelligible. Alonso argues that we must read Borges within history and within his situation as a writer on the periphery of the world literary and capitalist system if we are to grasp and understand his literary production. The point can be put more directly this way: the best approach to reading Borges and, therefore, teaching Borges is to recognize him not as an exemplar of open-ended linguistic play apt to be evoked at any moment for nearly any purpose but instead as the producer of a historically situated engagement with literary form. This engagement is shaped by the specific relationship Borges creates with the art of the past as he seeks to confront and meet the needs of the historical moment as he understands them. This critical approach enables us not only to develop a better understanding of specific works Borges wrote but also to analyze more fully and critically the centrality that has been ascribed to Borges in a wide array of debates about literature.

Below I argue that, rather than *a* course *on* Borges, an approach that focuses on Borges's narrative variations can assist in reorganizing our understanding of the world literary system and open up novel ways of teaching literature across a variety of courses for undergraduate students. I discuss three kinds of courses: an intermediate literature survey in Spanish, a global comparative literature course in English, and an advanced Argentine literature course in Spanish.

Intermediate Literature Survey in Spanish

Students often encounter Borges in intermediate surveys taught in the target language. Here students are generally minors or majors in Spanish and are often less interested in the literature itself than they are in improving their spoken Spanish in order to achieve personal or career goals. Because many of these students are motivated by the career-boosting possibilities that fluency in Spanish promises, there are often some who are variously skeptical of or frustrated with having to take a literature course. It is, of course, absolutely the case that knowledge of non-English languages is a distinguishing factor for graduates on the job market, but this goal of increasing job marketability often obscures students' understanding of the relevance and purpose of studying literature. In other words, the skepticism or frustration of some students is sometimes rooted in the desire for what they understand as more practical information or useful language skills.

I foreground these generalized understandings of Spanish language study and the related perceptions of literature courses directly in the course description. On the one hand, we want students to examine critically the notion that literature is an elitist endeavor that has little to do with matters of everyday life. On the other hand, in recognizing the relevance of literature to matters of daily life, we do not want to annihilate the specificity of the literary. We want students to improve in their reading, writing, speaking, and listening in Spanish, but we don't want the focus on those language skills to eclipse their ability to understand the wide array of debates that structure the field of literary and cultural studies in the Spanish language. To address these dilemmas, the first of Borges's narrative variations—the swapping of two diametrically opposed beings—can be useful for syllabus design. Student perceptions about the relationship between the development of language skills (often understood as useful, practical, or non-elitist) and courses in literature (sometimes understood as pointless, an unnecessary obstacle, or elitist) can be integrated directly into the course and examined critically by utilizing Borges's literary production.

I begin the semester with a short text by Borges: the prologue to *El informe de Brodie* (*Brodie's Report*; *OC* 2: 701–02; *CF* 345–47). While this text does, of course, make use of some of Borges's favorite tropes, I choose to begin the class with this text because its relative brevity and use of the narrative of swapping opposites enables students to use the course context to examine critically their own suppositions about studying the Spanish language and literary works written in that language. In the prologue, Borges examines his own literary production, explaining how he sought to execute "la redacción de cuentos directos" 'the writing of plain tales' as well as narratives that are "escritos de manera directa" 'composed in a plain style' (*OC* 2: 701; *CF* 345) rather than appeal to so-called Borgesian tropes. The goal of our analysis is not to contrast a tropological Borges with a nontropological Borges but instead to examine two key passages that help frame the course. After giving a mini-lecture to provide background explaining that Borges was not only seeking a new style but also seeking to return to previous themes, I ask students to analyze two passages: one in which Borges asserts that he is not "un escritor comprometido" 'an *auteur engagé*' (*OC* 2: 701; *CF* 345), "a politically committed writer" (my trans.), and another in which Borges cites the Argentine novelist Roberto Arlt's skepticism of the utility of *el lunfardo* in literature about the lives of working people. Noting in his citation of Arlt's point of view on *el lunfardo* that it was a literary strategy developed by playwrights, novelists, and tango lyricists to evoke the vocabulary and speech patterns of workers and the poor rather than an invention of workers and the poor themselves, Borges justifies both his own understanding of *el lunfardo* as "una broma literaria" 'a literary put-on' (*OC* 2: 702; *CF* 347) and his decision to excise it from his stories about the working class and poor in *El informe de Brodie*.

I ask students to work in groups to describe in their own words what Borges means by "escritor comprometido" and *lunfardo*. Once they have developed some basic ideas, we discuss them as a class, organizing the class responses on the board under each of the two topics. I then ask the groups to return to their discussions to consider why Borges might emphasize that his stories avoid utilizing *el lunfardo* and why he emphatically asserts that they cannot be categorized as politically committed. The point we emphasize in these discussions is that *el lunfardo* emerged through the production of art and art commodities created to circulate within particular market niches. Students are generally able to conclude that *el lunfardo* is not directly useful for understanding the whole of working-class language since, as Borges notes, this specialized vocabulary appears only in the slums of Buenos Aires as the by-product of workers' consumption of cultural commodities such as tango lyrics or *sainetes*, short theatrical works often set in tenements. Similarly, students are also generally able to recognize that "literatura comprometida," or "politically committed literature," at least as Borges presents it here, tends to have specific lessons or specific information that readers are meant to learn and is generally premised on the knowledge, narratives, and language that working people need to know in their daily lives in order to struggle against exploitation, make ends meet, and live together in a democratic community. For Borges, the solutions proposed in "la literatura comprometida," like *el lunfardo*, may or may not coincide with the actual strategies developed within working-class life, which Borges seeks to represent in his fictional narratives written in this "plain style."

With these two ideas in mind, I ask the groups to consider one last question: Why would Borges consider his "plain style" a useful tool for addressing the deficiencies he identifies with politically committed writers and *el lunfardo*? This conversation takes us back to the observations in the mini-lecture at the beginning of the class session. Using a "plain style" is a strategy by which Borges gains literary elbow room to write a good story rather than get arcane details right: "I don't have to become a historian or newspaperman. I can just dream away. And if the facts are essentially true, I don't have to worry about the circumstances" (Borges, "Post-Lecture Discussion" 719). By engaging in this conversation, by the end of the class session, we have reworked the notion of "la utilidad" 'practical information'—knowing certain vocabulary words or learning sets of information predetermined as useful but that may or may not correspond to the so-called real world and that may be less useful than getting to the truth a good story conveys. Borges's swapping variation becomes an effective way to engage students with a wide variety of academic and professional goals and helps them understand how an exploration of Latin American literature across various historical eras, cultural contexts, and literary genres can fall under the category of "utilidad" despite its lack of direct utility in a nonacademic workplace.

Global Comparative Literature Course in English

Borges is often taught in translation in world literature courses or in introductions to comparative literature. Indeed, works by Borges are featured in both *The Norton Anthology of World Literature* and *The Longman Anthology of World Literature*, both of which are popular textbooks for these kinds of university courses (Puchner et al.; Kadir and Heise). Both anthologies include "The Garden of Forking Paths" and "The Library of Babel," though the *Longman* also includes several other texts by Borges. Because the course described in this section, like the one in the target language, seeks to introduce students to a breadth of works rather than focus on just a few, I tend to organize a course like this one in a similar way: by utilizing one of Borges's narrative variations as a tool for thinking about and organizing our approach to a wide variety of texts. The course I teach focuses on the literatures of the five language traditions taught in my department: Spanish, French, German, Japanese, and Arabic. At the outset of the course, we discuss ways we might approach comparing and organizing an understanding of such a wide diversity of works. In the first session of class, we read several very short works: Franz Kafka's "The Trees," Augusto Monterroso's "The Dinosaur," and a fragment of Valeria Luiselli's *Tell Me How It Ends* (40–42). In each of these, there is a central image each author utilizes to organize and make sense of the world: "tree trunks in the snow" (Kafka, "Trees"), "the dinosaur was still there" (Monterroso), and the narrative scaffolding of "Border, Court, Home, Community" (Luiselli 41). In groups, students discuss how each image produces a particular way of organizing and understanding a narrative or collection of narratives, their internal relations, and their relations to one another. This conversation sets us up to work with an essay by Gail Finney titled "The Reign of the Amoeba," in which Finney uses a visual shorthand to describe four different institutional models for organizing the production of scholarship in comparative literature: the wheel, the tandem, the umbrella, and the grab bag. Students describe these models, and then they discuss how each image produces a different account of the relationships between literary works from multiple language traditions.

By engaging in this initial utilization of a central image as a tool for critical practice, students are prepared to read two short stories by Borges for the second day of class: "The Library of Babel" (*CF* 112–18) and "The Aleph" (*CF*

274–86). These are texts that explore the process and effects of gaining (or failing to gain) a total and absolute knowledge. By placing Borges in dialogue with the texts just mentioned, the total library and the Aleph can be grasped not only as Borges's reflection on (and horrified reaction to) the possibility of gaining total and absolute knowledge but also as a tool for reflecting on the relationship between the literary traditions we will study in the class. As one might suspect, this conversation leads us directly to "The Argentine Writer and Tradition," where Borges lays claim to "toda la cultura occidental" 'the whole of Western culture' (*OC* 1: 442; *SNF* 426) as the Argentine tradition. While we do cover the specific arguments he makes in the essay, the goal is not to focus students' attention solely on Borgesian tropologies or on what Borges contributes to world literature. Instead, we focus on his observation, for example, that *Don Segundo Sombra*, the novel that many Argentine nationalists of the early and middle twentieth century considered Argentina's "tipo de libro de nacional" 'characteristic national book' (*OC* 1: 441; *SNF* 424), is, in fact, a book that is the product of a direct dialogue with Mark Twain's *Huckleberry Finn*, Rudyard Kipling's *Kim*, and the aesthetic approaches to narrative developed in the French salons of Montmartre. In other words, we use the essay not simply to focus on Latin America but also to interrogate the underlying organizations and structures that studying a literary work can reveal. That is, we consider what it would mean to understand a "characteristic national book" as a particular set of relations between a multiplicity of traditions, a perspective that would require a reassessment of standard national-language approaches to literature, or what David Damrosch calls an awareness of the "presence of the world within the nation" (134). This enables the course to progress from Borges to a sustained engagement with, for example, the relationship between the literatures of France and francophone Africa, between internal regions within the Arabic-speaking world, or between Japan and the West, with a focus on how an imaging of modes of organization interfaces with the imaging of relations between national literary traditions as exemplified in the wheel, the tandem, the umbrella, and the grab bag described by Finney.

Advanced Argentine Literature Course in Spanish

The final kind of course I want to discuss is an advanced Argentine literature course. Borges, as might be expected, is an integral part of the course, and we read a significant number of his stories during the semester. But as with the other courses, the goal is not to develop a stronger grasp on Borgesian tropes but instead to utilize both of his narrative variations as tools to understand what kind of problem is presented by Argentine literature. The choice to read numerous works by Borges is not arbitrary but instead is driven by Borges's particular approaches to what would seem to be nationally specific elements of Argentine culture. Tango music or gauchos, for example, do function as solutions to the problem of marking the distinctness of the Spanish American (or Argentine) situation, but these are available as potential solutions elsewhere as well, not just in

Argentina. In other words (and again echoing "The Argentine Writer and Tradition"), a work need not be uniquely Argentine or be reducible to Argentina's national borders in order to be fully Argentine. This observation obviously reconfigures what it might mean to study Argentine literature, and it opens the door to a productive set of complications to identifying our object of study.

In the first weeks of class, we read sections of a series of radio conferences Borges gave in 1965 on the topic of tango (*El tango*). These came during his time collaborating with the tango composer and performer Astor Piazzolla, a collaboration that produced both the record *El tango* and Borges's poetry collection *Para las seis cuerdas* (*For the Guitar*). In these conferences, Borges develops parallels between Argentine gauchos and Montana cowboys and between Argentine tango and US jazz. His goal in developing these parallels is to articulate a continuity between two distinct phenomena (which echoes the swapping variation) that, at the same time, avoids collapsing all distinctions into a singular sameness (which echoes the totality variation). In this way, we arrive at the notion that one of the key problems Borges identifies in his approach to Argentine literature is that, through the particular literary forms they create, authors must formulate their status as simultaneously being fully Argentine and not being (or not only being) Argentine (i.e., not being reducible to whatever elements have been ascribed to an idea of Argentina in a given historical moment). While we explore this through classic themes in Argentine literature, I also help students begin to see that Borges arrives at solutions that parallel those that modernist visual artists like Frank Stella developed.

Engaging with the scholarship of art historians like Michael Fried, students and I work together to see in what ways Borges's approach to short fiction parallels Stella's approach to painting in works like *Moultonboro III* or *Chocura IV*.[1] Stella seeks to make his painting reducible neither to the shape of the support nor to the shapes painted on that support. He insists, instead, that his painting be understood as a unified whole constituted by the relationship between these elements, a whole that defeats any demand from a viewer that a painting have or be a unique shape. Stella's *Irregular Polygons* are discussed in Fried's essay "Shape as Form: Frank Stella's *Irregular Polygons*," which students read along with some pre-reading materials that provide an overview of Fried's thought and the necessary vocabulary to engage in discussion in Spanish on these topics. Stella utilizes the basic tools of painting to confront and solve for the time being or as never before what shape in painting makes possible by simultaneously being and not only being a shape. Similarly, Borges utilizes variations on the basic tools of narrative to articulate as never before what being Argentine makes possible for literary form and what literary form makes possible for notions of what is characteristically Argentine (i.e., simultaneously being and not being—or not only being—Argentine). This is something we explore by reading modernist visual art with a text like "Una tarde con Ramón Bonavena" ("An Evening with Ramón Bonavena"), written by Borges and Adolfo Bioy Casares (Borges et al.,

Obras completas [1979] 306–10; Borges and Bioy Casares, *Chronicles* [1976] 25–32). Students use Fried's essay to interrogate how Ramón Bonavena, the artist at the center of the story, conceives of his art. These visual parallels to the literary questions Borges and Bioy Casares are parodying in their story give students the opportunity to recognize that the aesthetic issues explored in the story expand beyond the supposedly provincial space of a 1960s Greater Buenos Aires.

Borges in the Basic and Intermediate Language Classrooms

I have argued that the best way to teach Borges is not *a* course *on* Borges. Instead, his works can be used as a tool for producing a critical engagement with the world literary system and its political realities. However, the kinds of activities that enable instructors to teach Borges in this way do not need to wait for advanced students, nor must they be relegated to courses in English translation. Indeed, Borges can very easily be integrated into the basic and intermediate language classroom, and the themes he explores can function as one possibility for engaging students early in their studies with the exciting and complicated ideas Borges makes available. This is, in fact, part of my own experience with Borges. My earliest encounter with Borges's work was in a basic language classroom, where my high school teacher Mary Ann Naser-Hall assigned us Borges's short text "Los dos reyes y los dos laberintos" ("The Two Kings and the Two Labyrinths"; *OC* 1: 1053; *CF* 263–64) not as a way to introduce Borgesian tropologies but instead as a strategy for using targeted grammar and vocabulary to draw and narrate our own interpretations of those labyrinths. Similarly, I can remember an early course I took with Dianna Niebylski at the University of Kentucky where we worked out the relationship between several M. C. Escher drawings and several Borges stories, eventually developing our own account of the narrative structure of Borges's stories. Inspired by and grateful for these experiences, I want to end this essay by giving one concrete example of how the totality variation could be integrated into a basic or intermediate language classroom.

In a basic language course, a fragment of "The Aleph"—the famous paragraph in which Borges attempts to express the totality he saw (*OC* 1: 1067–68; *CF* 282–84)—could be presented with some pre-reading activities in order to prepare students to create their own topically focused aleph utilizing the preterit and imperfect to structure their narrative description of an aleph focused on a specific vocabulary topic. This activity could be followed with a question that poses in basic form one of the themes Borges explores in the text: Does our topically focused aleph give the class access to a total knowledge of the topic? Why or why not? While this discussion of "The Aleph" cannot and will not exhaust analysis of the story, it does enable a level-appropriate and course-objective-appropriate introduction of the questions Borges poses in his work. And in this way we can meet the challenge of teaching Borges by engaging his questions and solutions in many different contexts, which can serve to reach students whenever and wherever we have the opportunity to teach them.

NOTE

1. The Museum of Modern Art has a freely available copy of William S. Rubin's book on Stella (for *Moultonboro III*, see Rubin 120). The Whitney Museum of American Art has freely available images of works like *Chocura IV* from its 2016 retrospective ("Frank Stella"). Various videos are available on *YouTube* so that students can see the size of the paintings in their exhibition space.

Borges and Identity Politics

Carol Mastrangelo Bové

Teaching Jorge Luis Borges's "Death and the Compass," "The Garden of Forking Paths," and "Emma Zunz" in the context of identity politics can be an effective pedagogical strategy today (*CF* 147–56, 119–28, 215–19). These three short stories in particular elicit reflection in students on complex questions of ethnicity and gender, though Borges may not have been writing with the concept of identity politics in mind given that it did not emerge until the late 1970s. I use the term *identity politics* to refer to "joint political action by individuals who feel themselves united by membership in a marginalized social category (ethnicity, gender, class, religion) that gives them common political interests" (Mohanty 1130).

I focus on critical readings of Borges's work that call attention to ethnicity and gender in vastly different, even contradictory, ways in order to engage students' thinking. I also examine the stories as translated versions of the original texts—in other words, I emphasize the role of the translator in shaping meaning, as understood in more recent developments in translation studies. Thus, I provide context for the stories as translations by familiarizing students with critics who discuss the original texts—which the teacher and students may not be able to do—and compare different English translations. Such a comparison enables students to understand more fully the political implications of race and gender in the translations of Borges's writing by considering the impact of the translator's choices. Finally, I examine genre theory's connections to identity politics using Borges's short stories as examples. For instance, teaching "Emma Zunz" as detective fiction enables a discussion of the genre's typical depiction of women as femmes fatales and shows how Borges's depiction of his protagonist and her struggle with marginalization differs. (See the appendix for prompts for discussion, oral reports, and papers.)

Focusing on a variety of readings—my own and those of literary critics and translators—uncovers ambiguity and nuance in Borges and mitigates a problem that often emerges in teaching literature, especially this writer and these stories. Students from a variety of disciplines tend to seek a monolithic message in a literary text. They often, for example, discuss the fact that Erik Lönnrot is overly confident in his skill as a detective in "Death and the Compass" and conclude that the principal import of the story is cautionary, warning against overconfidence. The ways in which Borges's stories subtly evoke questions of gender and ethnicity often perplex students, and many are initially unaware of the presence of such questions, particularly in "Emma Zunz." This is one of Borges's most difficult narratives and is also rare in its presentation of a female protagonist. Students tend to see it, for instance, as a story of revenge without sufficiently attending to the text's references to gender and sexuality or how gender and sexuality shape the daughter's plan to avenge her father's death as well as the overall meaning of the story.

This methodology does not use identity politics to produce didactic readings that teach a moral lesson condemning racism and sexism. Rather, the goal is to create a greater awareness of the nuances and ambiguities in Borges. In asking students to go beyond monolithic interpretations of the stories, instructors also find opportunities to discuss issues of identity politics and multiculturalism, ideas that are often applied in a reductive manner in and outside the academy to many of the best literary texts, where ambiguity and questioning often prevail over an unqualified message. In other words, class discussion broaches the issue of the repetitive and reductive qualities of some readings that bring the context of identity politics to a short story in a way that neglects the nuances of the narrative considered in its entirety.

As in "Death and the Compass," the political themes in "The Garden of Forking Paths" pose special challenges for students, which the pedagogical strategies proposed here can address. Borges foregrounds the issue of racism in the protagonist Yu Tsun's revelation that he has taken on the job of spying for the Germans to demonstrate his worth as a Chinese individual (*CF* 121). Students often do not perceive or understand the possible meaning of the ironic juxtaposition of the theme of anti-Asian racism and the brilliance of Yu Tsun's ancestor Ts'ui Pên.

After some introductory discussion of students' personal interpretations of "The Garden of Forking Paths," a good pedagogical strategy is to present two excellent but different, contradictory critical readings of the tale in order to have students engage more deeply with the story's subtexts, especially the implications for Chinese culture and Orientalism. They then begin to see other elements at work in the content and form of the narrative, and they become more likely to grasp the strength of Borges's writing in raising questions about marginalized Asian cultures, a topic particularly relevant in the United States today considering the coronavirus disinformation that has led to racist and xenophobic attacks against Asian individuals. The daunting problems brought to light by the Me Too movement and by the persistence of antisemitism also make clear the relevance of these stories in class discussion of the other two narratives.

Before discussing Borges's importance in confronting contemporary social issues, I thus begin class as many instructors may already do, by having students discuss their understanding of character, plot, literary methods, and underlying questions in the stories. In my course on detective fiction—which includes both more standard texts like Edgar Allan Poe's "Murders in the Rue Morgue" and a less usual title, Julia Kristeva's *The Old Man and the Wolves*—students come to recognize, often on their own, that the genre frequently lends itself to social critique. These introductory discussions might also focus on characteristics of a variety of artistic genres, including not only detective fiction as a subcategory of fiction but also the short story, the novel, and film. My students have the option to write their own short story in the early weeks of the course, an opportunity that invites a comparison of the genres of detective fiction and literary criticism, for example. We then move beyond discussions of genre to a consideration of two different readings of a particular story.

The opposing interpretations enable students to see previously unrecognized elements in the story, helping them add nuance and complexity to their own theses. Furthermore, they learn in this way how ambiguity in literary texts compels readers to examine their assumptions and, in doing so, to think more deeply about ethnicity, gender, and politics. One reading of "Death and the Compass," for instance, sees the story as a critique of antisemitism to the extent that Lönnrot focuses on Jewish mysticism in his overconfident, botched attempt to solve the murder. He implies that it is the Hasidim who have been killing Jewish victims. There is textual evidence to make such a reading credible, given that the detective obsessively pursues this possibility and speaks of his suspicions, while the police commissioner, Treviranus, demonstrates antisemitism in describing the Jewish faith as superstition. Providing biographical context enables students to read the story in light of Borges's stance against fascism. While such commentators as Gene Bell-Villada and Ilan Stavans examine the topic of the Jews in the tale, like most others they do not address the issue of identity politics or deal at length with racism (Bell-Villada [1981] 63–247; Stavans, "Borges"). Instructors can productively address these issues in class through a discussion of Lönnrot's obsession with Jewish mysticism and his attitude toward the Jews.

While we know, because of years of research on Borges, that Borges, as a person, and his stories are not antisemitic, it is pedagogically productive to present a second interpretation, very different from the first. According to this reading, the story itself is antisemitic in that many of the Jewish characters are either killed or are criminals, in particular the antagonist Scharlach, the murderer who captures and kills the detective. Discussing this reading of the plot and its subversion of the usual events in detective fiction becomes a teachable moment that clarifies the form of a short story and its impact on content. I discuss with the class how Borges subverts the genre that normally has the detective capture the criminal and how this subversion shapes a reading that sees antisemitism in the story. In this interpretation, Borges subverts the genre as he shapes an antisemitic narrative. Here an effective approach is to have class discussion attend carefully to the narrative's language in order to determine which reading is most accurate. In other words, is the story's critique of antisemitism in Lönnrot's focus on Jewish mysticism more credible than its prejudicial depiction of several Jewish characters, especially Scharlach, as criminals? John Beverley's discussion of Borges as "perhaps the most fascinating Latin American literary intellectual of the twentieth century" (93) emphasizes both his relevance to identity politics and the problematic nature of his politics, particularly in connection with "the reactionary and often racist positions" in his biography (94).

The presentation and discussion of the few critics who do broach the question of antisemitism make the point that students need to be able to identify reliable scholarly sources, as I emphasize in the pedagogy proposed throughout this essay. Some class time will for this reason focus on helping familiarize students with other readings and incorporating those readings in their essays. Geoffrey Shullenberger's "Borges's Jewish Uncanny and the Psychoanalytic Other: Uses of Paranoia in 'La muerte y la brújula'" is among the best, presenting the question of antisemitism in a complex, compelling way. Undergraduate students will likely need some help in understanding Shullenberger's reading. While Shullenberger argues overall that Borges's "Death and the Compass" reveals antisemitism, he also shows how the story is caught within antisemitism to the degree that it puts forward the nationalist idea that Jews and Jewish thought threaten the social order and the rational in the first half of the twentieth century in Argentina. In other words, for this critic, the story is both critical of antisemitism and antisemitic to the extent that it presents a nationalist notion prejudicial to Jews.

Alfred Mac Adam's article on translation and Borges, "Translation as Metaphor," helps the instructor convey these multiple meanings in "Death and the Compass." At the same time, it allows a recognition of the story as translated text and serves as a springboard for engaging students in thinking about the tale as a translation. The instructor can ask the class to read the first paragraph in Spanish and in two different English translations. For example, the Spanish "temeraria perspicacia" (*OC* 1: 892) describing Lönnrot in the opening sentence becomes "rash mind" in Norman Thomas di Giovanni's version (Borges, *"The Aleph"* 41) but is translated more literally as "reckless perspicacity" in Andrew Hurley's version (*CF* 147). Mac Adam finds the first inadequate to the original, implying that di Giovanni's phrase makes Lönnrot less of a target of Borges's critique of the detective in the story as a whole: he is "more like an impulsive adolescent than a man guilty of pride" (752). Discussing Mac Adam's comment may lead students to consider Lönnrot's fascination with Jewish mystical thought in a positive light, as one Jewish student in my class observed. Comparing di Giovanni's and Hurley's versions would thus prompt students to consider in more depth the two readings I have suggested and their vastly different takes on the theme of antisemitism in the story.

Published just one year before "Death and the Compass," "The Garden of Forking Paths" can elicit intense, relevant discussions of identity politics in many types of courses and particularly in those focused on the short story, detective fiction, or both. The same can be said about "Emma Zunz," which does not so much subvert the genre of detective fiction as create a new form of it.

In "The Garden of Forking Paths," a gun appears twice (*CF* 120, 127)—smoking in the second instance—and two murders occur (119, 127), the second remaining a mystery until the end, when Yu Tsun, the first-person narrator in most of the story, reveals that he will kill Dr. Albert to reveal to the German leader the name of the French town harboring the artillery supply. The detective, who otherwise does not appear in the story, is, in this reading, the reader who must solve the case. The instructor can easily elicit this idea from students, as I have often done in my classes. The instructor may also guide class discussion in this direction, an effective strategy to employ in teaching the detective fiction genre.

Racism surfaces early on in the narrative, in Yu Tsun's revelation that he is spying for the Germans during the First World War in order to prove his worth in the face of prejudice against the Chinese, as mentioned earlier. Solving the case may lead the reader to at least two different interpretations. One might conclude that Yu Tsun has acted courageously, confronting Orientalism, and has followed through on his plan to create a positive identity for himself by acting according to his principles as, for example, an existentialist worldview demands—that is, the Sartrean idea that one's actions determine identity. Another interpretation mobilizes the anti-war context provided by Yu Tsun's early observations: that the world has become increasingly violent to the point where peace is no longer possible ("pronto no habrá sino guerreros y bandoleros" 'soon there will be nothing but warriors and brigands' [*OC* 1: 869; *CF* 121]). In light of these comments on a world at war and of Yu Tsun's contrition in the final lines, the protagonist's murder of Dr. Albert is a terrible mistake. Albert is the scholar who makes clear to Yu Tsun the brilliance of Chinese culture—that is, of his ancestor Ts'ui Pên's novel. This reading fills Borges's conclusion with irony: the murder marks Yu Tsun, a Chinese professor of English who values literature and deplores war, as a violent man who in a sense destroys Chinese culture by killing the eminent sinologist. From this perspective, the story raises the question of self-loathing in a marginalized individual.

In discussing the conflicted character at the center of this story, one could highlight the excellent critical readings of Borges that students will find helpful in examining his writing. In a chapter titled "The Labyrinth of Trenches without Any Plan" (*Out of Context* 39–55), Daniel Balderston draws a parallel between the Chinese Yu Tsun and the Irish Madden (the captain working for the English who arrests Yu in the end) as acting at least in part in response to colonialism and imperialism. For Thomas O'Grady, who builds on Balderston's reading, both characters are conflicted in their projects to serve Germany and England, respectively. Balderston's chapter also connects Borges's story to James Joyce's *A Portrait of the Artist as a Young Man*, especially in its exploration of simultaneous, labyrinthine time versus the teleological, chronological path taken by Yu Tsun and Madden in the murders they commit—the first of Albert, the second of Runeberg (the spy working with Yu Tsun). O'Grady's and Balderston's approaches suggest that Borges's story, considered as a whole, is more accurately understood as a critique of Yu Tsun's and Madden's engagement in assassination than as an affirmation of their motives for spying and murder. While Haiqing Sun's essay does not discuss colonialism, imperialism, racism, or identity politics per se, it, too, supports the view that Borges's sympathies in this narrative lie more with civilization and art than with barbarism and war, as one might expect in a creative writer.

Violence and self-loathing also emerge in the eponymous character Emma Zunz, primarily in connection with her gender. Published in 1948, "Emma Zunz" resembles "The Garden of Forking Paths" to the degree that the protagonist commits murder for ostensibly ethical reasons only to experience regret and humiliation in the end. She feels these emotions both because of the sex act she engages in as preparation for the killing and because of the fact that her victim dies before hearing from her the reason for her act. That is, she punishes the textile mill owner for having unjustly accused her father of his own crime in stealing the factory's money. Many students perceive in the story the well-known conundrum of whether it is sometimes ethical to commit a crime—in this case, to murder Loewenthal, whom her father had denounced to her. But they often have difficulty interpreting the references to Emma's pathological fear of men and her sense that her parents' having sex was as humiliating for her mother as the sex she herself experiences with the sailor. This is difficult for both undergraduate and graduate students and for most readers to understand given the ambiguities and complexities of Borges's language.

It is not far-fetched to interpret the very strange characteristics of Emma as signs that she is mentally ill. The contradictions in her personality appear irrational. She prostitutes herself with the unknown sailor despite her fear of men to be able to accuse Loewenthal convincingly of having raped her once she has killed him. She goes to great lengths to avenge her father's death. She is convinced that he died by suicide after fleeing Buenos Aires, humiliated by the accusations against him and his term in prison. At the same time, another contradiction emerges in the narrative's portrayal of Emma: she notes similarities in the humiliating experience of sex with the sailor and her father's lovemaking with her mother, the third-person omniscient narrator tells us. The narrator's earlier comment made in connection with her lack of a boyfriend, that she feels a pathological fear of men, may well suggest an unstable psyche irrationally bent on murdering Loewenthal. She has, as several critics point out, no evidence for his theft other than her father's word. She nevertheless pursues the mill owner's murder. Eynel Wardi discusses Emma's pathological state in her psychoanalytic reading of the story, which requires more contextualization for undergraduates than for graduate students given the complexity of Wardi's reading.

One reading of mental illness in the story is that Emma's experience of sexuality as a traumatic event is connected both to her parents' past sexual experiences and to her own sexual experience with the sailor. In other words, the source of her fear of men is the belief that sex can be painful and humiliating for women. This is one plausible interpretation of the ambiguous references to Emma's attitude toward her father and its impact on her terror, her lack of a boyfriend, and, most important, her decision to kill Loewenthal.

An alternative reading sees the story as a narrative not about a mentally ill woman but about a woman who is resisting heteropatriarchy in its exploitation of women and the lower class. From this perspective, Borges creates a female protagonist, rare in his oeuvre, who represents an everywoman in her resistance to a heteropatriarchal culture that exploits marginalized groups. Loewenthal, the greedy, much hated owner of the textile mill, loves money more than his workers and women, including his own wife: "Había llorado con decoro, el año anterior, la inesperada muerte de su mujer—¡una Gauss, que le trajo una buena dote!—, pero el dinero era su verdadera pasión" 'he had decorously grieved the unexpected death of his wife—a Gauss! who'd brought him an excellent dowry!—but money was his true passion' (*OC* 1: 1017; *CF* 218). He represents, beyond the probable destroyer of Emanuel Zunz's reputation, the patriarch whose success depends on the exploitation of his male and female workers, including his wife. His portrayal as a "greedy Jew" also reintroduces the theme of antisemitism, enabling continuity in class discussion of "Death and the Compass" and "Emma Zunz." For Stavans, Emma's murder of Loewenthal "unsettles the stereotype of the money-grubbing Jew" ("Borges"): she is a Jew who resists injustice.

Both Bella Brodski and Stavans see Borges's story as highlighting a resistance to heteropatriarchy and its exploitation. In a convoluted essay—one that requires considerable explanation for undergraduates—Brodski connects the story to both feminist and deconstructionist theory, describing Emma as "an avenging angel" who expresses hatred for both economic and sexual exploitation (339). Stavans examines the story through the lens of Borges's thinking on the Jews—that is, how the author's writing helps readers understand what it means to be Jewish ("Borges"). His examination reveals the strength of "Emma Zunz" and "Death and the Compass" in promoting the notion of human rights for all, in the indirect methods of the finest literature. Like Brodski, he provides insight into Borges's choice of the protagonist's name. Brodski points out that the name "Emma" connects Emma to her father, whose birth name was "Emanuel," thus highlighting the sense of personal humiliation she experiences because of his shame (339–40)—and, I would add, the feelings of sadness resulting from intercourse with the sailor as well as from her transformation into a murderer seeking a revenge whose success is questionable. Stavans points out that her name links her to famous Emmas of canonical literature, Gustave Flaubert's and Jane Austen's, who, like Borges's Emma, are strong-willed and refuse to conform to the male establishment ("Borges").

Both readings highlight relations of power and identity politics to the degree that sexuality and classism create serious problems for women and for all citizens, in both the psychological and social arenas. Students come to see that Borges is not preaching about the sexist and classist sources of psychic conflict and social inequality but is instead urging the reader to think about these sources and their impact in early-twentieth-century Buenos Aires. Teaching Borges in the context of identity politics leads to animated discussions of pressing contemporary problems, including those that the Me Too movement confronts as well as racism directed against Asians and Jews. Conclusions will remain tentative, however, given Borges's commitment to literature's strengths in conveying the ambiguities and imperfections of human language.

APPENDIX: PROMPTS FOR DISCUSSION, ORAL REPORTS, AND PAPERS

The following are three examples of prompts that can be used for class discussion, oral reports, and papers. The prompts are grounded in the two pedagogical strategies discussed in the essay—that is, they ask students to engage with conflicting critical readings and the idea of the story as translated text.

Examine the first paragraph of Hurley's translation of "Death and the Compass" (*CF* 147–48) in the context of Mac Adam's analysis of di Giovanni's translation.

Analyze the last paragraph of "The Garden of Forking Paths" (*CF* 127–28) in light of the conflicting readings—that is, Yu Tsun as existential hero versus Yu Tsun as guilty murderer.

Consider the paragraph in "Emma Zunz" in which Emma compares sex with the sailor to her father's intercourse with her mother (*CF* 217). How does the passage shape the overall meaning of Emma's revenge for her father's downfall? Wardi's article will be helpful here, as will Donald Shaw's review of Hurley's translation of "Emma Zunz," which implies that a terrified Emma may well be unstable (Review).

Literary Visuality and Islam in Borges

Max Ubelaker Andrade

When students contextualize the references to Islam in Jorge Luis Borges's short stories using Borges's literary ideas (especially those involving visuality), they can explore a crucial dimension of the author's work, one that is connected to some of Borges's most influential work and the author's own complex relationship with blindness. One of the challenges of this contextualization is that the "Islam" that Borges fashions in his stories is an idiosyncratic version of the religion that is uniquely attuned to his creative project. This means that while it can provide a valuable window into the author's strategies of literary representation, the historical religion is often not represented in an accurate, rigorous way. Borges's references to Islam tend to rely, for example, on an exaggerated, ahistorical emphasis on prohibitions of visual representation (and attendant examples of iconoclasm and aniconism) that, as Finbarr Flood has noted (641), does not account for the great diversity of historical, political, and cultural contexts in which they occur (or do not occur). *Iconoclasm* here refers to the intentional destruction or alteration of certain kinds of visual representations for theological reasons; *aniconism* is the general practice of avoiding these visual representations. The "Islamic" aniconism and iconoclasm in Borges's stories are usually paired with forms of interpretation or contemplation that take place in the absence of representational images, often in larger contexts of storytelling and prayer. Even when there are no specific misrepresentations involved, the "Islam" that readers encounter in Borges's stories is a system of belief primarily concerned with the issues of representation, interpretation, and imagination that are of particular interest to the author; it does not tend to appear as a religion particularly connected to political, social, or regional realities.[1]

When students are guided to notice this strategic pattern, they will be able to identify how Borges uses the altered theology of his version of Islam in a way that turns it into what I have elsewhere referred to as a "literary theology" (Ubelaker Andrade, *Borges* 27–48): a way for literary characters and narrators to begin to engage with the fictional nature of themselves and their reality—especially in terms of their relationship with visuality and the uncanny presence of a reader.[2] The prohibitions of visual representation (and the attendant emphasis on textual interpretation) are often used to unsettle the stability of the visual dimension of his fiction, revealing it to be an unstable product of a reader encountering the artifice of language. In class, this reframing of theology can be traced to early essays such as "After Images"[3] and "Narrative Art and Magic" as well as to the ideas of Borges's friend and mentor Macedonio Fernández. Borges's strategic use of "Islam" appears in stories such as "The Mirror of Ink," "The Masked Dyer Hakim of Merv," "Tlön, Uqbar, Orbis Tertius," "The Aleph," "Averroes's Search," "The Zahir," and "Tafas: One of Our Brushes."[4] While a course on Borges could incorporate all these texts, I focus my attention here on the most canonical stories, "The Aleph" and "The Zahir," given that they are likely to be useful for a wide variety of approaches.

It is also important for students to understand that alongside Islam, which most often provides the theological source material for Borges's subversions of conventional literary visuality, other religious traditions—including Judaism, Buddhism, Gnosticism, and Christianity—are similarly transformed or reframed. When students comprehend that the strategies that Borges built around his version of Islam earlier in his career were extended, in "Ulrikke," to seventeenth-century Puritan Christianity (given its own traditions with iconoclasm, aniconism, and sacred text), they are better able to engage with the complexities of Orientalism and less inclined to formulate a simplistic understanding of Islam (or of Borges's approach to it). The essay closes with suggestions on how to further connect Borges's emphasis on literary visuality with the author's approach to blindness.[5]

Pedagogical Approaches

As Sylvia Molloy has written, Borges's texts are designed to create a ludic, challenging process of interpretation in which readers work through the contradictions, gaps, and ambiguities using their own tools, skills, experiences, and references, a process that can take time and run counter to desires for flowing reading experiences (1–2). For this reason, it is important to create a class structure that incentivizes multiple readings, discussions, and periods of research and reflection for each story. When students can share their reflections, questions, and doubts with one another (and receive peer feedback) before each class session through discussion boards, they are more able to offer truthful, nuanced perspectives on their reading and research experiences in class. I encourage a facilitation model of teaching in which the instructor engages in a process of respectful, engaged active listening to draw out differences of opinion, insights, and moments of uncertainty in the first half of every session—followed by the introduction of prepared materials and additional contexts, questions, and information that build on specific student questions and ideas wherever possible. Requiring a reflection text after each class session also helps ensure that the insights developed through teaching are written down and built on further. Given the interdisciplinary nature of Borges's reach, I have found that creating options for students to develop final projects that include films, works of art, websites, and games works well when there is a written component explaining the links between what students have created and the texts discussed in class.

I recommend showing students how many of the texts that are referenced in Borges's stories are available for free, because of their publication dates, as scanned copies on sites such as *Google Books*. Additionally, students should be aware that the 1911 *Encyclopædia Britannica* was one of Borges's primary resources; they can refer to it as if it were his *Google*—as long as its material is properly contextualized with contemporary sources and approached with a critical perspective. It is available online on several websites, including *HathiTrust*.

"The Aleph"

When students first approach "The Aleph," they tend to focus on the vertiginous description of the visual encounter that the narrator (an author surrogate named Borges) has with the Aleph in Carlos Argentino Daneri's basement. Because the narrator draws specific attention to the challenges of representation involved in this description, discussions, at first, often follow this direction. I recommend touching on the less than positive effects of the narrator's experience before guiding students to the moment in which the narrator asserts that the Aleph at the center of the story was "false": "Por increíble que parezca yo creo que hay (o que hubo) otro Aleph, yo creo que el Aleph de la calle Garay era un falso Aleph" 'Incredible as it may seem, I believe that there is (or was) another Aleph; I believe that the Aleph of Calle Garay was a false Aleph' (*OC* 1: 1069; *CF* 285).

It is a statement that is relatively easy to bypass—especially given the difficulty in reconciling it with the description of the narrator's experience with the Aleph at the center of the story: What does it mean, exactly, for the Aleph to be "false"? The answer is not immediately clear, and even though the narrator states that he will explain himself ("Doy mis razones" 'Let me state my reasons' [*OC* 1: 1070; *CF* 285]), one only finds a set of fictional objects cited from a manuscript written by Richard Francis Burton in 1867. (This manuscript is an invention of Borges.) These objects include the magical mirrors of Iskandar Zu al-Karnyn, Tarik Benzayed, and Lucian of Samasota; the seven-ringed cup of Kai Khosrow; the mirrored lance of Jupiter; and Merlin's crystal ball. All are rejected by Burton, however, for being "meros instrumentos de óptica" 'mere optical instruments' (*OC* 1: 1070; *CF* 285). The idea, therefore, is that the Aleph of Daneri is false because it—like the other rejected fictional objects—provides an optical experience.

Yet since the Aleph itself is described in wholly visual terms, what can it possibly mean for its optical nature to render it false? What would be left of the Aleph without its visual component? Importantly, the story continues with a description of another object in Burton's manuscript that is emphatically not seen: a stone column in the Amr Mosque of Cairo that holds the universe in its interior. The text explains that while no one can see this universe, the individuals who bring their ears close to its surface can, in time, perceive its muted rumbling. Here we are presented with an emphatically nonvisual object that nevertheless provides a form of connection with the entire universe. The implication is that the unseen object in the column of the Amr Mosque is the true Aleph, while the optical Aleph is false. Yet the story ends without providing a clear resolution regarding what that might mean.

After students discuss different possibilities, it is important to introduce two key pieces of extratextual information. The first is that the Amr Mosque mentioned by Borges has an unusual architectural feature: its initial lack of a concave mihrab. A mihrab is, traditionally, the empty, concave space situated within the wall of a mosque; it points—from the perspective of the worshippers inside—to qibla: the direction of Mecca. At this mosque, a different, unknown structure (also referred to as a mihrab) originally served to indicate the direction of Mecca (Whelan 209–10). It was specially marked by four columns. In 710–11, however, Kurra ibn Sharlk removed this unknown marker and erected a new southern wall with a concave mihrab. The old mihrab, however, was not forgotten; to commemorate its importance the four columns that enclosed it were kept and their capitals were gilded (Whelan 210; Corbett 773). The space occupied by the Amr Mosque's original (and, today, invisible) mihrab was, in this sense, quite literally enclosed within the four pillars.

Two of Borges's favorite texts may have provided him this key information; it is a good idea to provide copies of these pages for student use during the class session. First, the 1911 *Encyclopædia Britannica*'s general entry on mosques features only one illustration on its initial page: the architectural plan of "Mosque of 'Amr, Old Cairo" (Phené Spiers 899). The entry describes both the function of a mihrab and how the columns and capitals of the Amr Mosque were taken from ancient buildings. While there is no mention of the transformed mihrab in the encyclopedia, Edward William Lane's *An Account of the Manners and Customs of the Modern Egyptians*, which was well known to Borges, describes it in detail. The text explains how the four pillars that mark the absent mihrab were gilded and that "there were no gilt pillars in the mosque except them" (349).

The second key piece of information is that in the original manuscript of "The Aleph," the word *Aleph* did not, at first, appear. Instead, in the published critical edition of the manuscript, one can see that Borges originally wrote the word "mihrab" instead: "Aclaró ~~que un mihrab~~ que un Aleph es uno de los puntos del espacio ~~en el cual están contenidos~~ q. contiene todos los puntos" '[Carlos Daneri] explained ~~that a mihrab~~ that an Aleph is one of the points in space that contains ~~in which~~ all points ~~are contained~~' (Ortega et al. 39; my trans.).

These two aspects of Borges's story establish a link between the Aleph of Daneri and the true Aleph of the Amr Mosque. It is important to have students discuss the possible relationship between the visible Aleph described at the center of Borges's story and the mihrab that, crossed out in the original manuscript, was moved to the story's postscript as the true, nonoptical Aleph. The similarities are numerous: both are empty spaces found in buildings that invite prolonged contemplation. They are meant to be visually addressed. One points to a universe without a fixed center (viewed from infinite perspectives), while the other points to the center of the Islamic universe (from the privileged perspective of a mosque's interior). Yet there are also clear differences. A mihrab simultaneously points one's gaze toward Mecca and also blocks that gaze. Instead of instantly delivering a rapturous vision, it forms part of a set of devotional practices designed to invite contemplation and imagination in the absence of icons.[6]

Drawing a connection between this tension and Borges's "After Images" (*SNF* 10–12) can create context for this theological reframing.[7] The essay shows a young Borges wondering how it might be possible for someone to enter and persist within the artificial space of literature and interact with the peculiarities of their own fictionality. It suggests that this act of creation, which he describes in theological terms, would represent a more radical possibility than simply creating surprising juxtapositions of images from the recognizable universe. While a literary text does not offer entertaining stimuli directly to the eyes, Borges reminds us that to read is to conjure a visual world using the power of the imagination—without direct optical stimuli. Fashioning a fictional world takes time, skill, and mental effort, while the Aleph of Daneri delivers everything at once to any individual who is capable of sight: it is a relatively passive experience. The page of text that students are reading, like the mihrab, attracts the gaze of a reader and simultaneously blocks that gaze, requiring a sustained practice of contemplative imagination to create a visual (though not an optical) reality.

One can further offer the idea that in the context of fiction, the nonoptical mihrab is truthful regarding the nature of the universe that the characters inhabit. It successfully allegorizes the experience of the actual reader of the story—its truth is the truth it tells about its medium. This, of course, was precisely the goal described by Borges in "After Images."[8] From this perspective, the optical Aleph in Daneri's basement is false because it offers a mode of engaging with the universe that, in relying on a passive, optical experience, is completely incompatible with a literary world composed of the encounter between a reading mind and a page of text. While a fictional context does not allow for the direct, optical apprehension of the universe, that does not mean that it is devoid of visuality. It is, however, a visual context that must be imagined into existence. Daneri's Aleph is rejected not because it is visual but rather because it is merely optical. In delivering the universe to the beholder without requiring any effort, it is devoid of the creativity that reading and writing literature requires.

Working with students to tease out the entangled, overlapping concepts of the "visual" and the "optical" is worthwhile in this discussion—especially given how the visuality of imagination is accessible to many readers who are not sighted.[9] While Borges was able to see when he composed "The Aleph," he was also aware that he would likely one day be blind. That he would create a story about an object that offers perfect, total sight—which subtly reveals itself to be a trap, a hindrance—should, I believe, be in direct conversation with the author's relationship with blindness, especially given how the unseen Aleph in the column of the Amr Mosque is approached through touch and listening—two of the ways that people who cannot see are able to read.

A discussion of this aspect of the true and false Alephs allows students to return to other moments in the story with a different level of understanding. For example, the extended section in which Daneri is mocked for his ineptitude acquires new significance when students realize that he and his poetry have been influenced by an unfettered access to the addictive, effortless Aleph. One possibility for students to consider is that his work is unsuccessful (and laughable) because of the atrophying effect that the Aleph, which delivers a perfect visual experience of the world, has had on his mind. This is also a useful place for students to reflect on the relationship between current technology (and the access to the universe that it allows) and the experience of Daneri. This is especially true since Daneri himself draws a connection between his literary project and the capacity of the technology of his own era to bring the world—or at least representations of it—directly to the consumer (*OC* 1: 1062; *CF* 275–76).

Another relevant aspect of the story is the place of portraiture and the representation of faces. This is a special area of focus given that in many cases, iconoclasm in Islam was used to preserve art while making sure that it complied with the applicable prohibitions. Two of these iconoclastic gestures were the abrasive erasure of the face of a represented person or animal and the drawing of a line across their neck—the idea was to render the representations powerless while also preserving their essential forms (Flood 647). When students return to the beginning of the story, they should be able to notice a conspicuous parade of portraiture: Daneri's home is filled with representations of Beatriz Viterbo (the recently deceased woman—Daneri's cousin—whom the narrator describes being enamored of). Her visual representation sets up the final gesture of the story: the erasure of Beatriz's face in the memory of the narrator. After the overdose of optical visuality and the narrator's hope that forgetting might cleanse his mind, this erasure, which is in line with the iconoclasm of the author's "Islam," can certainly be approached as a release from a mode of visual representation that is content to simply mimic the existing world.

Rejecting mimicry in art was especially important to one of Borges's most influential mentors, the Argentinian poet, novelist, and philosopher Macedonio Fernández. Borges, recalling his early years as a writer, explained, "Yo, por aquellos años lo imité hasta la transcipción, hasta el apasionado y devoto plagio. Yo sentía: Macedonio es la metafísica, es la literatura" 'I, in those years, imitated him to the point of transcription, to the point of impassioned, devoted plagiarism. I felt: Macedonio *is* metaphysics, *is* literature' (qtd. in Isaacson 71–72; my trans.). Macedonio doubted that fiction based on the direct representation of everyday fears, desires, pleasures, and difficulties could have the liberating effects that he was interested in. Instead, such works of realism could reinforce social and metaphysical norms while delivering experiences that could not help but pale in comparison with the real thing. Providing students with selections from his writings—especially *The Museum of Eterna's Novel*—can further develop the literary context of Borges's "Islam." "[E]l horror del Arte" '[T]he horror of Art,' Macedonio writes, "es el relato y la descripción, la copia como fin en sí" 'is storytelling and description, the copy as a final goal' (Fernández, *Teorías* 236; my trans.).[10]

"The Zahir"

After working with "The Aleph," students will be well prepared to unearth some of the tensions between Borges's ideas about visual representation in literature and more conventional desires for alluring visual displays. Teodelina Villar, like Beatriz Viterbo, is directly connected to portraiture—she is a fashion model whose shifting yet orthodoxic relationship with her visual representation is described in theological terms.[11] The discovery of the explicitly "Islamic" Zahir after her death introduces the idea that certain objects, when seen, can (like the Aleph) be traps.[12] In the story, this Zahir is a simple coin that, once viewed, progressively takes over the viewer's mind. Students are often drawn to discussions of how this object comes in and out of view, operating in different dimensions—the narrator, for example, tries to distract himself from the coin by composing a story but ends up writing, inevitably, about the powerful allure of the treasure (of coins) belonging to a mythical Germanic dragon; when he is busy thinking about these coins (while trying to avoid thinking about coins), he subconsciously traces one with his footsteps, circling back to where he started. In a sense, Borges uses the limit of the Zahir's curse to create different, unexpected variations, improvising on a theme; to read the story is to develop a challenging double vision in which the coin (its possible images, meanings, and contexts) is superimposed on the logic of the text.

The creative tension between language and the imagined image of the coin also appears in a riddle found in the initial description of the titular Zahir, which is a good focal point for students to investigate using the tools at their disposal: "En Buenos Aires el Zahir es una moneda común de veinte centavos; marcas de navaja o de cortaplumas rayan las letras N T y el número dos" 'In Buenos Aires the Zahir is a common twenty-centavo coin into which a razor or letter opener has scratched the letters N T and the number 2' (*OC* 1: 1037; *CF* 242). I discovered that when one allows the "N" and "T" etched on the coin to refer to "Nuevo Testamento" 'New Testament,' the number *twenty* (as it is a twenty-centavo coin) leads us to the twentieth chapter in the New Testament. The "2" etched into its face directs us to the proper verse: Matthew 20.2. This is the precise moment in which Jesus describes the divine reward offered to his followers by comparing it, surprisingly, to a single coin.

Sharing this link with students allows them to discuss how the passage might relate to Borges's larger strategies. At the same time, it is a connection that provides a sense of what is possible when one explores the author's references. The parable of the coin involves workers who, despite laboring for different amounts of time, are all paid a single denarius. The story serves as an answer to Peter, who asks how they will be repaid for having given up everything as disciples. In this sense, the coin stands in for the divine gifts of salvation. In having infinite value, it is not exchanged for labor like normal coins—it is the same for all regardless of how long someone has held their faith or how much they have sacrificed. It is important to point out the ease with which, in this Christian parable, a denarius—a coin that features the representation of a person's face (Caesar's, most likely either Augustus's or Tiberius's) on one of its sides—is used to allegorically illustrate the divine reward of God. (Showing students images of these coins helps accentuate the point.) This theological use of visual portraiture stands in stark contrast to the ideas that Borges associated with his literary theology and recalls the centrality of the icon in much of Christianity.

At the close of "The Zahir," the narrator, noticing that he is succumbing to the power of the coin, expresses the hope that the mental repetition of the image of the coin will somehow allow him to consume it, just as Sufis use the repetition of certain words to transcend their own limits.[13] In an echo to the riddle etched on the coin's surface, the narrator (whose name is also Borges) hopes that he might find God on the other side of the coin. In this way, a Sufi tradition of textual repetition is joined with the possibility that incessantly returning to an imagined image might lead to a similar encounter with the sublime. A coin, adorned with the visual representation of a human being, establishes a conceptual bridge between the Bible and Islamic mysticism.

What can this bridge between iconicity and aniconism tell us? One possibility is that Borges was never interested in simply deposing a visual literary regime with the radical elevation of textuality: the literary theology he fashions complicates the icon instead of destroying it. The idea, instead, may have been to disrupt his readers' relationships with visual and literary norms, unsettling their desires for visually alluring experiences while directing their attention to the medium of the written word and the generative possibilities of reading. "The Aleph" and "The Zahir" can be approached as Borges's attempts to follow his own advice in "After Images" by transforming theological ideas to explore fiction from within (as a character named Borges instead of as an essayist or academic).

"Ulrikke"

While Borges emphasizes Islam's iconoclasm and aniconism in an unpublished essay manuscript, "Místicos del Islam" ("Mystics of Islam"), he also asserts that Islam and Christianity (with their final judgments, heavens and hells, demons and angels, and solitary, personal Gods) are, with the exception of the role of Jesus Christ, not particularly different from each other. "Ulrikke" can show students how Borges uses practices of iconoclasm and aniconism in seventeenth-century Protestant England in a way that establishes a connection with the "Islam" of his earlier stories. I present it here not as a direct example of Borges's "Islam" but rather as a story that complicates and enriches how students approach questions of Orientalism and of the author's relationship with Islam. Understanding that Borges is working between theological traditions—seeking practices and ideas that he can reframe in his literary project—is especially useful for students who might approach these traditions as separate and irreconcilable.

The narrator of the story is a Colombian professor named Javier Otárola. He first sees a woman he calls Ulrica in England's walled city of York, next to the Five Sisters, a set of nonfigurative stained-glass windows in the York Minster cathedral. Otárola describes them as "esos vitrales puros de toda imagen que respetaron los iconoclastas de Cromwell" 'those stained-glass panes devoid of figural representation that Cromwell's iconoclasts left untouched' (*OC* 3: 19; *CF* 202). Despite this initial encounter, he explains that they did not meet until the following day when he saw her, first from behind, as she was talking to someone else. When he finally does encounter her face-to-face, the description is detailed but immediately subverted by the admission that it draws, in truth, from later memories. The simple act of seeing or describing Ulrica is, in other words, deferred, interrupted, confused, and made unusually complex. Even her name signals that the version of Ulrica we encounter is filtered through the narrator's perspective: her true name is Ulrikke, but he uses a version of it that he finds easier to pronounce.[14] Christian iconoclasm and aniconism combine to provide a framework for the story's refusal to acquiesce to the visual expectations of the reader: we are asked to work with a nonfigurative text that asserts its authority while denying the possibility of an objective, unfiltered account. (The first line of the story installs this tension by proclaiming that "[m]i relato será fiel a la realidad o, en todo caso, a mi recuerdo personal de la realidad, lo cual es lo mismo" '[m]y story will be faithful to reality, or at least to my personal recollection of reality, which is the same thing' [*OC* 3: 19; *CF* 418].)

After following their conversation on a walk through the woods, the story ends in the room of an inn that is wallpapered in an arabesque style that at once echoes Borges's "Islam" and emphasizes the literary, textual character of the story. The florid wallpaper is by William Morris, an artist strongly influenced by Persian designs (Sasso 68) who, as Alice Petersen points out, is also the translator of *The Saga of the Volsungs*, a text referenced throughout the story by the characters and quoted for its epigraph (329). The story ends with an erotic encounter between the two characters; we read that "secular en la sombra fluyó el amor y poseí por primera y última vez la imagen de Ulrica" 'secular in the shadows love flowed, and I possessed for the first and last time the image of Ulrica' (*OC* 3: 21; my trans.).[15]

The notion that the narrator would focus on possessing the image of Ulrica can be disorienting; it is a peculiar choice of words that can serve as an opening for students to discuss the strategies used in the text. The story of this possession is set up, as noted, by a series of descriptions that, one after another, challenge expectations associated with everyday sight and traditional visual representation. Beginning with the Five Sisters aniconic framing of his first glimpse of Ulrica and the arabesque-covered room, there is also a gradual shift away from sight, with the white snow accumulating outside and, inside, the shadows taking the place of the inn's interior. Even when we are given a traditional description of Ulrica's appearance earlier in the story, the narrator complicates it, subverting the origin of its creation. Finally, Otárola's concluding assertion invalidates this previous, rather formulaic visual description—the first account is not, we are told, her actual, true image. This true image is, strikingly, not optical: a mental figure composed in darkness, informed by touch, intimacy, and a connection discovered through conversation. It is also ephemeral; if the image is "possessed," then this possession lasts only for a moment. (Ulrica asks, at one point in the story, if anything can truly be possessed or lost: "Inglaterra fue nuestra y la perdimos, si alguien puede tener algo o algo puede perderse" 'England was ours and we lost it, if one can possess anything or if anything can truly be lost' [*OC* 3: 19; my trans.].)

Perhaps one final aspect of the story deserves mention: it is difficult to sense whether the Spanish word "secular" in the last sentence is principally intended to signify "secular" or "ancient," yet for a story that draws, as this essay shows, from a long-standing practice of reshaping theological traditions, the idea that the true image of Ulrica arises in a secular context of human relation is worth considering.

Reading "The Aleph" and "The Zahir" through the lens of this later story can lead to new questions regarding Borges's approach to both "Christianity" and "Islam." It can also open discussions about Borges's female characters and their relationship with visual allure, especially given how the text draws attention to both the authority and the instability of Otárola's perspective. The nature of this dominance provides different possibilities for discussion as Otálora's image of Ulrica is joined with the representations (textual and otherwise) of Teodelina Villar and Beatriz Viterbo. "Ulrikke" is, additionally, a story that Borges wrote when he was blind. To deepen an understanding of his relationship with blindness, Borges's essay "Blindness" (*OC* 3: 415–23; *Seven Nights* 107–21) is a useful text for students to consider alongside the story "The Maker" (*OC* 2: 273–74; *CF* 292–93) and the poems of *In Praise of Darkness* (*OC* 2: 613–55). In distinct ways, these texts reject the notion that blindness is a curse, an impediment, or a simple lack of ability, suggesting instead that blindness can be approached as another mode of being in the world, one that holds its own generative possibilities of imagination, insight, and creation.

After working with "The Aleph" and "The Zahir" in the ways articulated in this essay, students will be able to perceive how Borges's "Islam" subverts conventional approaches to the allure of seeing, critiquing a cultural obsession with optical spectacle and possession that creates its own impediments, exclusions, and limits. In the encounter with the Aleph encased in the pillar of a mosque or the contemplation of a coin that overtakes the language used to evade its image, these stories gesture to a shifting, unstable visuality that is built in the territory of one's own imagination and understanding.

NOTES

1. To make the distinction between the religion and Borges's fictional version of it clearer, the word *Islam* will appear in quotation marks where appropriate.

2. When exploring connections between these strategies and Orientalism, it is important for students to consider how Borges might or might not be engaged in a "Western style for dominating, restructuring, and having authority over the Orient" (Said 3). While Borges utilizes an idiosyncratic version of "Islam" to explore his own literary ideas regarding visuality and literary imagination, to what degree does his use of the writings of Orientalists such as Edward William Lane and Ernest Renan reinscribe Orientalist patterns into his texts? To what degree do they disrupt or reinforce Orientalist perspectives on their own terms? Robin Fiddian's *Postcolonial Borges: Argument and Artistry*, Ian Almond's "Borges the Post-Orientalist: Images of Islam from the Edge of the West," Alex Gasquet's *Oriente al Sur: El orientalismo literario argentino de Esteban Echeverría a Roberto Arlt*, and especially Sonia Betancort's *Oriente no es una pieza de museo* are useful texts to consider in this exploration.

3. When using English translations, I strongly recommend comparing them with the original Spanish texts to help guide students through any issues created by the choices of the translators.

4. Note that Norman Thomas di Giovanni translated "Un pincel nuestro: Tafas" as "Tafas, A Talented Brush," which omits the assertion of belonging from the title (Borges and Bioy Casares, *Chronicles* [1976] 107).

5. For a more scholarly approach to the ideas referenced in this essay, see chapter 1 of Ubelaker Andrade, *Borges* (9–60), which also provides a detailed analysis of the stories mentioned above that amplify and build on Borges's strategic use of "Islam" in a diverse set of literary experiments. The book's epilogue (129–37) also features a description and analysis of an unpublished essay manuscript by Borges ("Místicos del Islam" ["Mystics of Islam"]) that can be useful as an account of Borges's understanding of Islam, especially in terms of how he connects it with Christianity and its own traditions of mysticism.

6. To better understand the spherical form of Daneri's Aleph and consider some of its nonoptical antecedents, students should read Borges's 1951 essay "Pascal's Sphere" (*SNF* 351–53), which offers a progression of aniconic representations of divinity that extends to Xenophanes.

7. Students may be interested in contrasting Borges's approach with that of José Ortega y Gasset, whose "The Dehumanization of Art" was published in 1925, the same year as Borges's "After Images," especially given that Ortega approaches modernist art with evocations of iconoclasm. See Ubelaker Andrade, *Borges* 149–51.

8. It can also be useful to assign Borges's "Narrative Art and Magic" (*SNF* 75–82), which suggests that the logic of magic—or theology—applies to the context of literature in a way that does not transfer over to the chaos and complex causality of the everyday.

9. For nuanced, deeply researched work on the relationship between visuality and blindness, see Kleege, "Blind Imagination" and *More Than Meets the Eye*.

10. I am not aware of English translations of Macedonio's *Teorías*.

11. Even the character's name combines fashion with theology: "Teo-de-lina" can be read as "the god of cloth" given the regional use of "lina" as a skein of wool—a possibility strengthened by Borges's manuscript "Místicos del Islam," which states that the etymology of "Sufi" is "vestido de lana" 'dressed in wool' (my trans.). "Teo-de-lina" and "vestido de lana" may form a punning pair connected to clothing, wool, and Islamic mysticism.

12. Note that Borges did not know Arabic and would not have been well-versed in its nuances, though he did take a few introductory language classes close to the end of his life. For possibilities regarding the textual origin of the word *Zahir*, see Ubelaker Andrade, *Borges* 161–63.

13. For an analysis of the links between Alfred Tennyson, Ibn Khaldoun, Sufi mysticism, and the repetition of one's name, see Ubelaker Andrade, "Tennyson," which presents a page of manuscript notes written by Borges close to 1947.

14. Andrew Hurley's use of the name "Ulrikke" throughout his translation erases this important distinction. Changing the title to "Ulrica" would, for example, emphasize that the reader only learns about the titular character through the narrator; she does not directly speak for herself in the text. This strategic admission is important given the story's references to feminism and the questions of possession and perception that their relationship involves.

15. Published English translations are not useful here because of their specific word choices.

Borges's Lens: The Symphony of a Rhizomatic Course

Rhona Trauvitch

In the spring of 2016 Florida International University housed a copy of Shakespeare's First Folio. A news article proudly proclaimed, "FIU is the only site in Florida to host the Folger Shakespeare Library's national traveling exhibit *First Folio! The Book that Gave Us Shakespeare*" (Gonzalez). February became a festive month featuring exhibitions, lectures, performances, open mic nights, screenings, and even an Integrated Computer Augmented Virtual Environment (I-CAVE) that transported visitors to the Globe Theatre of Shakespeare's time. As part of this celebration, I offered a special topics course that juxtaposed the work of the Bard with that of his contemporary Miguel de Cervantes and of the writer for whom Shakespeare and Cervantes perhaps formed the pillars of literature: Jorge Luis Borges. Borges's stories, poems, and essays are suffused with references to Shakespeare and Cervantes; several of his pieces are explicitly about them. Even writing of his that does not explicitly mention them foregrounds themes and tropes that shine in their work. Borges's oeuvre can be viewed as a microcosm of the influence Shakespeare and Cervantes have had on authors and readers for four centuries.

In what follows I describe the design choices that I made in order to construct Shakespeare and Cervantes by way of Borges, a course that is at its crux a conversation—across nations and generations—among the three literary greats and my students. My task was to create an environment that allowed students both to recognize the many connections among the three writers' words and worlds and to discover new associations. By sharing this pedagogical approach, I hope to provide instructors and students with a collection of ideas about how to pursue a multivocal Borges course.

Background: How to Build a Multivocal Course

While I had researched and taught the works of Borges for several years, I had only minimal background on Shakespeare and Cervantes. I reached out to four colleagues with this very expertise: the Shakespeare scholars Carmela McIntire and James Sutton and the Cervantes scholars Ricardo Castells and Ilan Stavans. At the time, McIntire and Sutton taught with me in Florida International University's Department of English, Castells taught in the university's Department of Modern Languages, and Stavans taught European studies, Spanish, and Latinx and Latin American studies at Amherst College.

Each was instrumental in my conceptualization of the course. During our conversations, my colleagues helped pinpoint connections between Shakespeare and Borges or between Cervantes and Borges and thus originated some of the ideas noted in the reflection prompts that cap each reading assignment, which I describe in more detail below. I would ask them whether certain Borgesian themes appear in Shakespeare's plays and Don Quixote's adventures, and they would locate parallels that allowed me to shape the course's structure. These colleagues also added their voices, quite literally, to the symphony: McIntire, Sutton, and Castells each visited our class to give talks and engage students in discussion, and students watched a video of an earlier lecture by Stavans. In these ways and more, as much as this course is about several people, it is also the creation of several people. Such teamwork is ideal—if not imperative—in the production of an intertextual course like this one. Or, as Borges might observe, the polyphony of the object mirrors the polyphony of the subjects.

Setup: How to Arrange a Rhizomatic Course

The whirlwind of connections among Borges, Shakespeare, and Cervantes is dizzying. In what order should the interrelations be presented? How to incline toward harmony and not cacophony? I sought a schema that would tame the disorder but keep the currents of inspiration strong—a method to the madness. It would be counterintuitive to group the material by author or chronologically. Those layouts suggest linearity, whereas the intertextuality of this course looks more like a network of organized chaos, how some might describe a rhizome.

In *A Thousand Plateaus*, Gilles Deleuze and Félix Guattari characterize the rhizome as follows: "any point of a rhizome can be connected to anything other, and must be. This is very different from the tree or root, which plots a point, fixes an order" (7). Furthermore, "[a] rhizome may be broken, shattered at a given spot, but it will start up again on one of its old lines, or on new lines" (9). Deleuze and Guattari further distinguish the rhizome as a form that "ceaselessly establishes connections" (7) and observe that "[m]ultiplicities are rhizomatic. . . . [T]he laws of combination . . . increase in number as the multiplicity grows" (8). Indeed, each connection between and among our three writers engenders new connections; this growth pattern is what makes such a course possible. Viewing the course's layout as a rhizome helps us understand the complex relationships among the many nodes of connection as well as the pathways that link them.

To identify major nodes, I drew inspiration from an observation made by Harold Bloom in *How to Read and Why*: "'Tlön, Uqbar, Orbis Tertius' begins with a disarming sentence (in Andrew Hurley's eloquent translation): 'I owe the discovery of Uqbar to the conjunction of a mirror and an encyclopedia.' That sentence is the purest Borges: add a labyrinth to a mirror and an encyclopedia, and you would have his world" (58). In other words, labyrinth-mirror-encyclopedia is the Borgesian thematic trifecta. I could see several manifestations of these themes in Shakespeare's and Cervantes's work, and my colleagues added to these examples their own insightful readings: Portia's labyrinthine use of the law in *The Merchant of Venice*, the labyrinth of Don Quixote's adventures, and the labyrinth in Don

Quixote's mind; the mirroring suggested by the play within *Hamlet* and in Don Quixote's quest to imitate the knights-errant of chivalric novels; Prospero's encyclopedic knowledge, which drives the events of *The Tempest*, and the listing and cataloging prominent in the first several chapters of *Don Quixote*. These are just a few of the rhizome's myriad links. It became evident that in the role of nodes, the parts of the trifecta have the capacity to generate a multitude of connections among the three writers' stories. Accordingly, I split the course into three modules: Labyrinth, Mirror, and Encyclopedia.

Literal labyrinths, mirrors, and encyclopedias are not necessarily found in each of Borges's, Shakespeare's, and Cervantes's narratives—though, sometimes, they may be. In addition to locating literal manifestations, I therefore searched for thematic and structural expressions of each part of the trifecta. *Labyrinth*, *mirror*, and *encyclopedia* were to be broadly interpreted; students were asked to use their detective's magnifying glass and discover traces of the trifecta—whether obvious or clandestine—in our reading.

To pave the way for this investigation, I recommend providing students with a list at the start of each module, one made up of synonyms of—and concepts related to—the theme of each module. For example, synonyms for *labyrinth* include *entanglement*, *intricacy*, *perplexity*, *puzzle*, and *web*; related concepts include twisting paths, confusion, and complexity. These lists prompt students to adopt a broad interpretation of our themes, which in turn facilitates the detection of these themes in the texts. Each module concludes with a prompt that highlights specific connections among the texts studied in that module. These prompts encourage students to reflect on certain questions and issues as they complete their reading and are meant to guide students in navigating the material as it relates to the course as a whole.

In week 2, for example, students read Borges's "The Garden of Forking Paths" (*CF* 119–28) and "The Immortal" (183–95) alongside Shakespeare's *Twelfth Night* (*Complete Works* 719–42), and I asked them to consider the following:

> While the labyrinths in "The Garden of Forking Paths" and "The Immortal" are rather obvious (albeit, in the case of the former, not necessarily straightforward), the labyrinth in *Twelfth Night* is not literal. In Shakespeare's play it is the plot that is labyrinthine, with all its twists and turns, general confusion, and "topsy-turvydom" (*Complete Works* 719). Note in particular the path Viola takes. At the conclusion of the soliloquy at the end of act 2, scene 2, she states, "O time, thou must untangle this, not I. / It is too hard a knot for me t'untie" (lines 40–41). What kind of labyrinth is Viola knotted into?

In week 8, students read Borges's "On Exactitude in Science" (*CF* 325) and "Pierre Menard, Author of the *Quixote*" (88–95) and, from the second part of *Don Quixote*, "Prologue to the Reader" (Cervantes 455–58) and chapters 2 (469–73), 59 (842–49), 62 (864–75), and 72 (924–28). Secondary readings included Mark

Currie's introduction to *Metafiction* and Patricia Waugh's essay in the same collection. During this week students received the following prompt:

> This week you are reading about metafiction in Currie's introduction and Waugh's essay. Metafiction relates to mirroring in that it involves fiction that is, in a sense, self-aware. Notice how metafictional *Don Quixote* becomes when Cervantes deals with the publication of the "false *Quixote*" (455n1) by a man known as "Avellaneda." In the *Don Quixote* chapters you're reading this week, Don Quixote (the fictional character) reads the (actual) "false *Quixote*," changes his itinerary because of the "false *Quixote*," and confronts a character from the "false *Quixote*"!

In week 12, students read Borges's "The Aleph" (*CF* 274–86) and "The Zahir" (242–49), Shakespeare's *Macbeth* (*Complete Works* 969–93), and Michael LoMonico's *The Shakespeare Book of Lists.* Students were asked to consider the following:

> Encyclopedias list, catalog, and enumerate. To describe the Aleph and the Zahir, Borges turns to listing. LoMonico draws attention to two lists in *Macbeth*: "When Malcolm tells Macduff of Macbeth's vices" and the "list of ingredients and a recipe" (16). What do Borges's lists in "The Aleph" and "The Zahir" accomplish? What is accomplished by Shakespeare's lists?

Pairing primary sources (see the appendix) and incorporating secondary materials that provide context and guidance also help students discover and make connections among the narratives. In terms of secondary materials, I incorporated the following: *Borges' Short Stories*, by Rex Butler (sections that consider the assigned Borges stories); the introduction to *The Shakespeare Book of Lists*, by LoMonico (13–17); *Jorge Luis Borges*, by George R. McMurray (the introduction [xvii–xxviii] and sections devoted to the assigned Borges works); *Quixote: The Novel and the World*, by Stavans (ch. 1 [3–25], chs. 3–7 [37–116]); and writings by Bloom (the section about Borges in *How to Read and Why* [56–60], the introduction from *Shylock* collected in *The Merchant of Venice* [198–205], and the introduction to *The Merchant of Venice* [xi–xiv]), Currie (Introduction), Alberto Manguel (*With Borges* 60–65), and Waugh. Of these, sections from Butler, McMurray, and Stavans as well as the short introductions that precede each of Shakespeare's plays in *The Complete Works* served as regular primary source accompaniments.

The appendix shows that among the readings assigned in weeks 14 and 15 are chapters of *Don Quixote* that students had already read earlier in the semester. Cervantes's novel is long, and it would be challenging to read all of it even if the entire semester were devoted only to this one novel. Why, then, would I ask students to reread some of the chapters rather than read more of them for the first time? As noted earlier, this sort of rhizomatic, polyphonic course precludes a linear progression. Accordingly, and in the spirit of Borges's "Kafka and His

Precursors," I include junctions at which students can revisit certain texts in light of new information. I believe that it is an important exercise both in close reading and in literary interpretation to reread a piece in a new context. Reading a given narrative using a different framework and looking for new clues, one gleans even more from the text. For example, approaching the first several chapters of *Don Quixote* in search of the encyclopedic (lists, catalogs, intertextuality), students discover a different realm from the one they explore when approaching these same chapters with labyrinths in mind.

Assessment: How to Design Assignments That Contribute to the Symphony

Students completed five types of assignments throughout the semester. Some called for group work, others were to be done individually, but each was open-ended enough to necessitate the students' design. That is, students always had several options to choose from. I describe each type of assignment in turn below.

In Class

This course met twice per week, on Tuesdays and Thursdays. Forty-one students enrolled and were randomly placed in twelve groups of three or four. Every Tuesday a different group would moderate class discussion on the assigned Borges stories, and every Thursday we would engage in a structured, class-wide discussion of the paired Shakespeare play or *Don Quixote* chapters assigned that week.

By Monday night of each week, each member of the given week's moderating group would post a question or a prompt pertaining to the assigned Borges reading on our course's *Blackboard* discussion page. On Tuesday I would project the moderators' prompts onto the classroom's screen, and the group would draw on these prompts to moderate class discussion. In the assignment guidelines, I asked students to think of prompts that would encourage their classmates to respond thoughtfully and analytically—to be creative. Also, though each post was graded individually, I asked moderators to collaborate with their group members before posting in order to make sure that the questions covered a range of topics and were not repeated, and—if two or more narratives were assigned—that the prompts addressed all the narratives due that Tuesday.

To incentivize reading, avoid repetition, and open the floor to as many participants as possible, I provided a common structure to each of our Thursday class-wide discussions. For Thursday, students were asked to read a Shakespeare play or chapters from *Don Quixote* that paired with the given week's Borges stories insofar as they all relate to the given module (the appendix lists these pairings). In class, I projected onto the screen a six-way split of the reading due that day, assigning each of the six sections to two groups. Students spent the first several minutes of class discussing their particular section with their groupmates, listening to one another's ideas, and coming up with two or three topics to broach with the rest of the class once we returned to a class-wide discussion. While these topics had to relate to their specific sections, they were otherwise open. Whatever they did, students were asked not to summarize their sections.

This structure incentivizes reading: because students do not know ahead of time which sections they will need to focus on in class, the hope is that they will read everything assigned in order to be prepared. Assigning specific sections to specific groups avoids repetition; without this, students may all choose to discuss the same two or three topics. Finally, this structure opens the floor to as many participants as possible because each group gets a turn to speak (but not everyone from each group is required to speak, which allows those who prefer not to speak in a class-wide discussion to limit their speaking to their group).

Outside Class

Outside class, students collaborated with their groupmates to create a presentation using *Prezi*, which they presented to the class during week 9. As was the case with most of the assignments in this course, students were given certain parameters, but they could take their research in any direction within these parameters. In creating their presentations, each group was allowed to choose any subject pertaining to the material we had covered thus far in the course. *Prezi* would be the medium through which each group presented its subject, which could take the form of a comparative analysis, an argument, and so on. Coediting in *Prezi* allowed all members of the group to work on the presentation concurrently, making it possible for them to collaborate in real time from different locations.

For their final assignment students were challenged to individually write one act of a play that scholars believe Shakespeare was involved in writing. This lost play, about a character in Cervantes's *Don Quixote*, is called *The History of Cardenio*. In the guidelines for the final project, I reminded students that earlier in the semester they had read a chapter of Stavans's *Quixote* that, in an approach we can call "meta," recounts the history of *The History of Cardenio*. I also provided them with a list of *Don Quixote* chapters in which Cardenio makes an appearance. I suggested they read (or reread) these chapters to collect information about the character so that they could write a convincing and accurate (in other words, consistent with his story) act of *The History of Cardenio*.

The final project consisted of two parts: one act of the play and a reflective commentary. For the first part of the assignment, I asked students to envision how Shakespeare would have contributed to or written *The History of Cardenio*. Would the play encompass all of what we know of Cardenio from *Don Quixote*? Would it focus and expand on just one episode of Cardenio's story? Once students envisioned this play, I asked that they choose one segment of it and recreate it. This could be the first act, a middle act, or the last act. I noted that since they were writing just one of the play's acts, what they wrote did not have to contain a whole story. Rather, it should be a comprehensive segment of the whole story.

I listed four requirements for this first part of the final: the act must take the form of a play, not that of a short story or a chapter of a novel; it must incorporate Shakespearean stylistic elements; it must include at least one Borgesian theme; and it should consist of between thirteen hundred and sixteen hundred words. The second and third requirements encouraged students to assimilate what they had picked up on over the course the semester. Since they had read several of Shakespeare's plays, they would have gleaned his style and penchants. Students were not asked to attempt to sound exactly like Shakespeare or write in his English; rather, they were invited to integrate Shakespearean elements such that their act read more like Shakespeare than, say, Aeschylus, Lorraine Hansberry, or Tim Burton. Since they had also read many of Borges's pieces and used his work as their guiding lens throughout the course, I asked that they blend into the act a Borgesian motif—perhaps one of the elements of the trifecta or another ingredient that is seen as quintessentially Borges. The theme could appear as an object (e.g., as characters making their ways through a physical labyrinth) or as part of the narrative's structure (e.g., as the characters' experiencing labyrinthine emotions)—this is purposefully open to interpretation.

For the reflective commentary, I asked students to discuss their writing and thought process and to expound on their aesthetic decision-making and other choices they made in creating their acts. The second part of the final had three requirements: First, students had to clearly and explicitly explain which Shakespearean stylistic elements they incorporated in their acts, how they did so, and why they chose these particular elements. Second, they had to clearly and explicitly explain which Borgesian theme or themes they incorporated in their acts, how they did so, and why they chose those themes. Third, their reflection had to consist of between five hundred and eight hundred words. In explaining how I would assess the final project, I told students that though I believed it was not possible to grade creativity, I would assign a grade that reflected the degree to which they were able to create a project that followed the guidelines—specifically, the listed requirements.

The national tour of Shakespeare's First Folio occasioned a course that I would have otherwise probably not developed. Those who teach Shakespeare were encouraged to offer their courses during the semester of the Folio's visit. I found my way to Shakespeare's work through Borges and rounded out the conversation with Shakespeare's contemporary and another of Borges's inspirations—Cervantes. The resultant special topics course is paradigmatic of the way Borges's work can be juxtaposed with that of so many others. His proclivity for intertextuality and the way his writing seems to seep into other texts suggests the feasibility of more courses that feature the rhizomatic symphony among Borges and numerous other writers.

NOTE

I dedicate this essay to Sandy, Jamie, Alexander, and Nicholas: thank you for being our Miami family.

APPENDIX: PAIRINGS OF BORGES WITH SHAKESPEARE OR CERVANTES

Unless indicated otherwise, all selections from Borges are from *Collected Fictions*. All works by Shakespeare are from *The Complete Works*.

	Labyrinth	
WEEK	**Borges**	**Shakespeare or Cervantes**
2	"The Garden of Forking Paths" (119–28), "The Immortal" (183–95)	*Twelfth Night* (719–42)
3	"The Theme of the Traitor and the Hero" (143–46), "Ibn-Hakam al-Bokhari, Murdered in His Labyrinth" (255–62)	*The Merchant of Venice* (453–79)
4	"A Problem" (308–09), "Death and the Compass" (147–56), "The House of Asterion" (220–22)	Part 1 of *Don Quixote*: "Prologue" (3–9), "To the Book of Don Quixote of La Mancha" (11–18), chapters 1–8 (19–65)
5	"The Secret Miracle" (157–62), "The Two Kings and the Two Labyrinths" (263–64)	Part 2 of *Don Quixote*: chapters 1–14 (459–548)
	Mirror	
WEEK	**Borges**	**Shakespeare or Cervantes**
6	"The Circular Ruins" (96–100), "The Man on the Threshold" (269–73), "Mirrors" (*Selected Poems* [Coleman] 105, 107)	*Hamlet* (681–718)
7	"Parable of the Palace" (317–18), "Covered Mirrors" (297–98), "Everything and Nothing" (319–20)	*Richard II* (339–67)
8	"On Exactitude in Science" (325), "Pierre Menard, Author of the *Quixote*" (88–95)	Part 2 of *Don Quixote*: "Prologue to the Reader" (455–58), chapters 2 (469–73), 59 (842–49), 62 (864–75), 72 (924–28)
11	"The Approach to Al-Mu'tasim" (82–87), "Parable of Cervantes and the *Quixote*" (315)	Part 2 of *Don Quixote*: chapters 12 (526–32), 49 (772–82), 67 (898–902); part 1 of *Don Quixote*: chapters 4 (35–41), 25 (190–204), 26 (205–12), 48 (414–21)
	Encyclopedia	
WEEK	**Borges**	**Shakespeare or Cervantes**
12	"The Aleph" (274–86), "The Zahir" (242–49)	*Macbeth* (969–93)
13	"Shakespeare's Memory" (508–15), "Funes, His Memory" (131–37), "John Wilkins' Analytical Language" (*SNF* 229–32)	*The Tempest* (1221–43)
14	"The Library of Babel" (112–18), "The Congress" (422–35)	Part 1 of *Don Quixote*: "Prologue" (3–9), "To the Book of Don Quixote of La Mancha" (11–18), chapters 1 (19–24), 3 (29–35), 6 (45–52)
15	"The Book of Sand" (480–83), "Blue Tigers" (494–503)	Part 1 of *Don Quixote*: chapters 32–35 (266–313); part 2 of *Don Quixote*: chapters 62 (864–75), 72 (924–28)

Borges and Film: Reading Movies, Watching Stories

Pablo Brescia

Like many Latin American writers of his generation, Jorge Luis Borges was attracted to and influenced by what was at the dawn of the twentieth century a new communication medium—film. This attraction peaked between 1930 and 1950, before he went blind around 1954.[1] In a 1974 interview, he stated, "Siempre lo vi desde su costado narrativo" 'I always saw cinema from a narrative point of view' ("Conversación" 133; my trans.). My lessons on Borges and film begin with this remark, which shows that the Argentine author did not think of himself as a movie critic or use film terminology in his writings but rather saw film as a new and exciting way to tell a story, a source of fictions where he could find entertainment, emotion, pleasure, and—perhaps more importantly—varied affinities with his literary poetics. Judging by the numerous adaptations of his works and references to him or his stories in movies, throughout the twentieth and twenty-first centuries, movie directors have been receptive to the Borgesian literary system, and this archive provides great opportunities for getting students excited to read Borges in relation to film. Spectator, reviewer, and screenplay writer, Borges had even tried acting when he was seventy-six years old, playing the protagonist of his story "The South" in an episode of a documentary entitled *Borges: A South American Destiny* (Pisani). I have suggested and expanded on elsewhere four main areas of inquiry to study the connection between Borges and film: his role as a film reviewer, his works as a screenplay writer, cinema's influence on him, and Borges's influence on cinema (Brescia, "El cine," "Citizen Borges," and "Máquinas"). In this essay I offer some strategies for further exploring the last two areas, which offer the most comprehensive and engaging material for approaching the author's connection to film.[2]

Reading Movies

Between 1925 and 1944 Borges commented on, among other films, *City Lights*, *King Kong*, *The Docks of New York*, *Battleship Potemkin*, *The Thirty-Nine Steps*, and *Citizen Kane*.[3] Free from canonic expectations—the cinema was a young art at the time—he opined candidly, and his reviews illustrate a style that came to be known as Borgesian. Take this observation about his favorite director, Josef von Sternberg: "El laconismo fotográfico, la organización exquisita, los procedimientos oblicuos y suficientes de *La ley del hampa*, han sido reemplazados [en *Marruecos*] por la mera cumulación de comparsas, por los brochazos de excesivo color local" 'The terse photography, exquisite direction, and oblique yet suitable methods of *Underworld* have been replaced here [in the movie *Morocco*] by hordes of extras and broad brushstrokes of excessive local color' (qtd. in Cozarinsky, *Borges y el cine* 29; *SNF* 144). In class we discuss Borges's method of focusing on narrative design and thematic elements in films, praising some (i.e., "oblique yet suitable methods") and rejecting others (i.e., "excessive local color") according to his own artistic views.

To start class discussion, we read together the essay "Narrative Art and Magic," where Borges sets forth his literary poetics:

> [E]l problema central de la novelística es la causalidad. Una de las variedades del género, la morosa novela de caracteres, finge o dispone una concatenación de motivos que se proponen no diferir de los del mundo real. Su caso, sin embargo, no es el común. En la novela de continuas vicisitudes, esa motivación es improcedente, y lo mismo en el relato de breves páginas y en la infinita novela espectacular que compone Hollywood con los plateados *ídola* de Joan Crawford y que las ciudades releen. Un orden muy diverso los rige, lúcido y atávico. La primitiva claridad de la magia. (*OC* 1: 405)
>
> [T]he main problem of the novel is causality. One kind of novel, the ponderous psychological variety, attempts to frame an intricate chain of motives similar to those of real life. This type, however, is not the most common. In the adventure novel, such cumbersome motivation is inappropriate; the same may be said for the short story and for those endless spectacles composed by Hollywood with silvery images of Joan Crawford and read and reread in cities everywhere. They are governed by a very different order, both lucid and primitive: the primeval clarity of magic. (*SNF* 80)

I then ask students the following: How is fiction like life? How is it different? What do you look for in a novel, story, or movie? Do you prefer art that reflects life or art that understands its created nature? We follow up by discussing how, as a reader and as a writer, Borges privileges "plots of design," wherein texts are self-contained and display a planned causality, as opposed to "plots of process," where causality is more haphazard.[4] Film—a modern medium capable of great reach—can create such magical causality, constructing a verisimilitude that does shy away from its artifice. The adventure novel, short stories, and movies are the kinds of narrative vessels where, as Borges says in the essay, "profetizan los pormenores, [y es un proceso] lúcido y limitado" 'every lucid and determined detail [can be] a prophecy' (*OC* 1: 406; *SNF* 82).

After reading the essay, we probe what Borges saw or could see in the movie screen and how it relates to his essays and stories. We use two films from around the time when he was watching and writing about cinema: a very famous one, *The Wizard of Oz*—which, apparently, he never watched—and a favorite of his, *Underworld*. In *The Wizard of Oz*, the protagonist, Dorothy, runs away from her farm in Kansas because her beloved dog, Toto, is about to be put down. As she makes her way back home, a tornado hits, and she takes shelter in her bedroom; the window breaks and knocks her unconscious. The house is sent spinning into the air and lands in Munchkinland, in the Land of Oz, a shift epitomized in the phrase "Toto, I have a feeling we are not in Kansas anymore" (00:20:56). Up to this point, the images have a sepia tone, but Technicolor—as it was called at the time—becomes the distinctive feature of the film once Dorothy and Toto arrive in Munchkinland. It is a musical, a comedy, a fantasy, and an adventure movie.[5] Students instantly recognize the film. Borges would have been especially fond of a favorite motif of his, the dream-versus-reality framework, where the characters in sepia—the evil Almira Gulch; the workers Zeke, Hunk, and Hickory; Dorothy's aunt and uncle; Professor Marvel—get transformed with the use of color and thanks to Dorothy's wish fulfillment into the Wicked Witch of the West, the Cowardly Lion, the Scarecrow, the Tin Man, and the Wizard himself. These correspondences foreshadow movements in plot through "lucid and determined" details, as Borges puts it in his essay.

This is a perfect movie to pair with Borges's classic story "The South." As the protagonist, the librarian Juan Dahlmann, rushes up the stairs to read the *Arabian Nights* in his room, he hits himself in the head with an open window, ending up in a hospital. From then on, readers fluctuate, just like in the case of *The Wizard of Oz*, between dream and reality, with the protagonist purportedly taking a trip to the countryside, where he will be involved in a fight. Having seen the movie and read the story, I ask students to search for correspondences between the reality and dream sequences. In "The South," the cab, the train, the nurses and medics, and a needle get reimagined in the other half of the story. Students will recognize, for instance, that the owner of the *pulpería* ("tavern") in the second half of the tale resembles one of the male nurses in the first half and that the needle in the arm of Dahlmann in the first corresponds to the knife that he wields against his aggressors in the second. Indeed, the story itself points to the parallel design, declaring that "a la realidad le gustan las simetrías y los leves anacronismos" 'reality is partial to symmetries and slight anachronisms' (*OC* 1: 916; *CF* 175) and signaling a possible passage to an alternate dimension: "Nadie ignora que el Sur empieza del otro lado de Rivadavia" 'Everyone knows that the South begins on the other side of Avenida Rivadavia' (*OC* 1: 916; *CF* 176). This is the equivalent to Dorothy's famous utterance in *The Wizard of Oz*, "I have a feeling we are not in Kansas anymore." In this way students are also exposed to Borges's favorite literary topics and ideas through movies.

Once we show in class how to establish a connection between Borges and cinema, we move on to what the Argentine writer did watch. *Underworld* was a model for subsequent gangster movies. In the opening scene, a stumbling drunkard witnesses an explosion in a Chicago bank and recognizes the gangster "Bull" Weed, who comes out with a case full of money. A shooting with the police ensues, and Weed throws the bystander into his escape car. Together in a hideout, "Bull" angrily declares that alcohol makes "bums and squealers" (00:03:24), to which the other man responds, "I may be a bum, but I am not a squealer. I might say, sir, that I am a Rolls-Royce for silence" (00:03:38). This points to the main theme in the film: loyalty. In "Narrative Art and Magic," Borges says that "[t]odo episodio, en un cuidadoso relato, es de proyección ulterior" '[e]very episode in a careful narrative is a premonition' and provides the film as an illustration of this point: "El diálogo inicial de *La ley del hampa* versa sobre la delación, la primera escena es un tiroteo en una avenida; esos rasgos resultan premonitorios del asunto central" 'The opening dialogue of *Underworld* concerns stool pigeons; the opening scene, a gunfight on an avenue: these details prefigure the whole plot' (*OC* 1: 406; *SNF* 81).

Borges liked von Sternberg's skillful and dynamic editing, used in the beginning of *Underworld* to signal the passage of time and introduce the main characters ("Bull" and "Rolls Royce," Feathers—the female love interest of both—and "Buck" Mulligan, Weed's rival). He also admired how lighting conveyed distinct emotions, and he enjoyed the close-ups of faces, of small details like a flower, or of gestures, which narrate through images "esa épica de la acción pura y elemental protagonizada por hombres que no se compadecen de su propia muerte" 'epic action, pure and elemental, with protagonists who do not pity their own deaths,' as he says in a 1974 interview ("Conversación" 135; my trans.). In *Underworld*, among many "epic" moments, love and loyalty triumph, and "Bull" becomes an unlikely hero. How does this relate to Borges? We may go back to "The South," specifically to the scenes of the accident and the duel. Following a basic discussion of the notion of montage—the association of two or more images designed to cause the viewer to perceive a movement in plot, an idea, or an emotion not present in the individual images—students break into groups and deconstruct both scenes in specific sequences, creating a sort of storyboard using pictures they may find on the Internet:

> [Á]vido de examinar ese hallazgo, no esperó que bajara el ascensor y subió con apuro las escaleras; algo en la oscuridad le rozó la frente: ¿un murciélago, un pájaro? En la cara de la mujer que le abrió la puerta vio grabado el horror, y la mano que se pasó por la frente salió roja de sangre.
> (*OC* 1: 915)

> [E]ager to examine his find, he did not wait for the elevator—he hurriedly took the stairs. Something in the dimness brushed his forehead—a bat? a

bird? On the face of the woman who opened the door to him, he saw an expression of horror, and the hand he passed over his forehead came back red with blood. (*CF* 174–75)

La lámpara de kerosén pendía de uno de los tirantes; los parroquianos de la otra mesa eran tres: dos parecían peones de chacra; otro, de rasgos achinados y torpes, bebía con el chambergo puesto. Dahlmann, de pronto, sintió un leve roce en la cara. Junto al vaso ordinario de vidrio turbio, sobre una de las rayas del mantel, había una bolita de miga. Eso era todo, pero alguien se la había tirado. (*OC* 1: 918)

The kerosene lantern hung from one of the beams. There were three customers at the other table: two looked like laborers; the other one, with coarse, Indian-like features, sat drinking with his wide-brimmed hat on. Dahlmann suddenly felt something lightly brush his face. Next to the tumbler of cloudy glass, on one of the stripes in the tablecloth, lay a little ball of wadded bread. That was all, but somebody had thrown it at him. (*CF* 178)

Then we examine students' storyboards and discuss them. As we go back to the montage of the accident—the sensation of being brushed by something, the terrified face, the bloody forehead—we see an essential event that projects a strong visual impact, narrated with the photographic skill that Borges admired in his favorite directors.[6] As for the duel, the ridiculousness of the challenge—drunkards throwing breadcrumbs—makes it all the more humiliating. It is the creation of an atmosphere ("kerosene lantern," "cloudy glass," the tension among the men at the *pulpería*) that provides the desired epic effect that Borges found so enticing in Hollywood movies. In the imminent confrontation of the story, we identify von Sternberg's gangsters with the creole version in "The South," the *compadritos*, or young thugs. Students learn how attention to detail—in their own storyboards and in Borges—makes it possible to narrate through images.[7]

By examining how Borges reads movies, students see that his valuation of the screen is twofold: he considers cinema to be, on the one hand, an archive of themes akin to his literary interests and, on the other hand, a novel way to explore the *ars combinatoria* of narrative time and images needed for fictional discourse.

Watching Stories

By the 1950s, the Borgesian literary system counts as its central themes the inner workings of literature and the nature of knowledge, the multiplicity of identity, and the philosophical dimensions of time and space and explores motifs such as dreams versus reality, labyrinths, mirrors, libraries, duels, and doubles.

To further understand the connection between such a system and film, we watch Orson Welles's *Citizen Kane*, considered by experts to be the best movie in the history of cinema. I ask students to become movie critics and write a review of the film following some of the models provided on *Rotten Tomatoes.* The catch? Students must write the review as if they were Borges. Most of them by now notice his unique ways of watching and, trying to imitate him, offer commentary not only on themes but also on structure. We break into small groups, and, as I introduce them to Borges's own review of *Citizen Kane*, we talk about the differences and similarities between what they wrote and Borges's text. In the review, his ambivalence about the movie is apparent, recognizing Welles's skills—"hay fotografías de admirable profundidad" 'the cinematography has a striking depth,' he states—but saying it suffers from "gigantismo" 'giantism,' "pedantería" 'pedantry,' and "tedio" 'tedium.' Ultimately, he gravitates toward what he sees as a binary design in plot construction. He judges the first storyline a "banal" appeal to sentimentality over a childhood sled but the other storyline "a la vez metafísico y policial" 'a kind of metaphysical detective story,' presenting spectators with "la investigación del alma secreta de un hombre, a través de las obras que ha construido, de las palabras que ha pronunciado, de los muchos destinos que ha roto" 'the investigation of a man's inner self, through the works he has wrought, the words he has spoken, the many lives he has ruined' (qtd. in Cozarinsky, *Borges y el cine* 65; *SNF* 259). Borges sees in some parts of *Citizen Kane* the kind of fiction he likes and engages in a dialogue about narrative strategies as well as themes and motifs such as time, identity, and the labyrinth.

How does Welles create this identity puzzle? First, the inquiry into the meaning of "Rosebud" (the last word a dying Charles Foster Kane utters) is led by Thompson, an investigative reporter who, like the viewer (and many times like the reader in Borges's stories), must trace steps and put together pieces. Second, Kane's life is reconstructed through a multiplicity of points of view and narrative modalities, from the purportedly objective view of the *News on the March* clip to the subjectivity of memory—embodied in the diary of Thatcher (Kane's caretaker when he was a child) and the interviews with Kane's friends Leland and Bernstein; his ex-wife, Susan; and his butler, Raymond—to the omniscient narrator, the camera-eye that at the end reveals the meaning of "Rosebud." By discussing the movie together with students' reviews and Borges's take on the film, we conclude that this game of shifting narrators, so common in modern literature, questions the reliability of single accounts in fiction (and perhaps in life) and provides a kaleidoscopic collage emphasizing the elusiveness of Kane's authentic identity. How is this done? With the free use of the flashback technique, one of *Citizen Kane*'s most acclaimed innovations. Welles reverses the chronological order of storytelling from the start: the first event shown in the movie is Kane's death in his Xanadu mansion, and from then on, we see his life as an enigma in overlapping sequences. As Borges himself says in his review, this approach was not new—"el procedimiento es el de Joseph Conrad en *Chance* (1914) y el del hermoso film *The power and the glory*" 'the same technique was used by Joseph Conrad in *Chance* (1941) and in that beautiful film *The Power and the Glory*' (qtd. in Cozarinsky, *Borges y el cine* 64; *SNF* 259)—but it was assembled with an astonishing effectiveness that, together with the cinematography, marked a new direction in moviemaking and the history of cinema.[8]

Next we consider how *Citizen Kane* can help us understand Borges. The similarities in terms of narrative strategies, themes, and motifs are plentiful, but I ask students to read Borges's story "The Other Death" and to focus on the identity theme. Students quickly see that it also deals with a reconstruction of an identity—a puzzle—from different viewpoints and using different recollections and timelines. According to Colonel Dionisio Tabares, Pedro Damián behaved like a coward in the battle of Masoller and ran away to the province of Entre Ríos; however, for Dr. Juan Francisco Amaro, Damián died like a hero in that same battle. The narrator—who has just received a translation of Emerson's poem "The Past"—investigates like the reporter in *Citizen Kane* and entertains several hypotheses of what really happened with Damián. Finally, he offers his version of the events: at the hour of his death, Damián relived the battle and was able to modify the past and thus "en 1946, por obra de una larga pasión, Pedro Damián murió en la derrota de Masoller, que ocurrió entre el invierno y la primavera de 1904" 'in 1946, by the grace of his long-held passion, Pedro Damián died in the defeat at Masoller, which took place between the spring and the winter of 1904' (*OC* 1: 1021; *CF* 227). Students may notice that the colonel's and doctor's memories tell only one side of the story (and history) and that the overlapping of memories, testimonies, and the narrator's speculations are not enough to find out the truth, pointing once again to two topics dear to Borges and also present in Welles's film: personal identity as a complex puzzle, on the one hand, and the intricate workings of the layers of time, on the other. "Modificar el pasado no es modificar un solo hecho; es anular sus consecuencias, que tienden a ser infinitas" 'To change the past is not merely to change a mere single event; it is to annul all of its consequences, which tend to infinity,' says the narrator in "The Other Death" (*OC* 1: 1024; *CF* 227).

When watching films, Borges read them as if they were literature.[9] Students can reverse the procedure and watch his stories as if they were movies. After admitting that his investigation was a failure, Thompson says in *Citizen Kane* that discovering the meaning of "Rosebud" did not amount to much because "I don't think any word can explain a man's life" (1:54:28). Many of Borges's stories engage in an exploration of this idea, perhaps first enunciated in "The Nothingness of Personality," a short essay from 1929: "No hay tal yo de conjunto. Equivócase quien define la identidad personal como la posesión privativa de algún erario de recuerdos" 'There is no whole self. He who defines personal identity as the private possession of some depository of memories is mistaken' (*Inquisiciones* [Debolsillo] 82; *SNF* 4). Each life is configured as one of Borges's favorite motifs, the one he also sees in *Citizen Kane*. He gives the movie a thumbs-up in his personal dictionary of symbols: "En uno de los cuentos de Chesterton—'The Head of Caesar', creo—el héroe observa que nada es tan aterrador como un laberinto sin centro. Este film es exactamente ese laberinto" 'In a story by

Chesterton—"The Head of Caesar," I believe—the hero observes that nothing is so frightening as a labyrinth with no center. This film is precisely that labyrinth' (qtd. in Cozarinsky, *Borges y el cine* 65; *SNF* 259).[10]

Borges at the Movies (Redux)

The adaptations of Borges's works since the 1950s and his continued presence in movies (whether movies that were adapted from his stories or essays or in which he himself appears as a character or reference)[11] indicate that the output of Argentine and international films that refer to him has been steady. Another important question for students may thus be the following: What has cinema done with Borges's ideas? As a final strategy to engage with this connection, I ask them to read Borges's essay "Kafka and His Precursors" and his story "The Garden of Forking Paths" and watch Christopher Nolan's movie *Interstellar*. Borges's continued relevance for contemporary film can be seen in his presence in Nolan's movies, from *Memento* to *Inception* and *Interstellar*,[12] an influence the director has acknowledged on multiple occasions.

In "Kafka and His Precursors," Borges explains his idea of what a precursor is—an artist who alters not only future literary and cultural traditions but also past ones (*OC* 2: 80–81; *SNF* 363–65). This notion is useful not only when one reads him and tries to understand his views on art but also when it comes to considering his actual and potential relationship to film. These connections find an excellent illustration in "The Garden of Forking Paths," an espionage tale set during the First World War whose characters include Yu Tsun, a Chinese professor of English who spies for Germany; Richard Madden, an English captain who is chasing him; and Dr. Stephen Albert, an eminent sinologist who is studying a novel by Ts'ui Pên, who happens to be—here we have again the Borgesian correspondences—an ancestor of Yu Tsun. Ts'ui Pên's novel, described as "un invisible laberinto de tiempo" 'an invisible labyrinth of time,' is entitled *The Garden of Forking Paths*, and it presents "infinitas series de tiempos, en una red creciente y vertiginosa de tiempos divergentes, convergentes y paralelos. Esa trama de tiempos que se aproximan, se bifurcan, se cortan o que secularmente se ignoran, abarca todas las posibilidades" 'an infinite series of times, a growing, dizzying web of divergent, convergent, and parallel times. That fabric of times that approach one another, fork, are snipped off, or are simply unknown for centuries, contains all possibilities' (*OC* 1: 873; *CF* 126–27).

I ask students to focus specifically on the passages where Yu Tsun and Albert discuss the novel. Then we watch *Interstellar*'s Tesseract scene (2:20:12–2:24:07). In it, the montage shows an astronaut falling—the connection with the iconic *2001: A Space Odyssey* is obvious—a girl combing her hair, a small library, talk of a "fifth dimension," and a message that needs to be sent in Morse code. The protagonist of the movie, Cooper, is a farmer-astronaut living in 2067, and an environmental crisis has ravaged Earth, propelling a search for inhabitable planets, wormholes and black holes, and a spaceship named *Endur-*

ance. The film includes several references to Borges, among them a library that houses *Labyrinths*, the first published English-language collection of Borges's texts. Toward the end of the film, Cooper is inside Gargantua, a black hole, where he finds the Tesseract, a cube within a larger cube that in the movie represents the three physical dimensions in addition to time constructed by beings—the evolved humans from the future—who live in a five-dimensional reality. We then briefly discuss Barry Vacker's notion of the "cosmic sublime" an existential and aesthetic experience related to the paradoxical feelings humans experience when contemplating life in the universe.

The film's references to themes and motifs in other stories by Borges such as "The Library of Babel" and "The Aleph" are clear, but this "labyrinth of time" contains a representation of all times in a bedroom in which Murphy—Cooper's daughter—will grow up to save the world by becoming a genius physicist who solves the quantum gravity problem. In class we come full circle and, following "Kafka and His Precursors," ascertain not only how much Nolan is like Borges but also how much Borges is like Nolan. In short, the Tesseract scene is the enactment of the many philosophical corollaries of not only Ts'ui Pên's *The Garden of Forking Paths* but also the story "The Garden of Forking Paths." As Yu Tsun says in the story, "Me pareció que el húmedo jardín que rodeaba la casa estaba saturado hasta lo infinito de invisibles personas. Esas personas eran Albert y yo, secretos, atareados y multiformes en otras dimensiones de tiempo" 'I sensed that the dew-drenched garden that surrounded the house was saturated, infinitely, with invisible persons. Those persons were Albert and myself—secret, busily at work, multiform—in other dimensions of time' (*OC* 1: 873; *CF* 127). We end the discussion with a return to the notion of the cosmic sublime and the idea of the existential vertigo created by the *mise en abyme* structures in both Borges's story and Nolan's movie.

Because of their linguistic and literary sophistication, Borges's texts may be a challenge for students and even somewhat alien to their lives and literary experiences. Yet when they persist, they find that, like any movie or book that matters, they need to watch or read again to realize the depth of meaning that Borges brings to issues close to our life experience, such as the nature of reality, identity, or time. Borges's relationship to film was important to his literature and in his life. His stories can be read in a variety of contexts: philosophical, historical, political, aesthetic. To these we must add the cinematographic and, once again, follow his idea of a precursor: film modifies our understanding of Borges, and Borges modifies our views on film.

NOTES

1. Borges kept going to the movies so that he could at least listen to the dialogue and the music, as Gonzalo Aguilar and Emiliano Jelicié explain in *Borges va al cine*. They offer a list of the films he listened to once blind, among them works by Federico Fellini, Luchino Visconti, and Alfred Hitchcock and even *West Side Story*.

2. The scholarship on the relationship between Borges and cinema has been steadily increasing since the publication of Cozarinsky's *Borges in/and/on Film*. This book and Aguilar and Jelicié's *Borges va al cine* would complement students' reading of Borges's stories.

3. Most of these notes, published in newspapers and cultural magazines such as *Sur*, were first gathered by Cozarinsky. Some of them are included in *Selected Non-fictions*.

4. I borrow this useful distinction from Cook's *The Meaning of Fiction*.

5. The literary reference for Borges in this context would be, of course, *Alice in Wonderland*.

6. For an analysis of Borges's views on montage, see González.

7. In the preface to *Historia universal de la infamia* (1935; *A Universal History of Iniquity*), Borges mentions von Sternberg as an influence (*CF* 3). In the preface to the second edition (1954), he declares the book "no es otra cosa que apariencia, que una superficie de imágenes; por eso mismo puede acaso agradar" 'all just appearance, a surface of images—which is why readers may, perhaps, enjoy it' (*OC* 1: 593; *CF* 5). That "surface of images" is, of course, cinema.

8. Students can be asked to pay attention to those Borgesian stories where time is of the essence and to see if they find any filmic footprints. In "A Survey of the Works of Herbert Quain" (*OC* 1: 857–60; *CF* 107–11), a story framed as a review of a dead writer's novels, Borges presents a time that runs backward and applies it to Quain's novel *April March*, and in "The Secret Miracle" (*OC* 1: 900–04; *CF* 157–62), a multilayered fantastic, metafictional tale set during the Second World War, he experiments with the freeze-frame by magically stopping the execution of Jaromir Hladík.

9. Intending a pun, David Oubiña says that Borges was "corto de vista" 'shortsighted' given that "ve los films *sub especie literaria*, no solo porque utiliza un saber aprendido en los libros sino, ante todo, porque proyecta la literatura sobre ellos. El escritor-espectador ve todo el cine como si fuera un medio hecho de libros ilustrados. Es decir: lee lo literario en ellos" 'his gaze is limited by his interests. He sees films *sub especie literaria*, not only because he uses knowledge learned from books but also because he projects literature onto them. The writer-viewer watches cinema as if it were a medium made of illustrated books. That is, he reads the literary in them' (138; my trans.).

10. For another take on the relationship between Borges and *Citizen Kane*, see Accaria. In his conversations with Richard Burgin in 1968, Borges stated, "I saw *Citizen Kane* when it first came out. I did not like it. I thought it was an imitation of Joseph von Sternberg . . . Later I watched again and said to myself: 'Well, Orson Welles has invented modern cinema'" (*Conversations* 84).

11. Some of Borges's texts that have served as the basis for film adaptations include "Emma Zunz," "Man on Pink Corner," "The Story from Rosendo Juárez," "The Interloper," "The Gospel according to Mark," "The South," "The Theme of the Traitor and the Hero," "The Immortal," "The Dead Man," "The Wait," "Story of the Warrior and the Captive Maiden," and "Death and the Compass." Most adaptations are not especially memorable, but some of the films that use Borgesian ideas provide material to study how cinema watched Borges, so to speak, and tried to translate his work onto the screen.

12. For more on Borges's influence in Nolan's films, see Pontes Velasco; Zavaleta Balarezo; and Simorangkir.

Borges and Translation Studies

Emron Esplin

In his now famous tome *After Babel: Aspects of Language and Translation*, George Steiner claims, "Arguably, 'Pierre Menard, Author of the *Quixote*' (1939) is the most acute, most concentrated commentary anyone has offered on the business of translation. What studies of translation there are, including this book, could, in Borges's style, be termed a commentary on his commentary" (73). Steiner also quotes the tantalizing opener from Borges's essay "Las versiones homéricas" ("The Homeric Versions")—"Ningún problema tan consustancial con las letras y con su modesto misterio como el que propone una traducción" 'No problem is as consubstantial to literature and its modest mystery as the one posed by translation' (*OC* 1: 413; "Homeric Versions" 69)—as one of the three epigraphs to his book and offers his own translation of this mysterious claim, which I return to below. By the late twentieth century, Steiner was not the only reader who was taking Borges seriously as a translation theorist (whether through argumentative prose or through fiction). The claims that Borges made to level the playing field between so-called originals and their translations in "Pierre Menard," in a trio of essays on translation that he published between 1926 and 1936—"Las dos maneras de traducir" ("Two Ways to Translate"), the aforementioned "Las versiones homéricas," and "Los traductores de *Las 1001 noches*" ("The Translators of *The Thousand and One Nights*")—and in a short article titled "Sobre el 'Vathek' de William Beckford" ("On William Beckford's *Vathek*") were radical in the first half of the twentieth century, but they became mainstream to more than one strain of contemporary translation studies and translation theory in the following years.

Borges's ideas on translation are so germane to the twentieth-century growth of the field of translation studies that Borges can be offered as a central thinker in both lower-division and upper-division university courses on translation studies—from courses that serve as an introduction to the field to specialized courses on Borges and translation. In this essay, I show how Borges's thoughts on what he calls "two types of translation" resonate with historical ideas of translators and translation theorists and how his open denial of the source text's supposed superiority over the target text foresees concepts that are essential to various schools of translation studies in the twentieth century. I demonstrate, through analysis and a sample syllabus, how Borges's works can be used as bookends in an introductory course on translation studies in English and as a common thread that runs through and connects the material within that same course.

The Introductory Course and the Syllabus

The syllabus I provide is a slightly adjusted version of a syllabus I use in an introductory course in translation studies, with a specific focus on literary translation, that I have taught various times (see the appendix). It is designed for a fifteen-week course that meets twice a week, and it provides days (thirty in total) rather than dates. I have purposefully left three days open to allow for adjustments for exams, student conferences, peer review workshops, or other activities. For each day, I supply the topics of study and the daily readings. I have not provided sample assignments, but I have had the most success in this course when requiring students to write descriptive translation studies papers—papers that analyze (in descriptive and analytic rather than prescriptive terms) one or more target texts in English alongside one or more source texts or papers that examine two or more English-language translations of a specific text if the student cannot access the source text in the source language. Of course, students who are fledgling or practicing translators can also offer a translation of a short literary text for their final project. Bracketed annotations make explicit, for the instructor, how Borges is connected to a specific day's readings and discussions. I have not provided comments in brackets for days in which Borges's texts or texts about Borges are included in the daily readings (eight class periods) since the connections to him become clear in my analysis below, and I have not left bracketed comments for the days in which the subject matter does not easily connect to Borges (six days).

The course calendar is designed to follow two well-known books that were created to introduce readers to the field of translation studies—Lawrence Venuti's edited volume of primary texts on translation from ancient times to the twenty-first century, *The Translation Studies Reader*, and Anthony Pym's succinct *Exploring Translation Theories*.[1] The calendar includes all of Pym's book but only about a third of Venuti's, leaving room for adjustments based on the emphases that individual instructors would like to offer. The calendar also contains several other readings that the instructor can provide to students (typically in a course packet), including various texts by Borges. In general, the theoretical readings follow a chronological path that is interrupted every few class periods by case studies that require students to read multiple translations of one text in order to compare how different translators have wrestled with the specific work. Each case study is connected to a text that Borges either approached in his own fiction (the Bible) or examined closely in his writings on translation (the *Iliad* and the *Thousand and One Nights*). After covering a great deal of historical ground through the theoretical readings and the three case studies, the course ends by examining Borges's own translation praxis and by analyzing several competing translations of a select number of Borges's stories.

Borges as Bookend and Through Line

Borges begins and ends this introductory course in translation studies, and he serves as a through line for the entire semester. On the first day of class, before any readings have been assigned, I introduce students to the complexities of translation by discussing with them the opener of Borges's essay "Las versiones homéricas" and its English translations. This enigmatic assertion and the disparate ways it has been translated into English create immediate talking points about issues of syntax, word choice, length, and register that emphasize for students, from the start, that translation is not a simple matter. I use a visual slide to juxtapose the source text with its two published English translations (by Eliot Weinberger and Suzanne Jill Levine, respectively) and with the version that Steiner offers in *After Babel*. The slide looks something like this, but sections of the translations are color-coded to mark thc four main issues we discuss about this quotation:

> "Ningún problema tan consustancial con las letras y con su modesto misterio como el que propone una traducción" (*OC* 1: 413).
>
> "No problem is as consubstantial to literature and its modest mystery as the one posed by translation" (Borges, "Homeric Versions" [trans. Weinberger] 69).
>
> "No problem is more essential to literature and its small mysteries than translation" (Borges, "Some Versions" [trans. Levine] 1136).
>
> "No problem is as completely concordant with literature and with the modest mystery of literature as is the problem posed by a translation" (Steiner xxi).

At the level of syntax, all three English translations turn Borges's phrase (it is not really a sentence since the main clause lacks a verb) into a complete sentence by adding "is." Each of the translators, with this addition, performs one of what the translator and translation theorist Antoine Berman calls "deforming tendencies" (Venuti, *Translation Studies Reader* [*TSR*] 250)[2]—in this case "clarification" (252)—by making the phrase understandable in English. Without "is," Weinberger's and Steiner's translations would leave the reader waiting for the end of what feels like a convoluted introductory clause, while removing "is" from Levine's rendition would make the phrase read like a quip or a brief response to a question that the reader did not know had been asked. Adding "is" makes the sentence work in English, but such clarification, as Berman suggests, "aims to render 'clear' what does not wish to be clear in the original" (252), or, at least, it reveals a difference in expectations between typical readers of Spanish and English.[3]

We then move to the question of word choice, focusing specifically on Borges's use of "consustancial," "letras," "modesto," and "propone" and on the translators' translations of these particular terms. Because of the limited space, I examine only the trickiest of these terms here, *consustancial*, although we also ask similar questions in class of the other three words. This word's English cognate—*consubstantial*—shares the same etymology, the Latin *consubstantialis*, and the two words have similar primary definitions: "Perteneciente a la propia naturaleza de alguien o de algo e inseparable de ella" 'Belonging to someone's or something's own nature and inseparable from it' ("Consustancial";

my trans.) and "Of one and the same substance or essence; the same in substance" ("Consubstantial"). Both words are laden with religious meaning; the secondary definition of *consustancial* refers directly to the trinity in the Catholic faith, and the secondary definition of *consubstantial* references the Godhead.[4] But the word is not well known in English outside a religious context, and it can send a reader to their dictionary. Such an experience is not rare when reading certain English translations of Borges, but does the same thing happen with the reader of the Spanish-language source text? And what are we to make of Borges, an agnostic writing in a primarily Catholic country but a devourer of all literatures both sacred and profane, choosing this particular term? Should it carry religious weight with it into English or not? For Weinberger, the answer is yes, and he goes with the cognate. For Levine, the answer seems to be no, and she chooses the much more common "essential"—getting right at the Spanish term's secular denotation without any religious overtones. Steiner, in contrast, offers the alliterative "completely concordant," discarding the Spanish word's religious meaning but carrying over some of its (and Borges's) erudition.

Connected to word choice, we have the question of length, and the class confronts two more of Berman's "deforming tendencies" in the translators' approaches. Levine's translation is significantly shorter than Borges's text (thirteen words to his eighteen), demonstrating what Berman calls "quantitative impoverishment" (*TSR* 254), while Steiner's shows what Berman calls "expansion" (252–53), because it grows from eighteen to twenty-three words and repeats both "problem" and "literature," even though in Borges's version each word appears only once and is later referred to by a pronoun. Weinberger's translation comes closest to Borges's text, with seventeen words and a similar length overall.

Finally, we discuss the issue of register. With her particular word choices—"more essential . . . small mysteries than translation"—and the shorter length of her translation, Levine lowers the register of this passage, making it clear and easy to read. Some readers of Borges (both in English and in Spanish) argue that such a shift in register demystifies Borges and alters the reading experience for the worse, while others claim that reading Borges in Spanish is not difficult and that certain English-language translations add a level of confusion that does not exist in his Spanish source texts. Weinberger's fairly literal word choices, "consubstantial . . . modest mystery . . . posed by translation" and similar length maintain a consistent register with Borges's source text, although the class wonders if "consubstantial" does different work in Protestant or secular contexts than "consustancial" accomplishes in a Catholic setting. Steiner's word choices—"completely concordant . . . modest mystery . . . as is the problem posed by a translation"—and his expansion of the passage's length both seem to try to raise the register while simultaneously secularizing it, which leaves his translation open to the inverse praise or critique that some readers of Borges would offer to Levine's approach.

Interestingly, even with all these differences, all three translations take the same general approach—one of domesticating rather than foreignizing, one that offers the sense of Borges's claim about the mysteries of translation rather than a word-for-word translation of his statement. The similarity in approach is most visible with the addition of "is," a domestication that tries to make Borges's claim sound like English, rather than a foreignizing approach that would not add the verb and, thus, make the translated text feel or look foreign in the eyes of the English-language reader. To add to this discussion of translation's complexity, I ask the class how the translations might differ if they were published in very different contexts—either in time or space. All three of these translations were published in the United States, although by translators with very different backgrounds from one another, within a fairly short period of time—Steiner's in 1975, Levine's in 1992, and Weinberger's in 1999. The class then takes the other path and offers its own, overly literal translation, one that lacks a main verb; translates "las letras" literally, as "letters" instead of as "literature"; and makes no clarification of prepositions connected to "propone." The final product looks something like this: "No problem as consubstantial with the letters and with their modest mystery as the one that proposes a translation." As students realize from this exercise, translation is much more complex than simply replacing a word from one language with its supposed equivalent in another. This literal translation is far more confusing, and far less poetic, than any of the three published versions.[5]

And so the course begins. I do not have the space here to explain how I run each class period connected to Borges, but I can briefly discuss the most significant recurring ideas in Borges's three primary essays on translation—"Las dos maneras de traducir," "Las versiones homéricas," and "Los traductores de *Las 1001 noches*"—that openly connect Borges to several of the classroom discussions beyond the days in which the class actually examines these specific texts. In each of these works, Borges proposes what the title of the first essay states as fact, the idea that there are two types of translation. In "Las dos maneras" he states, "Universalmente, supongo que hay dos clases de traducciones. Una practica la literalidad, la otra la perífrasis" 'Universally, I suppose there are two types of translations: one is the practice of literality, the other, paraphrase' ("Las dos maneras" 257; "Two Ways" 55). In the latter two essays, Borges juxtaposes these two types of translation by referencing the debate in the 1860s between Francis W. Newman and Matthew Arnold in which Arnold argued for periphrasis and Newman championed literal translation. While Borges never openly disparages either thinker and, instead, savors the "hermosa discusión" 'beautiful debate' between them (*OC* 1: 415; "Homeric Versions" 71),[6] his analyses of various translations in these essays reveal his penchant for liberal translations over literal ones. Borges's continued comparison of these two approaches to translation makes him a germane talking point during several of the class periods on the syllabus since the breakdown he offers resonates with other translation theorists and practicing translators, including Jerome, Friedrich Schleiermacher, Newman, and Arnold. His discussion of literal versus nonliteral translations is also relevant in twentieth- and twenty-first-century debates on foreignizing versus domesticating translations offered by scholars like Berman and Venuti, although Borges's proclivity for domesticated translations that openly demonstrate the cultural and literary context of the target culture certainly flies in the face of Berman's and Venuti's preferences for a foreignizing approach.

Apart from theorizing two types of translation, Borges also shows in all three of these pieces that he thinks quality translations are possible and that he does not inherently prefer source texts over target texts. In "Las dos maneras" he argues that texts change when they move to different spaces (from Argentina to Chile, for example) even when they do not change languages (256). In "Las versiones" he claims, "Presuponer que toda recombinación de elementos es obligatoriamente inferior a su original, es presuponer que el borrador 9 es obligatoriamente inferior al borrador H—ya que no puede haber sino borradores. El concepto de *texto definitivo* no corresponde sino a la religión o al cansancio" 'To assume that every recombination of elements is necessarily inferior to its original form is to assume that draft nine is necessarily inferior to draft H—for there can only be drafts. The concept of the "definitive text" corresponds only to religion or exhaustion' (*OC* 1: 413; "Homeric Versions" 69). And in "Los traductores" he passionately advocates for a domesticating translation praxis that would bring the fantastic tradition of German literature into play in a hypothetical German translation of the *Nights* (*OC* 1: 743–44; "Translators" 108–09). In short, in each of these works Borges begins to question the sanctity of so-called originals.

That questioning reaches a radical apex in 1939 with "Pierre Menard" and in 1943 with "Sobre el 'Vathek' de William Beckford." In the former, Borges's title character—a twentieth-century French poet—recreates (does not copy, but rewrites verbatim) a section of *Don Quixote*, and, famously, Borges's narrator suggests that Menard's identical passage "es casi infinitamente más rico" 'is almost infinitely richer' (*OC* 1: 846; "Pierre Menard" 94) than Cervantes's version, since the time and place of the writing have changed significantly and thus change the text. The secondary version, not the original, has more value. In "Sobre el 'Vathek'" Borges makes a similar claim, arguing, about the French version of the novel that Beckford composed in 1782, that "[e]l original es infiel a la traducción" '[t]he original is unfaithful to the translation,' in part because "el frances del siglo XVIII" 'eighteenth-century French' is purportedly "menos apto que el inglés para comunicar los 'indefinidos horrores' (la frase es de Beckford) de la singularísima historia" 'less suitable than English for communicating the "undefined horrors" (the phrase is Beckford's) of this unusual story' (*OC* 2: 99; "On William Beckford's *Vathek*" 239). With both of these pieces, Borges flips on its head the millennia-long favoring of originals over translations. In the former, he emphasizes how changes in context alter any text, even if the language (and even the very exact words) do not change. And in the latter, he hollows out the idea of fidelity to the point that it makes just as much sense for an original to be faithful or unfaithful to a translation as the other way around.

This idea clearly converses with two very different translation paradigms from the later twentieth century—Skopos theory and descriptive translation studies. The former started in the late 1970s with the work of Hans Vermeer, and it argues for the importance of a translation's purpose, or *skopos*, over the concept of fidelity to the source text. According to Vermeer, a translator and a client create a "commission" that clearly states the "purpose" of a specific translation, and the translator then acts as "an expert" to bring about that purpose (*TSR* 220). The purposes vary by client, translator, and context, and they are not beholden to the source text unless that is the stated goal of the client. Pym summarizes Skopos theory as "a paradigm that is based on a simple idea: a translation need not be equivalent to its start text" (*Exploring* 59). While Skopos theory offers a template for translators, descriptive translation studies proposes that readers and theorists of translation attempt to describe and analyze translations rather than prescribe what they should be. From James S. Holmes's naming of the academic discipline in 1972 to Itamar Even-Zohar's work with polysystems, and from Gideon Toury's studies of norms to André Lefevere's examinations of translations as "refractions" or "rewritings," descriptive translation studies sets out to examine what translations actually do in a given literary tradition rather than to judge how good or bad individual translations are based on any notion of fidelity to a source text. As Toury states, "[T]ranslations are facts of target cultures" (23). In short, both of these approaches—Skopos theory and descriptive translation studies—are target-oriented and refuse to place the source text on a pedestal, and, thus, they create clear points of comparison with Borges's appraisal of translations as texts that are every bit as worthy of study and praise as so-called originals.

While serving as a through line for the theoretical discussions of the course, Borges also informs the class's three case studies. I introduce each case study with works by Borges that comment on the translated text in question. For the first and third case studies—selections from the *Iliad* and the *Thousand and One Nights*, respectively—we discuss Borges's aforementioned essays on the translations of each of these canonical texts, and both case studies allow students to see vastly different approaches to translation and to then judge whether they prefer literal or liberal, word-for-word or paraphrase, foreignizing or domesticating. In the second case study, selections from the Bible, students read two of Borges's stories in translation—"The Gospel according to Mark" and "The Book of Sand." The former serves as a horrific literalist translation of Christ's crucifixion for the story's protagonist, Baltasar Espinoza ("Gospel" 401), and the latter hinges on its narrator's decision to trade his pension and "[a] black-letter Wyclif" Bible for an infinite book, a book of sand ("Book" 482). These stories demonstrate possible extreme points in our discussions surrounding a wide variety of approaches to Bible translation as seen through comparisons of Bible prefaces, translators' notes, and selected Bible passages. I have left this section of the syllabus particularly open since instructors may want to compare different passages depending on their own interests and on the availability of local experts (Bible scholars, Bible translators, or scholars of ancient texts) to visit the class.[7]

After following Borges through the course's theoretical readings and its case studies, the class finishes with a brief unit on Borges as its final bookend. We spend one day discussing Borges's work as a translator with the help of selected readings from Efraín Kristal's *Invisible Work: Borges and Translation* and Sergio Waisman's *Borges and Translation: The Irreverence of the Periphery*. Then we read multiple English-language translations of two or more specific works by Borges. Instructors can follow their own preferences when choosing which Borges texts to teach, but the following stories have the most available translations, and some of them offer very distinct approaches: "El jardín de senderos que se bifurcan" ("The Garden of Forking Paths"), "El Aleph" ("The Aleph"), "Pierre Menard," "Borges y yo" ("Borges and I"), "Las ruinas circulares" ("The Circular Ruins"), and "La muerte y la brújula" ("Death and the Compass"). Reading various translations of selected Borges texts provides another opportunity for the instructor to juxtapose different approaches to translation in practice, and it provides a unique moment in which students can see which, if any, of Borges's English-language translators translate his stories in the ways that he praises in his essays on translation or in the ways that he actually translates others' works.

Possible Course Adjustments

The syllabus I have offered can be used with students who have varied skills in languages other than English. When I have taught this class, I have usually had a few students who are advanced speakers of Spanish, a number of students who are speakers of other languages (Japanese, Mandarin, Italian, French, and Portuguese, to name a few), and a few monolingual students. The course readings and the types of assignments that I use function well for each of these groups, but, not surprisingly, some students who can work in more than one language and literary tradition often take their final papers to a higher level because they have access to the source texts. The basic template I have offered in this essay can be adjusted if all students in the course have advanced language skills beyond English, or it can be altered if the instructor has specific expertise in any subfield within translation studies or experience with literary traditions outside English studies.

One hypothetical version of this class would be a more advanced course for students who know both Spanish and English and have some basic experience with translation studies. This course could be titled Borges and Translation Studies, and rather than working its way through Pym and Venuti, it could offer only the chapters and essays most closely related to Borges from each of those texts. Doing so would open up several class periods in which students could study Borges's work as a translator—reading Kristal's and Waisman's monographs in their entirety and analyzing selected translations performed by Borges alongside the source texts. Those works could include Walt Whitman's *Leaves of Grass*; Virginia Woolf's *A Room of One's Own*; Langston Hughes's "I, Too," "Our Land," and "The Negro Speaks of Rivers"; Edgar Allan Poe's "The Purloined Letter"; and many others, depending on the instructor's expertise and students' interests. Then the class could conduct in-depth comparative readings of a number of Borges's most well-known stories that have been translated into English multiple times, and, unlike the introductory course, students' experience with Spanish would make it possible to include Borges's source texts. In short, a course like this would enable similar discussions of Borges's connections to translation theories of the twentieth century while also allowing students to see more clearly whether Borges puts his theories into practice when he translates and to explore how Borges's translators treat his works as sacred originals, as start texts from which to form merely another draft of a work, or as something in-between.

NOTES

I would like to thank Margarida Vale de Gato and Daryl Hague for their helpful suggestions as I revised this essay.

1. Between the time in which I originally wrote this essay and its publication in this volume, Pym released the third edition of *Exploring Translation Theories*. This new edition contains several significant changes and new chapters. I still teach my course using the second edition, but the third edition can also be used with slight modifications to the sample syllabus.

2. Unless otherwise indicated, references to Venuti's *Translation Studies Reader* are to the fourth edition.

3. Referring to Berman's "analytic of translation" (*TSR* 249) on the first day of class prepares students for the discussion of ethical and non-ethnocentric translation practices that students will encounter in later course readings by Venuti and Berman.

4. The *Oxford English Dictionary* states that *consubstantial* was "[o]riginally a term of Theology" and shows ninety-three years between the word's first theological use and its first secular use ("Consubstantial").

5. This exercise itself is reminiscent of Borges, who makes a similar move in the conclusion of "Las dos maneras" (259).

6. In "The Translators of *The Thousand and One Nights*," Esther Allen offers "beautiful exchange" as a translation of "hermosa discusión" (*OC* 1: 732; Borges, "Translators" 95).

7. Bible translation has been an extremely fruitful topic in the field of translation studies. This unit could be extended to include other texts by Eugene Nida and responses to and critiques of his work. The topic of Bible translation provides an opportunity to discuss the increased nuances of the term *equivalence* that students will have explored a few class periods earlier.

APPENDIX: SYLLABUS FOR INTRODUCTORY COURSE ON TRANSLATION STUDIES

DAY 1. Introductions, Syllabus, Translation Studies

In-class exercise with three published translations of the first sentence of Borges's "Las versiones homéricas" (Borges, "Homeric Versions" 69 and "Some Versions" 1136; Steiner xxi)

DAY 2. Translation Studies, Translation Theory, The 3% Problem

Lawrence Venuti, introduction to *The Translation Studies Reader* (1–9)

Venuti, "How to Read a Translation"

DAY 3. Translation Studies, Translation Theory, The 3% Problem
Anthony Pym, chapter 1 of *Exploring Translation Theories* (1–5)
Esther Allen, "Translation, Globalization, and English"

DAY 4. Word-for-Word versus Sense-for-Sense
Jerome, "Letter to Pammachius," translated by Kathleen Davis (Venuti, *Translation Studies Reader* [*TSR*] 29–38)
Friedrich Schleiermacher, "On the Different Methods of Translating," translated by Susan Bernofsky (*TSR* 51–71)
[Borges's "Las dos maneras de traducir" (next class period) can be referenced here in connection with both texts, as can his translation essays on Homer and the *Thousand and One Nights*.]

DAY 5. Word-for-Word versus Sense-for-Sense, The Newman/Arnold Debate
Borges, "Two Ways to Translate," translated by Suzanne Jill Levine
Francis William Newman, "The Unlearned Public Is the Rightful Judge of Taste"
Matthew Arnold, "The Translator's Tribunal"

DAY 6. Case Study 1: The *Iliad*; Versions of Homer through Borges
Borges, "Some Versions of Homer," translated by Levine
Borges, "The Homeric Versions," translated by Eliot Weinberger

DAY 7. Case Study 1: The *Iliad*
George Chapman, "To the Reader"
Alexander Pope, "Pope's Preface"
Newman, Preface
Richmond Lattimore, "A Note on the Translation"
Stanley Lombardo, "Translator's Preface"
[Borges's ideas on translations of the *Iliad* serve as background.]

DAY 8. Case Study 1: The *Iliad*
Chapman, "The First Book of Homer's Iliads"
Pope, "Book 1"
Newman, "Book 1"
Lattimore, "Book 1"
Lombardo, "Book 1"
[Borges's ideas on translations of the *Iliad* serve as background.]

DAY 9. Natural Equivalence, Directional Equivalence
Pym, chapter 2 of *Exploring Translation Theories* (6–23)
Pym, chapter 3 of *Exploring Translation Theories* (24–42)
[Students can also watch Pym's videos about equivalence on *YouTube* ("Pym," "Theories of Directional Equivalence," "Theories of Natural Equivalence," "What's Wrong").]
Eugene Nida, "Principles of Correspondence" (*TSR* 171–85)
[Borges's three essays on translation provide a counterpoint here.]

DAY 10. Borges on Translation
Borges, "On William Beckford's *Vathek*," translated by Weinberger
Borges, "Pierre Menard, Author of the *Quixote*," translated by Andrew Hurley

DAY 11. Purposes, Skopos

Pym, chapter 4 of *Exploring Translation Theories* (43–61)

Hans J. Vermeer, "Skopos and Commission in Translational Action" (*TSR* 219–30)

[Borges's ideas from "Pierre Menard" and "Sobre el 'Vathek'" foreshadow Skopos theory's emphasis on the target text's purpose over fidelity to the source text.]

DAY 12. Descriptive Translation Studies

Pym, chapter 5 of *Exploring Translation Theories* (62–85)

James S. Holmes, "The Name and Nature of Translation Studies" (*TSR* [1st ed.] 172–85) [Students should skim the essay and read pages 176–78 closely.]

Itamar Even-Zohar, "The Position of Translated Literature within the Literary Polysystem" (*TSR* 191–96)

Gideon Toury, "The Nature and Role of Norms in Translation" (*TSR* 197–210)

[Borges's ideas from "Pierre Menard" and "Sobre el 'Vathek'" foreshadow the target-oriented approach of descriptive translation studies.]

DAY 13. Translation as Rewriting, Making Originals

André Lefevere, "Mother Courage's Cucumbers: Text, System and Refraction in a Theory of Literature" (*TSR* 231–46)

Lefevere, chapter 1 of *Translating Literature* (5–14)

Karen Emmerich, "Difference at the 'Origin,' Instability at the 'Source': Translation as Translingual Editing"

[Borges's ideas from "Pierre Menard" and "Sobre el 'Vathek'" foreshadow the target-oriented approach of descriptive translation studies.]

DAY 14. Foreignizing versus Domesticating

Antoine Berman, "Translation and the Trials of the Foreign," translated by Venuti (*TSR* 247–60)

Venuti, "Invisibility" (*Translator's Invisibility* 1–34)

[Borges's three essays on translation can further inform this juxtaposition.]

DAY 15. Case Study 2: The Bible; Bible Translations in Borges's Fiction

Borges, "The Gospel according to Mark," translated by Hurley

Borges, "The Book of Sand," translated by Hurley

DAY 16. Case Study 2: The Bible; Guest Speaker

Bible prefaces [according to the instructor's or guest speaker's preferences]

"The Translators to the Reader" (translator's note or preface to the 1611 King James Version)

Donald Ebor, "Preface to the New English Bible"

David Bentley Hart, Introduction

[Other selected prefaces are available at www.biblegateway.com.]

DAY 17. Case Study 2: The Bible; Guest Speaker

Bible passages from several Bible translations [according to the instructor's or guest speaker's preferences]

DAY 18. Uncertainty

Pym, chapter 6 of *Exploring Translation Theories* (86–116)

Jacques Derrida, *Monolingualism of the Other* (1–11)

Derrida, "What Is a 'Relevant' Translation?" (*TSR* 373–96)

[Borges's thoughts on translation and on language in general are relevant to the discussion of uncertainty.]

DAY 19. Translation and Gender

Lori Chamberlain, "Gender and the Metaphorics of Translation" (*TSR* 261–75)

Sherry Simon, "Taking Gendered Positions in Translation Theory" (Simon 1–38)

[A discussion about the confusion surrounding who translated and who signed some of Borges's and his mother's published translations of specific literary texts might be useful here.]

DAY 20. Localization, Translation, and Technology

Pym, chapter 7 of *Exploring Translation Theories* (117–37)

Michael Cronin, "The Translation Age: Translation, Technology, and the New Instrumentalism" (*TSR* [3rd ed.] 469–82)

DAY 21. Cultural Translation

Pym, chapter 8 of *Exploring Translation Theories* (138–58)

Gayatri Chakravorty Spivak, "The Politics of Translation" (*TSR* 320–38)

DAY 22. Case Study 3: The *Thousand and One Nights*; Borges on Translators of the *Nights*

Borges, "The Translators of *The Thousand and One Nights*," translated by Allen (*TSR* 122–35)

DAY 23. Case Study 3: The *Thousand and One Nights*

Comparison of contents

Overview of different translations

Robert L. Mack, Introduction

Mack, "Note on the Text"

Edward William Lane, "Translator's Preface"

Richard Francis Burton, "The Translator's Foreword"

Isabel Burton, Preface

Husain Haddawy, Introduction

[Borges's ideas on translations of the *Thousand and One Nights* serve as background.]

DAY 24. Case Study 3: The *Thousand and One Nights*

Mack, "Arabian Nights' Entertainments"

Lane, Introduction

Richard Francis Burton, Introduction

Isabel Burton, Introduction

Haddawy, Prologue

[Borges's ideas on translations of the *Thousand and One Nights* serve as background.]

DAY 25. Borges as Translator

Efraín Kristal, "Borges's Method as Translator" (*Invisible Work* 87)

Sergio Waisman, introduction to *Borges and Translation* (11–17)

Waisman, "Borges and Domestication: Orientalism from the Margins?" (*Borges and Translation* 79–83)

DAY 26. Borges in Translation: "El jardin de senderos que se bifurcan"

Borges, "The Garden of Forking Paths," translated by Anthony Boucher

Borges, "The Garden of Forking Paths," translated by Donald A. Yates

Borges, "The Garden of Forking Paths," translated by Helen Temple and Ruthven Todd

Borges, "The Garden of Forking Paths," translated by Hurley*

[Other possible Borges pieces with several different translators include "Pierre Menard," "Borges y yo," "Las ruinas circulares," and "La muerte y la brújula."]

DAY 27. Borges in Translation: "El Aleph"

Borges, "The Aleph," translated by Anthony Kerrigan

Borges, "The Aleph," translated by Norman Thomas di Giovanni and Borges

Borges, "The Aleph," translated by Hurley

[Other possible Borges pieces with several different translators include "Pierre Menard," "Borges y yo," "Las ruinas circulares," and "La muerte y la brújula."]

* Di Giovanni's translation of this story as "The Garden of Branching Paths"—not available in the out-of-print translations that he published in collaboration with Borges—is another version that can be used on this day. However, it is very difficult to find because it was never officially published, and online copies are only sometimes available.

The Slyness of Borges

Christian Reed

My goal in this essay and its roster of projects is twofold: first, to actively enable teachers at the high school level, especially English teachers, to teach more works by Jorge Luis Borges and, second, to spark an interest in the pedagogical approach I outline, a variation on project-based learning, with teachers of Borges at the college level. What slyness has to do with this, we will see soon enough.

A *Difficult Humorist*

The slyness I describe is a phenomenon of humor, so let's start there. What kind of thing is a joke for Borges? A jokey answer would be—it's hard to tell. Inevitably, one finds one's favorite Borges jokes are one's own indeed. No one finds this out faster than a teacher in the classroom. You would not believe the shrugs I have seen at a phrase I find hilarious ("fecal necessities," from "The Library of Babel" [Irby, "Library" 51]) or the "mehs" I've been met with when I intone the pun "on the other hand" (at the crux of "Pierre Menard" [*CF* 94]). There is something funny about the way that Borges is funny. I've heard myself laugh at it alone.

In-jokes are Borges's favorite type of jokes. Jokes like his are averse to betraying their essence, which is to be private, and their metaphysical status, which seems to be subjective. In the pursuit of this truth, the joke declines, with killing tact, the laughter of others. It seems plausible in this context to speak of Borgesian "anti-comedy," which would not mean, of course, that Borges is not funny, but rather that his funny does not lie in the traditional binding sense of comedy, heard in the sister words *common* and *community*. What makes you laugh is only what makes you laugh. Borges is a difficult humorist.

The Upsurge of Interest

I mention this because lately, if belatedly, there does seem to be an upsurge of interest in the comic side of Borges among English-language readers. The discourse on Borges as comedian has come a long way since an early US reviewer of *Ficciones* wondered dismissively, "Is all this learned trifling mere trifling and nothing more?" (R. T. H. 53). The valence of such speculation had to be reversed, and so, in 1971, a critic of the stature of Alfred Kazin took meeting Borges very seriously; one "clever" is all he emitted. Even in 2004, a writer with the comedic chops of David Foster Wallace, in a searching reappraisal, stressed Borges's "mystical" side. A spate of recent treatments, however, shows a distinct emphasis on Borges's humor and the discernment in which it abounds.[1] I am thinking not only of the thoroughgoing *Humor in Borges*, by René de Costa; the dossier on humor in issue 12 of *Variaciones Borges*; and some bracing pieces written by Michael

Wood invoking "productive mischief" ("Productive Mischief," "Unreachable Real," "Borges"), an especially promising concept. More broadly, a host of quips swarm to mind, having sprung up lately in popular and critical treatments. There are a lot of these, and, on the whole, they are a lot of fun.[2]

For now, however, I limit my consideration to the consequences of this fine new enthusiasm for the classroom. How might it change how Borges is taught—and to whom?

The Sly Classroom

Let me jiggle the argument a bit. Its warrant is that the comedy of Borges is in the ascendant with critics. Its premise is that Borges is funny, but in a funny type of way. Presently it will insist that "sly" is a suitable name for the Borges type of funny. But first a question asserts itself: Say Borges is sly, who cares? Does it earn him any new readers? Who vibes with sly? My intuition is immediate. It is the very group I teach—adolescents.

Perhaps this is because slyness in its structure sets up an inverted image of regular classroom instruction (the dynamics of which have become very familiar to high school people). In both cases, the ruse and the classroom, there is one who is supposed to know and another who is supposed not to. The teacher imagines they teach; the student imagines that one day they may teach, but for today they'll be sly. "I know something you don't know" is the mantra common to both.

In a striking moment in "An Autobiographical Essay," Borges appears to recognize these possibilities and then give the matter a memorable twist. He imagines the home sneakily as a classroom, one in which "children educate their parents, not the other way around" (142). The saying is wise; its attribution is sly. Borges says he heard it from his father.

The logic is loopy: he taught me that I taught him that he taught me that. . . . But the circular formulation hints at a happy prospect, which I'll call the sly classroom. By means of slyness, Borges sets up an ideal of education as mutual education, a space in which each might learn about learning from each.[3] The ideal strikes us as beautiful because its consequence strikes us as true: one might well teach what one does not know. We could take this formula from a celebrated book by Jacques Rancière, or we could tack an alternate ending onto a slogan from John Dewey: learning is learning to think, for students as for teachers.[4]

We are coming around to the claim that slyness should be slyly taught. But let's pause first to consider what slyness actually looks like in Borges. Though "sly" may be a master term for this writer, he is too sly to use the word much himself. Still, we have the sense that for Borges the verbs "to tell" and "to insinuate" are rigorously synonymous. The preferred mode of observation in both essays and stories is the lateral glance. Everyone watches everyone sideways. The subjective omniscience of Funes, like the objective omniscience of the Aleph, are conveyed precisely through zigzag glimpsing (*OC* 1: 882, 1: 1068; *CF* 135, 283–84). Side-eye abounds, moreover, at the beginning of history (in

"A Defense of Basilides the False" [*OC* 1: 392; *SNF* 68]), as at its end, in that deadly story "Deutsches Requiem." There, the sideways, sly way of looking at the world is akin to the poetic practice of David Jerusalem, whom his tormentor describes as delighting in "cada cosa, con minucioso amor" 'every smallest thing, with meticulous and painstaking love' (*OC* 1: 1028; *CF* 232). The manner seems in some dim way to recall that of the fictitious editor of the text, who plays the Sub-Sub to its narrator's Ahab,[5] and to whom Efraín Kristal attributes "one of the highpoints, if not *the* highpoint, of moral literature in twentieth-century Latin America" ("Jorge Luis Borges's Literary Response" 360). Such courage does not betray its slyness. When the Nazi Otto Dietrich zur Linde is about to boast about how exactly he tortured Jerusalem, the editor intervenes—with an ellipsis, a footnote, and nothing more: "Ha sido inevitable, aquí, omitir unas líneas" 'It has been necessary to omit a few lines here' (*OC* 1: 1028; Kristal, "Jorge Luis Borges on War" 50:40–52:26; see also *CF* 232). If, in its structure, slyness insists, "I know something you don't know . . . ," here it attains its moral apex with the supplement "and for the sake of both our souls, let's keep it that way."

Slyness Calls for Slyness

Slyness thus has a rich but simple essence. What is it? I know something you don't know. We should see where that asymmetry goes. I'll see. And you? Oh, you'll see too. Perhaps its structure is simple so that it can seem deceptively simple. But its ethic is the same way. Slyness calls for slyness. In other words, the trick rebounds.

We take the axiom straight out of Aesop. Whenever there's a fox on the scene in a fable, it means not only that the fox will be tricky but also most likely that the fox will be tricked. In one fable like that, in the William Caxton translation, the moral runs as follows: "he that begyleth other is oftyme begyled hym self." Slyness calls for slyness. In this way, Borges ought to be answered by his new readers, earned on the sly, prank for prank. The style of his contrivances calls not only for a crafty reader but also for a trickster, positively. And so that's how I approach teaching Borges to younger readers.

But how exactly do I do it? The roster of projects presented below takes the question seriously. The prompts that appear there rely heavily on the word "project." However, I am not exactly using the term in the sense of the pedagogy called "project-based learning." That approach generally involves using real-life problems to capture student interest and develop skills; the resulting student projects are geared to look like real-life products. It is a refreshing departure from conventional schoolwork. But more to the point of Borges, for me, would be the way this same word, "project," is used by his contemporary Jean-Paul Sartre (as on page 39 of *Being and Nothingness*). For Sartre, "project" and "magic" almost rhyme. Our acts project our values, which may in turn lead us away from, not toward, the world as it is known. That's the case for Borges too. All of Borges's great characters become what they are because of the projects they undertake (think of "The Circular Ruin": I project, as I am projected). And the writings themselves, by a method that is well-known, mirror the process on another, stranger level ("he preferido la escritura de notas sobre libros imaginarios" 'I have chosen to write notes on imaginary books' [*OC* 1: 829; *CF* 67]).

Roster of Projects

Below are eight and a half unconventional projects I have assigned when teaching Borges at the high school level. Each is an invitation to slyness.

Tlönic Translation: Thinking like a Translator

On the fantastic planet Tlön, Borges imagines two languages. Neither makes use of nouns. The basis of one language is the impersonal verb (so that one says not "the moon" but "it mooned," not "one says" but "it's said"). The basis of the other language is the string of adjectives (so the moon might be "aerial-bright above dark-round" or "soft-amberish-celestial" or any other clump of qualities that it happens to evoke in the moment). Your challenge is to translate a paragraph-sized snippet from any text you have read for this course (minimum one hundred words) into the English equivalent of one of the two Tlönic languages. Your assignment should include the original text (retyped by you, not scanned or copy-pasted), your translation of it, and a brief "translator's note" in which you reflect on your method of translation and any gnarly problems that you faced. Compelling translations will aim to capture the spirit of the original, creatively preserving its pacing and emphasis rather than sticking strictly to the letter and grinding out a mechanical word-for-word rendition. You can trim, tweak, reorder, and artfully embellish material in the original text in order to make it work for Tlönistas.

Imaginary Place: An Imaginary Encyclopedia Entry

Design a counterfactual place based on a philosophical claim that can be stated in a single sentence. The claim should be drawn from or inspired by your readings for this class. You will craft an encyclopedia entry for the place that sums up key elements of the invented culture, much like the counterfeit entry for "Uqbar" in the *Anglo-American Cyclopedia* that kick-starts "Tlön, Uqbar, Orbis Tertius" (*OC* 1: 832; *CF* 69–70). I recommend starting from a philosophical premise that is strange to think but simple to say (e.g., "Far from mindless entertainment, film is the best teacher" or "Only through music can we perceive ultimate reality"). Then brainstorm rituals and social institutions that spring from and support your claim. The ways of being you describe ought to affirm and elaborate your premise. Finally, summarize your imaginary place by composing an encyclopedia entry (like those in Alberto Manguel and Gianni Guadalupi's *The Dictionary of Imaginary Places*) or an abbreviated *Wikipedia* page (including headings like "History," "Geography," "Politics," "Economy," and "Culture"). Your single-sentence premise should appear somewhere, perhaps somewhere unlikely or offbeat, in the entry you compose.

Fictional Newspaper: Conveying the Daily World of a Character

Imagine a full-page newspaper spread that could be read by a character in a Borges story. The section may be the front page of the paper (featuring the top stories of the day) or the front page of any section of the paper (sports, lifestyle and leisure, business, opinion, comics, etc.). The spread you work up should include the basic elements of a real newspaper: header (including paper title, section title, and date of publication); no fewer than four (partial) stories, each with a catchy and informative title; a visual element or elements with captions; and teasers for other stories or features that the reader can find elsewhere in the day's paper. The fictional newspaper should be an accurate and interesting image of the world in which the story takes place. Its goals are to promote interest in the Borges story and to facilitate an unexpected interpretation of it (or take on it). If the project is done with a partner, two full pages are expected, and the pages must be consecutive. You are encouraged but not required to submit supporting materials that may help the instructor understand your vision.

Newspaper Blackout Poem: A Secret Project Unlocked by Completing the Fictional Newspaper

Consider the phrase "la creación como hecho casual" 'creation as a chance act' (*OC* 1: 391; *SNF* 68) and then compose a blackout poem based on the fictional newspaper you submitted. Take a look at some examples of blackout poetry on Austin Kleon's website ("Newspaper Blackout Poems"). Kleon finds the poem lurking in a page of the newsprint by scratching out everything on the page that's not the poem. Your original poem, prose poem, or poetic utterance (akin to Kleon's) should be about an element of the newspaper's source text that you did not discuss in your newspaper. Append an "artist's statement" that sets out your method and intention and describes how your blackout poem illuminates a significant element in the source text.

Five Hundred to One: Unconventional Close Reading

One of the interesting characteristics of Borges's style is that he supercharges certain words, often unusual words, with meaning.[6] Your challenge is to spot one such keyword and explore its wealth of meanings in an analytic essay. You'll take one word and turn its analysis into the task of five hundred words or more. How does the entire text draw on—or draw out—different definitions of the term? How does Borges invoke denotative and connotative meanings? How does the word's context in the story involve its etymology, the history of its meanings (including outdated or obscure meanings), or both? How does the sound of the word relate to its meaning as such and its meaning in the source story? What does this word contribute to the overall meaning of the story or the reader's overall experience that its synonyms would not? Research into the original Spanish term, other translations, or both is encouraged; see the instructor if you need help making that happen.

Griddy City: A Wild-Card Project

Of Buenos Aires, Borges writes, "Four infinities meet at every crossroad" ("Buenos Aires" 14). This city strikes this sensitive observer as a sublimely grid-like space. Your challenge is to use that form of the grid, squares on squares, to explore the form and meaning of one distinctive aspect of life in this city, the country that surrounds it, or both. Your exploration may take the form of a visual study, a mathematical experiment, an intricate piece of text art, or even (ahem) a square dance. The only constraints on your imagination are, first, that the project be based on a distinctive and intriguing (to you) aspect of the cultural history of Buenos Aires and, second, that its premise or appearance be tied to the form of a grid. The fully realized project should include your finished grid and any supporting documents required to make sense of it, which should include an "artist statement" outlining your method and intention. An original title is vital.

Gamification: Multiplayer, Replayable Adaptation of the Premise of a Story

Convert a text by Borges, any text, into a game for up to four players. Games that can be played in the physical world are preferred, but it is possible that an e-game may get a green light, after a short formal proposal. Your pitch will need to convince me both that this is worth doing and that you can do it. The interpretive game you invent should be able to hold the attention of players for thirty to ninety minutes at a time. Enjoyable games make a point of including short- and long-term goals and rewards. Your game ought to work out—and play with—the cognitive puzzles and challenges posed by the text you have chosen, deepening players' understandings of story elements like character, plot, and theme. The game should be fully realized (able to be played) and include directions that make sense to the target audience. A one-paragraph "gamer's statement" should describe your inspiration. The game must be titled, the title must include a logo, and the logo must be consistent with the overall aesthetic (or look) of the game.

Necessary Monsters: An Exercise in Fantastic Zoology

Craft an entry for a future edition of Borges and Margarita Guerrero's *The Book of Imaginary Beings*. This book, written in the style of a field guide, is made up of short descriptions of creatures with magical properties. Read Borges's overview of the project (Borges and Guerrero, Foreword) and a few example entries. As you will see, the creatures it features have been culled from lore, literature, and myth. Some are ancient, and others modern. Some are well-known, others obscure. Some arise from a particular book, a particular writer, a particular culture; the origins of others are hazy. In every entry, the creature's key traits are presented in an admiring yet detached style. Concision is crucial, since field guides need to be light enough for users to carry around comfortably. The entry you compose should be based on a living or lifelike being with at least one fantastic property. You may target an individual being or a species of beings, but in each case it should speak directly to Borges's interest in "*necessary* monsters" (Borges and Guerrero, Foreword xii): the creature should really do a service for the psyche. Illustration in the style of Peter Sís for bonus points.

Tips for Teaching

With the roster above, my intention is to be generative. No sooner will you read my prompts than you will think, I can do better. I'm with you. Here are the tips I have to give.

Borges was a walker, and many of my ideas about Borges have surprised me while I have been out on a walk.

Talk to other people about what you're thinking of doing. Even more than a walker, Borges was a talker. When pitching an idea to someone, less context is better. The task should carry its measure and motivation within itself.

The flip side: imagine your prompt as it will be talked about by others. In particular, imagine its being talked about by students with fellow students. How might they explain what you're asking to a peer? What type of response might they receive? It is worth considering because if someone else helps your student out, that helps you out. And the obverse is true too.

Be able to point to something like the finished product in the world. However, if that product is too familiar, it will dull the imagination.

Shoot for prompts that are 150–200 words long. Know you will be asked to say it all in a single sentence a thousand times, for a thousand reasons. Do not rush that sentence. But do not trick yourself into thinking you'll get along without it.

Make sure the project has a written component. For visual or musical works, an "artist's statement" on method and intention works well.

Let students pick their own projects. I present several projects for students to choose from, each of which can be focused on any text we have read, with the intention of empowering whatever choices students make.

I have found it convenient to standardize my expectations about how long these things take. I say two to four hours. Students often track their progress.

The root of the word *project* is the same as *projectile*. The question your feedback answers won't be "Is this thing valid and consistent, like an argument?" but "What is striking to me about it?" and "What didn't land, and why?"

Think of the prompt as a challenge for students, even a dare, rather than a set of instructions. Learning is learning to think. Teaching that aspires to learning like that must have something sly about it.

NOTES

1. The emphasis on humor in recent criticism is distinct but not new. Gene H. Bell-Villada's *Borges and His Fiction* provided English-language readers an appreciation of Borges's humor in its literary context and an inventory of its various techniques and attitudes (Bell-Villada [1999] 47–48). The major concept in Bell-Villada's treatment of Borgesian humor is "high playfulness" (48), which is itself a highly playful alteration of Matthew Arnold's criterion for the best poetry, "high seriousness" ("Study" 310–11).

2. Around and around, the fine phrases turn. Their variety reflects the richness of the humor of Borges. An inventory of critical moves reveals the pivot to subtlety ("There is much humor in Borges, as well as a kind of whimsy" [González Echevarría]); the horizon, opening out ("a writer who endlessly teases himself and his readers" [Bernstein, "*Collected Fictions*"]); the turn to metacommentary ("not only witty himself but the cause that wit is in other men—and women" [Barnes 93]); the plain fact ("his coy sense of humor" [Couture 265]); baroque embellishment ("there is always something lusciously self-mocking in Borges' language" [Bernstein, "*Selected Nonfictions*"]); and even the first hints of fatigue setting in. "I found myself becoming tired of Borges," writes Geoff Dyer, "irritated by the effort demanded by the pleasure afforded."

3. My preference in this essay about slyness is to cite the slyest versions of things. But it is notable that Borges sets out this concept of teaching in a plain way too. In a series of interviews conducted by Fernando Sorrentino, Borges describes classroom learning as a process of collaboration: "I think this idea that the teacher is *always* the one that is older is totally false. I don't mean to say the opposite is the case either. But I know (and for many years I've had my professorship at the University, at the Argentine Association for English Culture, and at the Colegio Libre de Estudios Superiores), I know I've learned a great deal from those who were learning from me; that is, it's a process of collaboration" (*Seven Conversations* [2010] 48). Here, as in "An Autobiographical Essay," the older party does not necessarily have intellectual priority; instead, learning means working it out together, sometimes on the sly.

4. The biggest obstacle to teaching Borges to younger readers, namely the writer's massive erudition, is magically transmuted into an asset. The ideal reader of Borges, sure, knows a bit of Dante and Schopenhauer, or can google them, or whatever, but besides that knows mostly that they know don't know all that much.

5. Herman Melville's *Moby-Dick*, a favorite book of Borges's, appears to be at issue in "Deutsches Requiem." Otto Dietrich zur Linde is an avatar of Ahab, the monomaniacal captain, and the fictitious editor is a reincarnation of the Sub-Sub-Librarian, a comic persona who pops up in the prefatory material for Melville's text, having swum through libraries to put together the book's collection of epigraphs about whales and whaling

(8–17). It is clear from "Deutsches Requiem" which of these figures engages the sympathies of Borges: the librarian.

6. An illustration of this that I find teaches well is the reading of the word "rubric" that appears in Sylvia Molloy's *Signs of Borges* (38–39). The specific passage Molloy close-reads is from "The Theme of the Traitor and the Hero." The word "rubric," however, does not appear in Andrew Hurley's translation of that passage (*CF* 145), though it does appear in another from *A Universal History of Iniquity* (*CF* 38). It is from the latter passage that I launch the lesson. In the project, I have students work with the entries for their chosen words in the *Oxford English Dictionary* in order to see the ways Borges and his translators put polysemy to artistic use.

Borges and I, Et Alia: Exploring the Limits of Sovereignty in Borges's Work

Kate Jenckes

In both my teaching and writing on Jorge Luis Borges's work, I focus on Borges's interrogation of the oppositions between self and other and representation and reality as well as their implications. Although much of his writing focuses on highly mediated structures of thought, representation, and experience, including literature, philosophy, and unconventional perspectives on subjectivity, I endeavor to show how it concerns nothing less than the building blocks of personal and political sovereignty as well as their internal limits and contradictions. This amounts to a questioning of power that extends from such apparently innocuous structures as subjectivity, perception, and representation to political constructs that seek to control not only human beings but also time, history, and the nature of representation.

I teach an introductory class on Borges almost every year, oriented to the lower level of the Spanish major and minor. I have chosen to teach this way because it allows me to focus on the close reading of short texts and to introduce seemingly basic questions about the nature of Borges's work and how it might be relevant today. In other words, I use the class to promote the humanities to students who tend to be focused on more practical and preprofessional concerns, including improving their Spanish.

"Borges y yo" ("Borges and I") serves as a kind of welcome mat for the class, since it is easily accessible and tends to generate good discussion, allowing me to assess the level of the class both in terms of linguistic proficiency and analytic abilities. Students are quick to identify the text as a rumination on the differences between private and public personae, which they can identify with in relation to social media, college and job applications, and so forth. Some are content to settle on a value-based hierarchy, in which the immediacy of subjective experience is considered real, and mediation, including the public-facing proper name of Borges, is viewed as a false and hostile antagonist. Viewed this way, the vignette describes life as a kind of losing battle against the vitality and self-presence of subjective truth. I am sympathetic with the resistance this produces, but I encourage other interpretations by stressing some details in the text, including the questions raised by the allusion to Spinoza: "Spinoza entendió que todas las cosas quieren perseverar en su ser; la piedra eternamente quiere ser piedra y el tigre un tigre" 'Spinoza believed that all things wish to go on being what they are—stone wishes eternally to be stone, and tiger, to be tiger. I shall endure in Borges, not in myself' (*OC* 2: 299; *CF* 324). Spinoza's notion of conatus is more complex than Borges's shorthand invocation of it here, but the allusion is used heuristically to invite reflection on the nature of existence, consciousness, and time. Does stone wish to be stone? What is the nature of such wishing, and its implied agency, in such a sentence? What about in the implied parallel, that "I" wish to be "myself"? Is such a wishing imaginable outside of time ("eternally")? Questions such as these lead students to consider that the division implied by the title may be due less to a distinction between a true and false self and more to the inevitable effects of time and the mediated nature of consciousness. I also ask about the list of likes attributed to the *I* ("Me gustan los relojes de arena" 'My taste runs to hourglasses'), which are almost all forms of mediation (of time, space, meaning); the *I*'s fondness for vestibular spaces ("el arco de un zaguán y la puerta cancel" 'the arch of an entryway and its inner door'); and the notion that "lo bueno" 'the good'—not only good writing but also any worthwhile accomplishment—exceeds a proprietary structure of origin, which implies that just as *I* am not strictly, eternally *I*, so my writing is not strictly, eternally mine (*OC* 2: 299; *CF* 324). The text ends with an unresolvable tension between the self and a structural, internal otherness that includes transformation and emergence—"tendré que idear otras cosas" 'I shall have to think up other things' (*OC* 2: 299; *CF* 324)—as well as loss and confusion.

I pair "Borges y yo" with "El otro tigre" ("The Other Tiger"; *OC* 2: 316–17; *Selected Poems* [Coleman] 117–19), which is less inviting but can be seen as a kind of inversion of the first text. While "Borges y yo" addresses tensions implicit in understanding or representing the self, "El otro tigre" addresses the difficulties of understanding or representing the other. The figure of the tiger serves as an icon of vitality and distance from the lyric speaker's urban and bookish surroundings—that is, it emblematizes an external, flesh-and-blood reality beyond human construction and conceptualization. The poet dejectedly discards drafts of his efforts to imagine a tiger, but he ends with a resolve to continue searching for another tiger, or for a way in which the limited, temporal, and mediated lyric subject can relate to something outside itself in a way not fully determined by existing forms of knowledge and understanding.

Together, these two texts set the stage for an examination of Borges's work as driven by, on the one hand, a radical interrogation of the grounds and conditions of knowledge, including the autonomy and sovereignty of the subject and the transparent functionality of representation (including conceptualization) and, on the other hand, an imperative to think about the real world while acknowledging the limitations of our ability to do so. We begin with some essays from *Otras inquisiciones* (*Other Inquisitions*) that exemplify the relationship between knowledge and power implicit in the word *inquisitions*. "La muralla y los libros" ("The Wall and the Books") is exemplary in this regard. The essay describes the efforts of an ancient Chinese emperor (Shih Huang Ti) to assert political sovereignty through the construction of a border wall and the destruction of books, actions that can elicit comparisons with contemporary instances of border management, censorship, and historical revisionism. The essay can be read as an allegory of origins and boundaries, suggesting that Borges's recurrent interest in time and space is not merely play (as it is described in "Borges y yo," for instance) but concerns a critical attention to forms of history and territory, among other things. I ask students to analyze the essay's structure, which consists primarily of a series of conjectures (a string of maybes), and to compare it to the structure of sovereignty implied by the emperor's actions. This exercise has the benefit of encouraging students to articulate their difficulty with the dense prose and also to begin to analyze Borges's style, including its relationship to the nature of authorship and authority.

The final sentences of "La muralla y los libros" provide an enigmatic but critical definition of Borges's understanding of aesthetics. Although it presents a bit of a challenge, I ask students to consider the description of the "inminencia de una revelación que no se produce" 'imminence of a revelation as yet unproduced' (*OC* 2: 14; *SNF* 346) in relation to "Borges y yo" and "El otro tigre," on the one hand, and Shih Huang Ti's despotic control of history and territory, on the other. In the latter instance, the emperor's actions appear directed at producing the foundation and boundaries of knowledge and control. In "Borges y yo" and "El otro tigre," in contrast, Borges's literary personae struggle with the elusive nature of both self and other, both of which resist "revelation" or can be seen as doggedly engaging with the "imminence of a revelation," thereby performing the very essence of what Borges here calls the "aesthetic fact" (*OC* 2: 14; *SNF* 346). I stress that this "aesthetic" sense of imminent arrival or irreducible otherness is not limited to things conventionally understood as aesthetic, since it includes different forms of experience and encounter. I also emphasize the indeterminate temporality of such encounters, as described in the penultimate clause: "quieren decirnos algo, o algo dijeron que no hubiéramos debido perder, o están por decir algo" 'they want to tell us something, or have told us something we shouldn't have lost, or are about to tell us something' (*OC* 2: 14; *SNF* 346).

This segues nicely into the following readings on literature, including "Kafka y sus precursores" ("Kafka and His Precursors"; *OC* 2: 80–81; *SNF* 363–65), "Sobre los clásicos" ("On the Classics"; *OC* 2: 134–35), "Pierre Menard, autor del *Quijote*" ("Pierre Menard, Author of the *Quixote*"; *OC* 1: 842–47; *CF* 88–95), and "El libro de arena" ("The Book of Sand"; *OC* 3: 68–70; *CF* 480–83), which stage how even things that seem inert and fully present, such as words on a page, bear traces of an ever-transforming imminence that exceeds and unsettles stable frameworks of knowledge and sovereignty, including that of the reading or writing subject. This is followed by a short section on autobiography, including "El otro" ("The Other"; *OC* 2: 442; *CF* 411–17), "La nadería de la personalidad" ("The Nothingness of Personality"; *Inquisiciones* [Seix Barral] 93–104; *SNF* 3–9), "Líneas que pude haber escrito y perdido hacia 1922" ("Lines I Could Have Written and Lost round about 1922"; *OC* 1: 53; *Selected Poems* [Coleman] 31), and "Yo" ("I"; *OC* 3: 121; *Selected Poems* [Coleman] 347), which reinforces a sense of self based on encounters with internal alterity. Following this section is another short section on encounters with others, including "El etnógrafo" ("The Ethnographer"; *OC* 2: 627–28; *CF* 334–35) and "There Are More Things" (*OC* 3: 34–38; *CF* 437–42).

I wrap up the first half of the semester with "El Sur" ("The South"), which, combining elements from the last few sections, we read as a heteroautobiographical tale about the dangers of entrenching one's sense of self—and by extension, of the nation—in a static notion of the proper, as grounded by the paired figures of inheritance and property. Although literature is cast in this story as a danger and a distraction, I stress that the book featured in this story is linked to the wound that sets off the subsequent events, so while literature can support identitarian logic, it also has the potential to disrupt it (Dove, *Catastrophe* 79). The book in question, the *Thousand and One Nights*, can be seen as a cipher of Orientalism—that is, the idealization of non-Western culture as a foil for a Western sense of supremacy, which is reproduced in the nationalist idealization of rural culture in the story. (Students are usually eager to identify analogues.) However, the fact that the book is a compilation of tales from a variety of different cultures, translated, in this case, by a German Jewish Arabist (Gustav Weil), can be seen as undermining the purported homogeneity of culture along with any clear distinction between self and other (a gesture I subsequently link to a minor perspective in "El escritor argentino y la tradición" ["The Argentine Writer and Tradition"; *OC* 1: 438–44; *SNF* 420–27]). Furthermore, the frame narrative of the *Thousand and One Nights*, in which Scheherazade retells stories as a mechanism of survival, introduces a structure of incompletion and deferral. This allows for a possible rereading of the end of "El Sur" in which there is a possibility of life beyond the fatality of pure self-identity and its rejection of difference, figured first as infection and subsequently as the "Sur que era suyo" 'South that belonged to him' turning against him (*OC* 1: 918; *CF* 179). Such a possibility can be associated with the autobiographical dimension of this story, in which Borges describes how his mature period of writing began after a brush with death that resembles that depicted in this story ("Autobiographical Notes" 83–84). That is, "El Sur" constitutes a kind of origin story of writing in which fiction is linked to an experience of life that exceeds and unsettles a sovereign structure of self or the proper.

In the second half of the course, we move from a focus on the sovereignty of the subject to more impersonal constructions of sovereignty, including the ideals of absolute knowledge and totalizing control, which Borges's fictions push to dizzying extremes. Perhaps inspired by Franz Kafka's fictional description of an effort to perfect the Tower of Babel ("On Building" 239), several of Borges's fictions feature structures that can be read as "Babelic" efforts to acquire God-like powers of creation, perspective, and control (Jenckes, "Walls" 4). "La biblioteca de Babel" ("The Library of Babel") invokes such an association by name. In that story, the ambition to achieve totalizing omniscience is proportionate to its apparent impossibility. Thc tools of the pursuit of knowledge, in a dystopian combination of "walls and books," have replaced the natural world, leaving humans—far from the unified society that came together to build the biblical Tower of Babel—isolated, competitive, and irreparably mired in Babelic confusion. Their only creation seems to be that of dogma and political-theological schema designed to defend the existence of an order amid evident disorder.

The narration is structured to fascinate readers with the details of this peculiar world, to the point that they forget to question the objectivity of the narrator—a must in all of Borges's stories, which I repeat ad nauseam throughout the semester—or to look for signs of a repressive political structure, which is often underplayed by the narrator's bland recounting of them. The description of a book consisting entirely of the letters *M*, *C*, and *V* repeated over and over can be interpreted as a subtle indication of the tension underlying the apparently objective nature of the story's narration. Read out loud, *CV* sounds like the Spanish words *se ve*, "one sees" or "it is seen," while the repetition of *MCV* yields a version of *veme*, "see me," as if to admonish, *Consider the narrator, who is not as objective as you might think* (*OC* 1: 862; *CF* 114).

When the narrator affirms the existence of the *Vindications*—books that prefigure and justify individual lives, effectively microcosms of the presumed totality of the library—based on what he admits is dubious firsthand experience, we are, in effect, invited to examine the narration for other instances of bias, including an acceptance of the mechanisms of a political-theological authoritarianism. The belief in the library's totality—not only its presumed lack of limits but also the idea that everything, including the very nature of the possible, is already written and can be found on one of its infinite shelves—leads to a censorial defense of this belief, which includes ominous-sounding agents such as inquisitors, Purifiers, and the subtle introduction of an assumed orthodoxy as well as heterodox transgressors. Such "órdenes severas" 'strict orders' to preserve a political-theological sense of "Orden" 'Order' is perhaps most easily associated with the Spanish Inquisition, although Borges's interest in the relationship between belief and domination was more varied and included an enduring fascination with the origins of Christian orthodoxy and its exclusions (*OC* 1: 864, 865; *CF* 116, 118). The story can also be read in light of the rise of fascism, given the time of its publication (1941) and its echoes with other tales of totalitarianism, including "La lotería en Babilonia" ("The Lottery in Babylon"), "Tlön, Uqbar, Orbis Tertius," and "Deutsches Requiem." In "La biblioteca de Babel," the examples of heterodoxy provide hints of a different way of thinking: the heretics ponder the possibility that chance and disorder exceed and upend any order that might claim them, which changes the nature of the possible from something that can be apprehended to something that constitutively cannot, even by extreme ideal or institutional structures. In other words, as Jacques Derrida has noted of the fable of Babel, difference and dispersion condition and undermine the building of the tower of human unity and ascendency, just as they do the apparent monolingualism of its builders ("Des tours de Babel" 104). Although the idea of the primacy of difference is described in the story as a "divinidad que delira" 'hallucinating deity' (*OC* 1: 865; *CF* 117), it can also be associated with the very nature of life, for which so little allowance is made in the ordered hexagons of the library.

In "Tlön, Uqbar, Orbis Tertius" we note the shift from ancient and early modern theocratic bureaucracies governing the limits of orthodox belief to a project born of the Enlightenment, in which, in what might seem like a mash-up between *Minecraft* and continental philosophy, the design of an invented region and world begins to infiltrate reality. The plot, hidden in layers of narrative, is basically this: some philosophers, perhaps tired of only speculating about the world, decided to create their own, designing its language, academic disciplines, and other modes and structures that shape perception, such as art and subjectivity. Since their project is purely ideal, with no pesky reality to limit their design, it can be seen as a totalizing project, a secular version of the fable of Babel, in which the designers achieve not only omniscience and total control but also the (divine) power to create. The link between knowing and creating, or bringing things into being, is associated with a version of idealism summed up in George Berkeley's axiom, *Esse est percipi* ("To be is to be perceived"). If perception constitutes existence, then structures of knowledge can be understood as creating their objects, like God created the world.

A large part of the story is dedicated to a detailed description of the invented language, academic disciplines, and creative practices of Tlön, which can be understood as linking being and perception in ways that privilege subjective experience and immediacy over systematization and mediation: for instance, tactile geometry, creative arithmetic, language that rejects categorization and reflects lived experience, emphasis on the unrepeatability of the here and now and its lack of relation to the then and there. To get students over any initial bewilderment in the face of so many disconnected details, I ask them to write sentences in the two languages described in Tlön. We then talk about how these idiomatic peculiarities, as well as several other examples of Tlönian idiosyncrasies, relate to Berkeleyan idealism. Although the privileging of subjective experience is appealing up to a point, it soon becomes clear that it is posited as a source of totalizing knowledge—"el sujeto del conocimiento es uno y eterno" 'We must always remember that on Tlön, the subject of knowledge is one and eternal'—which contradicts the apparent rejection of systematization, described as "la subordinación de todos los aspectos del universo a uno cualquiera de ellos" 'the subordination of all the aspects of the universe to one of those aspects' (*OC* 1: 837, 836; *CF* 76, 74). The sovereignty of subjective perception moves subtly from a long list of amusing examples to the more sinister mention of doctrine and heresy, which can be seen as an indication that the project of Tlön is related to the evolving political-theological structure of power.

In the postscript, the history of Tlön is revealed as the imaginary invention of a multigenerational secret society that counted Berkeley among its members. It is picked up in the nineteenth century and gains the sponsorship of Ezra Buckley, a (fictional) US American prostitute- and slave-owning millionaire. Buckley's character brings what had previously been a philosophical game, albeit with inquisitorial leanings, into a more pointed critique of how idealism and materialism inform history. His last name, which in a Spanish inflection of Irish English is nearly homophonic with "Berkeley" and evokes the stereotype of US Americans reducing everything to a sense of value based on money ("bucks"), combines the Berkeleyan idealist notion of perception as intuition through sensation with the legal and materialist sense of perception as the collection of revenue from properties.[1] Buckley suggests that the exercise of constitutive perception in inventing a country had already been accomplished in the United States (students are often perplexed by this, but I think it is worthwhile to have them puzzle out the oblique reference to the settler-colonialist doctrine of manifest destiny), and he proposes expanding the project to the creation of a world. Buckley invested the spoils from the riches his expansionist perception had yielded him—"sus cordilleras auríferas" 'his gold-veined mountains'—into the invention of this world in which perception determines being (*OC* 1: 839; *CF* 79). The combination of extractivism and production, furthermore, is repeated in Tlön with the production of *hrönir* and *ur*, duplicated objects constituted by perception, whose process of production (which involves prisoners and students) suggests an alienation of the means of both production and perception. This shows how in the modern manifestation of Tlön the Berkeleyan tenet, *Esse est percipi*, is not a neutral theory of ontology but an ideological production of perception, which complements and reinforces the real, from American-style capitalism and historical revisionism to the structures of order-like symmetry mentioned at the end of the story, dialectical materialism and Nazism (*OC* 1: 841; *CF* 81). I ask students to think of contemporary examples of how perception can be said to produce reality, a task that has become frighteningly easy in recent years.

Although the story ends with the ominous idea that Tlön will take over the world, the description of the narrator's reaction—appearing at first glance to be an insouciant shoulder shrug—can be interpreted as providing a glimmer of possibility of a different relationship between perception and reality. His translation project involves linguistic difference and thereby resists the prediction that different languages will disappear (as a reversal of Babel). Furthermore, the text that he is translating, Thomas Browne's philosophical archaeology, *Urn Burial*, opens with the observation that "a large part of the earth is still in the urn unto us" (Browne), suggesting—contra Berkeley—that there is much that exists beyond our range of perception. The narrator's translation project can therefore be seen as a subtle evocation of Borges's own writing, including this story. This is, incidentally, one of the moments where I invite comparisons with "El otro tigre." The producers of Tlön are content to take their own images as reality (including, fittingly, transparent tigers), whereas Borges's fictional personae are depicted as involved in an uncertain labor of engagement with what lies beyond perception, concepts, representation, and so on, although the beyond (which is also inside us) can only ever be reached by means of the limits of the media available to us.

The tension between a totalizing figure and the act of writing is repeated in a number of stories, including "Funes el memorioso" ("Funes, His Memory") and "El Aleph" ("The Aleph"). Although we dedicate most of our class time to analyzing the details of the figures of totality featured in these stories and the significance of their settings—the prodigious memory of a rural teenager from the global periphery, a fantastic object found in the basement of a family home on the cusp of modernization—I also stress the relationship between the figure of totality and language, including the act of narration. In the opening sentence of "Funes el memorioso," for instance, the narrator alerts us to a fundamental difference between himself and Funes: he does not have the right to pronounce the "verbo sagrado" 'sacred word' *remember*, a right that belonged exclusively to Funes (*OC* 1: 879; *CF* 131). The reference to a sacred word evokes Funes's namesake, Irenaeus, an early theologian who posited the concept of the Christian logos as a word that encompasses all time and also formalized the distinction between Christian orthodoxy and heresy.[2] The narrator's repeated acknowledgment of the limits of his memory and language, although apparently a disadvantage, ultimately appears to constitute the condition of possibility of both thinking and life itself. This can be linked to the end of "Tlön, Uqbar, Orbis Tertius," where a word that is used to describe Funes's mind, *abarrotado*, meaning both "stuffed" and "barred," like a crammed prison, appears at the moment that reality gives way to Tlön.[3] The writing performed by the narrators of both stories, while ostensibly inferior to the fantastic forms of totality they confront, represents profane alternatives to such suffocating structures.

This model receives a twist in "El Aleph" (*OC* 1: 1061–70; *CF* 274–86), which features two different forms of totality: the narrator's determination not to change after the death of his beloved, and the eponymous Aleph, a point where all time and space coincide. The narrator's observation of the Aleph reveals the imperfection of his love, and while his feelings of awe and sadness are described as infinite, the spell of totality has been broken, and he returns to his imperfect, temporal existence. This reaction contrasts with that of his rival, Carlos Argentino Daneri, who has dedicated his life to converting what he has seen in the Aleph into a literary magnum opus, grandiloquently titled *La tierra* (*The Earth*). That this work wins a national prize, whereas the narrator's does not, can be interpreted as an indictment of the timeless and totalizing aspirations of a certain conception of literature, one that is notably distinct from the narrator's acknowledgment of the impossibility of describing the Aleph, which once again can be compared to "El otro tigre," among other texts that consider the nature of writing.

"El jardín de senderos que se bifurcan" ("The Garden of Forking Paths") and "Deutsches Requiem" bring some of Borges's recurrent concerns into relation with the two world wars. In the former story, the narrator describes the structure of enmity as relying on the suppression of time, space, and difference, elements whose complexity becomes palpable for him in the minutes before he reverts to wartime logic and kills the man who has helped him understand this complexity. In the latter story, the narrator describes how his philosophical inclinations were subsumed into Nazi ideology, which he defends to his death, even after the fall of Nazi Germany. Some of the details resonate with principles described in "La biblioteca de Babel," including the belief in a structure of order that transcends its parts, even its most fervent supporters. This belief is reflected in a sentence in "Deutsches Requiem," "Que el cielo exista, aunque nuestro lugar sea el infierno" 'Let heaven exist, though our own place be in hell' (*OC* 1: 1030; *CF* 234), which appears nearly verbatim in "La biblioteca de Babel" (*OC* 1: 865; *CF* 117). In the case of "Deutsches Requiem," as with "El jardín de senderos que se bifurcan," the character identified as an enemy represents an incommensurability to the logic of war. In "Deutsches Requiem," this concerns a Jewish poet interned in the concentration camp that the narrator administers. The narrator admires the poet's work, even though it runs counter to the racist, homogenizing order that he is committed to upholding. With evident appreciation, the narrator describes the poet's work as more attuned to singularity than Walt Whitman's poetry, held up as an exemplar of the singularity of experience. Nevertheless, he is committed to killing the poet as a means of eradicating a part of himself that resists his official belief in a totalizing order. The last line of the story, "Mi carne puede tener miedo; yo no" 'My flesh may feel fear; I *myself* do not,' suggests how this division persists even as the unifying "nuevo orden" 'new order' is proclaimed victorious (*OC* 1: 1030; *CF* 234). This sentence serves as an interesting counterpoint to other depictions of subjectivity in Borges, including the very different description of internal division in "Borges y yo."

I tend to end the class with "Del rigor en la ciencia" ("On Exactitude in Science"; *OC* 2: 339; *CF* 325), which lends itself nicely to comparison with many of the texts we have considered throughout the course. The map that coincides with its territory situates the ideal of Babel-like omniscience, and a perception that produces its object, in the historical context of Spanish American colonialism. The description of the map's disintegration highlights the gap between the timeless ideal of colonial territory and the temporality of material terrain, which can once again be connected to the representation of ideation (of life) and its limits in "El otro tigre," among other texts.

This brings me to some general comments about my approach to teaching Borges. The first is that I always begin by situating his work, including his reprehensible support for the Argentine military coup in 1976 as well as his later retraction. I explain that while it is important not to overlook this stance, at least for me, the opposition to structures of domination that appears throughout his writing outweighs his abhorrent but temporary siding with the wrong side of history. I allow that students may have a different perspective, and I invite them to bring this up at any time.

In a different register, I also find that it is best to address the peculiarities of Borges's style early on in anticipation of confusion or dislike, especially with students who have a weaker grasp of Spanish or a lower tolerance for literary complexity. Early in the term I discuss the elements of a conventional narrative, including a linear plot, reliable narrator, and resolution. I do this with the help of a video of a beginning Spanish speaker recounting the plot of "The Three Bears," which adds some lightness to the exercise. We then contrast this conventional structure with a story by Borges. Students tend to remark on the general lack of action, the tendency to enumerate, and, with some prodding, the unreliability of the narrator. Later, we talk about his proclivity for the short form, his resistance to developing psychological depth in his characters, and any clear distinction between "good guys" and "bad guys," even when he names his narrators "Borges." Toward the end of the first half of the semester, I assign stories by Edgar Allan Poe and H. P. Lovecraft, which allows students to sharpen their understanding of Borges's style and ethos in relation to writers that he invokes in his works.

My teaching style privileges an inductive process, based largely on discussion guided by open-ended questions and prompts. I therefore do not cover all the ground I describe above, although I do get to most of it in one form or another. Despite the complexity and seriousness of the subject matter, or perhaps because of it, I work hard to make the class material accessible and hopefully fun and appealing to students at different levels and with different interests. Depending somewhat on the mood of the class, I include a variety of media and, in some cases, creative activities to lighten the mood and help students approach the subject matter from different angles. For instance, I pair "La biblioteca de Babel" with the Jorge Luis Borges Google Doodle, available on *YouTube*, and ask about the implications of the trompe l'oeil that suggests that the library—which the search engine *Google* appears to claim as its own—is separate but also part of the strange city that appears to lie outside its windows ("Jorge Luis Borges Google Doodle"; Hillis et al. 117). Some other resources I have used are the *Borges animado* series created by MagrioAnimaciones, available on *YouTube*; some of the works included in *Painting Borges*, by Jorge Gracia; Paul Miller's film *Spiderweb*, based on "La muerte y la brújula" ("Death and the Compass"); a musical composition by Taylor Brook titled *El jardín de senderos que se bifurcan* (*The Garden of Forking Paths*); and the Chilean public art exhibit designed by Alejandro Beals and Loreto Lyon based on the same story (Palma). I occasionally present images related to different stories—from book covers and other resources—and ask students to reflect on what aspects of the stories they think the images are intended to highlight. This exercise provides a nice reprieve from text-focused discussion and allows students to see different points of emphasis and even different interpretations of a story in a single slide. In addition to papers and comprehension-check quizzes, I also assign a short annotated bibliography, for which students are required to find and summarize three articles on the same story, accompanied by a final reflection in which they respond to some of the ideas in the articles. I conclude the class with a required creative project that engages with some aspect of Borges's work, which can be done individually or in small groups. The creative project has yielded some flops, to be sure, but it is more successful than not, and at times it has produced truly stunning work, including original works of writing, music composition, choreography, game design, sculpture, photo-journals, computer programming, and even a meal.

NOTES

1. The Real Academia Española's *Diccionario de la lengua española* provides the following definitions of *percibir*: "Recibir algo y encargarse de ello. *Percibir el dinero, la renta*" 'To receive something and be responsible for it. *Receive the money, the rent*,' "Captar por uno de los sentidos las imágenes, impresiones o sensaciones externas" 'To capture by one of the senses images, impressions, or external sensations,' and "Comprender o conocer algo" 'To know or understand something' ("Percibir"; my trans.). The first sense also exists in English ("Perceive").

2. Borges describes this in "Historia de la eternidad" ("A History of Eternity"), emphasizing Irenaean doctrine as a matter of power more than as a matter of belief (*OC* 1: 381 and following; *SNF* 130 and following).

3. This repetition is unfortunately not evident in Andrew Hurley's generally excellent translations. In "Funes el memorioso," we read that "[e]l en abarrotado mundo de Funes no había sino detalles," which is translated by Hurley as "[i]n the teeming world of Ireneo Funes there was nothing but particulars" (*OC* 1: 525; *CF* 137). In "Tlön, Uqbar, Orbis Tertius," a proliferation of editions of "Mankind's Greatest Masterpiece" "abarrotaron y siguen abarrotando la tierra," which in Hurley's translation appears as "filled the earth and still do" (*OC* 1: 473; *CF* 81).

The Personal Narrative through Myth and Memory: Borges and Sandra Cisneros in Latina Literature and Prison Writing Courses

Audrey Harris Fernández

Over the course of my teaching career, I have taught Latina/o literature to many students who are first- and second-generation immigrants of Spanish-speaking Mexican and Central American descent. In 2018, with a grant from the Mellon Foundation, I led a creative writing workshop based on the writings of Jorge Luis Borges and Sandra Cisneros in the women's area of the CERESO prison in Mérida, Mexico. I have also taught in the Prison Education Program at the University of California, Los Angeles. As part of the program, groups of students travel by bus to local prison facilities to take classes alongside incarcerated individuals. Over and over again, when working with these groups, I have returned to Borges: in class we focus on the short-format style of *El hacedor* (*Dreamtigers*) as well as the innovative blend of myth and memory that he uses in his writing to express his sense of otherness as a blind man and as an Argentine of half-English, half-criollo descent; to illuminate the humble street corners of his own memories; and to tell the stories of local toughs and everyday heroes from his childhood neighborhood of Palermo, a once peripheral neighborhood located outside the city center of Buenos Aires.[1] I teach his stories alongside Cisneros's writings from *The House on Mango Street*, which blends real-life stories of immigrants from inner-city Chicago with fantasy and fairy tales, and elsewhere, to discuss the way authors can bridge space and time by borrowing inspiration from one another and building on one another's work. Often, after we read both Borges and Cisneros and discuss Borges's influence on the techniques in several of Cisneros's stories, I ask students to explore those devices in their own personal narratives, which draw on their own memories and local contexts.

Because the line between life and literature is porous in this class, I present both authors' biographies, beginning in the first class with Cisneros and focusing on points of intersection that bind the two writers. As a child, Cisneros, who is of Mexican American descent, traveled back and forth almost every year between Chicago and Mexico City, developing a fascination with Mexico and a lifelong love of travel (*House of My Own* 99). Like Borges, she grew up between two languages (though she writes in English, while Borges wrote primarily in Spanish): American English and the yearned-for Spanish, that language that she associated with her father's tenderness and with long summer vacations in Mexico City and Acapulco. English was the language of school, of teachers who made her feel tongue-tied, and of her mother's anger (359). Her education was primarily in English, and as a child she was a voracious reader of English literature, encouraged by her mother, who, Cisneros later stated, was a frustrated artist and intellectual (352) whose education ended at ninth grade. Meanwhile, Spanish was the language of her father's sticky-sweet endearments—"mi cielo" 'my heaven,' "mi vida" 'my life,' "mi reina" 'my queen' (353; my trans.). Though she continues to write in English, increasingly her writing has come to mimic Spanish grammatical structures, so that the English sounds more like Spanish.

Cisneros first read Borges in high school; there, as well as in college at Loyola University, Chicago, in the 1970s and later at the Iowa Writers' Workshop, Cisneros read Latin American literature in English translation. In *A House of My Own*, Cisneros writes of her awe-filled visits to Borges's public lectures in midwestern universities during his tours in the 1970s:

> I'm reminded too of the many occasions I was in the audience for the lectures of Jorge Luis Borges. Every time he came to Chicago, we thought it would be the last since he was so old. There would always be a huge wave of disciples, and *un silencio enorme*, a great silence, even before he opened his mouth and spoke. The master Borges was already an elderly man, and blind besides, which, as he himself admitted, inspired kindness. . . . [*E*]*l maestro* Borges sat on a chair and leaned, it seemed to me, on a cane. At least he is leaning on a cane in my memory. He spoke of marvels, things that cause astonishment, labyrinths, mirrors, stories that leave you with your mouth open, because he liked to tell those kinds of stories. . . . His work appealed to young writers. He was experimental and avant-garde. (38)

I often conclude my first lecture by reading from two short writings: "Poetry," an essay from Borges's *Seven Nights*, and "Letter to My Readers," a blog post by Cisneros that references that Borgesian text. Her blog post begins with this quotation from Eliot Weinberger's translation of "Poetry": "I believe that poetry is something one feels. If you don't feel poetry, if you have no sense of beauty, if a story doesn't make you want to know what happened next, then the author has not written it for you. Put it aside" 'Creo que la poesía es algo que se siente, y si ustedes no sienten la poesía, si no tienen sentimiento de belleza, si un relato no los lleva al deseo de saber qué ocurrió después, el autor no ha escrito para ustedes. Déjenlo de lado' (*Seven Nights* 65; *OC* 3: 398). The central essay of *Seven Nights* is on Buddhism. The side-by-side reading of "Poetry" and Cisneros's "Letter to My Readers" provides an early opportunity to discuss the deep influence of Buddhist principles in the works of both writers. These principles include the doctrine of *anatta*, or the "non-self"; reincarnation, or the idea that the human spirit may take on different material forms; and interbeing.[2] To conclude the lecture, I ask students what Borges means by describing the reading of literature as a practice of discovering beauty. I then ask them which authors or texts have imparted a sense of beauty to them, and why. Finally, I encourage students to discover what resonates for them in the texts we read in class. I ask them as they read to mark the places that make them feel something or that give them an experience of beauty. Close analyses of these passages, their formal devices, and the illuminations they impart should form the starting point of their literary analyses.

Our second class begins with the biography of Borges (again focusing on points of contact with Cisneros) and then considers the influence of the foreword to *Dreamtigers* on Cisneros's "A House of My Own," the introduction to the twenty-fifth anniversary edition of *The House on Mango Street*. Borges lived his formative years in Europe, for seven years from 1914 to 1921, sufficient time to instill in the emerging young writer a strong sense of a multinational identity. In "Autobiographical Notes," Borges recalls the many hours in his childhood he spent reading with his British paternal grandmother, Fanny Haslam, who taught him her native language and cultivated his love of English literature, particularly the adventure stories of Robert Louis Stevenson, Edgar Allan Poe, Charles Dickens, and Oscar Wilde; *Grimm's Fairy Tales*; and Richard Frances Burton's translation of the *Arabian Nights*. He first read *Don Quixote* in English translation. Later, at the age of nine, he published his first translation, a Spanish translation of Wilde's "The Happy Prince"—not coincidentally, his first publication trafficked in the English language.[3] He served as a visiting professor at the University of Texas, Austin, from 1961 to 1962 and found inspiration in and inspired many North American writers. In his famous 1951 lecture "El escritor argentino y la tradición" ("The Argentine Writer and Tradition"), he proclaimed that Argentine writers, rather than merely limiting themselves to regional and national subjects, "podemos manejar todos los temas europeos, manejarlos sin supersticiones, con una irreverencia que puede tener, y ya tiene, consecuencias afortunadas" 'can take on all the European subjects, take them on without superstition and with an irreverence that can have, and already has had, fortunate consequences' (*OC* 1: 443; *SNF* 426). Hence Borges avails himself of many classics from Western literature, such as the *Odyssey*, the *Iliad*, and the Bible, often borrowing themes, ideas, or lines from them and placing them in stories set in something resembling the pampas or the *arrabales*, the poor neighborhoods on the outskirts of Buenos Aires. He also combines an interest in the fantastic—defined by Tzvetan Todorov as "that hesitation experienced by a person who knows only the laws of nature, confronting an apparently supernatural event" (25)—and in metaphysics with a deep interest in the unique attributes of the Americas, including an interest in indigenous cultures and the *mestizaje*, or racial and cultural mixing, precipitated by the European conquest. Borges's interest in *mestizaje* is nowhere more apparent than in his writings about gauchos and *compadritos*, the urban descendants of the gauchos, often featured in his tales of knife fights. Borges uses the term "aindiado" 'man with Indian features' to describe the *compadrito* Juan Muraña, the hero of the story of the same name (*OC* 2: 720; *CF* 372), and Francisco Real, a knife fighter in "Hombre de la esquina rosada" ("Man on Pink Corner"; *OC* 1: 629; *CF* 47).[4] *Mestizaje* also appears in "Historia del guerrero y de la cautiva" ("Story of the Warrior and the Captive Maiden"; *OC* 1: 1009–11; *CF* 208–11), in which Borges compares his grandmother's story of displacement from England and marriage to an

Argentine general with the tale of an English captive who, after being carried off in an indigenous raid, falls in love with an indigenous chieftain and bears him children of mestizo descent.

The foreword to *Dreamtigers*, entitled "For Leopoldo Lugones," is a prose poem written in the style of a lucid dream, dedicated to the Argentine poet Leopoldo Lugones. In the piece, the narrator leaves the sounds of the plaza behind him and enters the space of the library. The brief mention of his departure from the street ("los rumores de la plaza quedan atrás" 'leaving behind the babble of the plaza') before the entry into the library, "el ámbito sereno de un orden, el tiempo disecado y conservado mágicamente" 'the enveloping serenity of order, time magically desiccated and preserved,' is the first of a series of telescoping movements, movements from the outside in, from present to past. Borges first describes the room through physical and emotional sensation: "De una manera casi física siento la gravitación de los libros" 'I feel, almost physically, the gravitation of the books.' He then looks to both sides and surveys "los rostros momentáneos de los lectores" 'the readers' momentary profiles' in an example of hypallage, where an adjective describing one object is displaced to another; it is his glimpse that is momentary, not the faces themselves. He describes them as illuminated by "lamparas estudiosas" 'officious lamps' and explicitly credits Milton for his use of this second hypallage. This clever wordplay introduces the destabilization of reality that sets the scene for the clearly fictional journey he narrates, to Lugones's office within the library, where he meets the dead author and presents the book we are about to read, to the master's approval. Auto-reflexively, he describes his own construction of this fantasy: "En este punto se deshace mi sueño, como el agua en el agua. La vasta biblioteca que me rodea está en la Calle México, no en la Calle Rodríguez Peña, y usted, Lugones, se mató a principios del 38" 'At this point my dream dissolves, like water in water. The vast library that surrounds me is on Mexico Street, not on Rodríguez Peña, and you, Lugones, killed yourself early in '38' (*OC* 2: 271; *Dreamtigers* 21).

Borges's foreword to *Dreamtigers* begins with the entry into the writing space, the homage to the master, and the sense of an offering to an awaiting reader. It is written in a disarming first person, directed to the second person (Lugones, though the reader also feels included in this respectful address), creating an immediate sense of intimacy and verisimilitude. The apprentice leaves behind the noisy streets and descends into the musty but hallowed library, a place of infinite return. The *Lunario* that Borges refers to in the foreword, as an inspiration for his use of hypallage, alludes to *Lunario sentimental*, Lugones's third collection of verse. Like *Dreamtigers,* it includes an assorted collection of short-form pieces of various literary genres.

In "A House of My Own," Cisneros employs many of the elements of *Dreamtigers*'s opening salvo. She begins by referencing a photo of herself in which she's sitting in her office in front of a typewriter: the entry into the writing space. She mentions the neighborhood outside—Chicago, 1980, Bucktown—and the masters who once populated it: "Nelson Algren once walked these streets. Saul Bellow's turf was over on Division Street, walking distance away" (*House on Mango Street* xii). Then she moves back inward, to the office and the "magical" objects it contains, where she can "be quiet and still and listen to the voices inside herself" (xii). Like Borges with his lucid dream, Cisneros describes the retreat into the writing space as a descent into the self and the imagination. The office is her canvas, "walls white as typing paper" (xiv), just as, for Borges, the library is the place where figures of speech flourish, where influences burn bright and inspire. She stares up at the walls, "inventing pictures in the cracks in the plaster, inventing stories to go with these pictures" (xv).

In contrast to the economy of style and imagery and themes in Borges's foreword to *Dreamtigers*, Cisneros evokes many worlds and several role models in her introduction, one of whom is Borges himself:

> The young woman in the photo is modeling her book-in-progress after *Dreamtigers* by Jorge Luis Borges—a writer she'd read since high school, story fragments that ring like Hans Christian Andersen, or Ovid, or entries from the encyclopedia. She wants to write stories that ignore borders between genres, between written and spoken, between highbrow literature and children's nursery rhymes, between New York and the imaginary village of Macondo, between the U.S. and Mexico.
>
> (*House on Mango Street* xvii)[5]

In her introduction, Cisneros guides the reader on a journey both physical and temporal in which she invites the reader to witness her encounter with not one (like Borges's Lugones) but two important mentors. First she describes a remembered encounter with Norma Alarcón, publisher of the independent Berkeley-based Third Woman Press, which provided a forum for Cisneros and other Chicana writers. She describes the encounter in the first person so that, as in Borges's lucid dream, past and present merge, and linear time becomes irrelevant, replaced by a perpetual present.[6] In the scene, Alarcón walks through the rooms of Cisneros's apartment and writing space. With awed admiration, she asks, "You live here . . . alone?" (xxiii). The young writer proves herself to the mentor, as Borges would have done with Lugones, defying expectations, stepping out from beneath her shadow. Cisneros addresses the next paragraph directly in the second person to Alarcón, as Borges directs his foreword to Lugones. She credits Alarcón for her encouragement; for introducing her to the Mexican writers Sor Juana, Elena Poniatowska, Elena Garro, and Rosario Castellanos; and for showing her "another way to be—*otro modo de ser*": "Until you brought us all together as U.S. Latina writers . . . until then, Normita, we had no idea what we were doing was extraordinary" (xxiv).

If Borges steps into the library from the noisy streets of Buenos Aires, which, along with the pampa, is a backdrop he will endlessly circle and mine, Cisneros steps into her apartment from the Chicago streets that smell of "beer and urine, sausage and beans" (*House on Mango Street* xxiv)—the multicultural, Mexican-influenced, and poverty- and desperation-steeped urban milieu that she will paint in *The House on Mango Street*. Later in the introduction, Cisneros mentions another backdrop to a subsequent office at her house in San Antonio, which points yet further south: "Trains moan in the distance all the time, ours is a neighborhood of trains. . . . [The San Antonio River] wends its way behind my house to the Missions and beyond until it empties into the Gulf of Mexico. From my terrace you can see the river where it bends into an S" (xxv). Here the homecoming is to Mexico itself, that land she writes within and against, finding it both apart from and inside herself.

I assign Borges's landmark essay "Narrative Art and Magic" as a companion to "For Leopoldo Lugones" and "A House of My Own." In this essay Borges enumerates the techniques employed in nineteenth-century romantic epic poetry to narrate fantastic events within a realistic narrative—techniques he employed to great effect in his own writings, which later had an enormous influence on the marvelous realism employed by the Latin American Boom generation and, later, by extension, in Chicana/o literature. These techniques include the following: the fantastic object is seen through hazy circumstances (such as mist or, in "For Leopoldo Lugones," the disorienting effects of dusk and nightfall); the description of the magical being is left to the reader's imagination rather than stated; direct descriptions of things are replaced by metaphors. Borges quotes Mallarmé: "nombrar un objeto es suprimir las tres cuartas partes del goce del poema, que reside en la felicidad de ir adivinando; el sueño es sugerirlo" 'naming an object . . . is to suppress three-fourths of the joy of reading a poem, which resides in the pleasure of anticipation, as a dream lies in its suggestion' (*OC* 1: 404; *SNF* 78). Rather than by logical cause and effect, the narrative is governed by what Borges defines as a magical causality of symbolism and suggestion, a destabilization of reality that ushers the reader into the realm of magic. Questions I ask students as we read "For Leopoldo Lugones" and "A House of My Own" include the following: How and where does Cisneros destabilize reality in her introduction? Where do we see the techniques outlined in "Narrative Art and Magic" employed in these two texts? What metaphors does Cisneros include in the description of her writing space, and how do they impart a sense of magic ("walls white as typing paper," magical objects, walls become canvases to invent)? How do Cisneros and Borges effect the movement from present to past in their respective texts? How do they blur the line between the living and the dead?

We notice how both texts end in direct address to someone who has died and how both effect an upward movement in their concluding lines. I remark on the strangeness of the fact that death ends the introduction and foreword (which more usually bear an association with new beginnings or an invocation of birth) to *The House on Mango Street* and *Dreamtigers* and ask students why this might be. Though answers may vary, students often discuss themes of spirituality and transcendence. I often conclude the lecture by stating that in both texts, literary creation itself is the magical event that transcends the temporal realm and blurs the border between the living and the dead.

That Cisneros paid close attention to *Dreamtigers* as she wrote *The House on Mango Street* is nowhere clearer than in her brief story "Hairs," which clearly takes Borges's clever "Las uñas" ("Toenails"), from *Dreamtigers*, as a model. These are both stories (or, more accurately, prose poems) that move from the inside out and with utmost economy from the microcosmic to the macrocosmic. They also both employ metonymy. In the Borgesian piece—one succinct paragraph with a page to itself—toes are personified as stubbornly independent and industrious workers: "No les interesa otra cosa que emitir uñas: láminas córneas, semitransparentes y elásticas, para defenderse, ¿de quién? Brutos y desconfiados como ellos solos, no dejan un segundo de preparar ese tenuo armamento" 'Nothing interests them but emitting toenails, horny plates, semitransparent and elastic, to defend themselves—from whom? Stupid and mistrustful as they alone can be, they never for a moment stop readying that tenuous armament' (*OC* 2: 277; *Dreamtigers* 26). Here Borges exhibits a playful attention to detail and an almost childlike wonder of the odd workings of the human body in one of its humblest incarnations. Like Borges's stubborn toes, the narrator's hair in "Hairs" is "lazy": "It never obeys barrettes or bands" (*House on Mango Street* 6). Meanwhile, her father's hair sticks up like a broom, her sister Nenny's is slippery, and Kiki, the youngest, has "hair like fur" (6). Her description of these varied strands, particularly the curly and textured, alludes to her family's mestizo ethnicity. In both stories, the elemental—toenails, hairs—expands outward, until at the end of the piece it encompasses the cosmic and the universal. Both stories reflect on the importance of individualism for building community and celebrate the absence of a single unifying order. Just as toenails, although integral to the whole, do not depend on other parts of the body (such as the mind or brain) to tell them what to do, hair types in Cisneros's story refuse to conform to one texture or style, even among siblings. When she describes her mother's hair, the description of its curls turns to the sweet smell of the hair, the feeling of being held by her mother as a child, and then the memory of sleeping next to her one rainy morning: "the rain outside falling and Papa snoring. The snoring, the rain and Mama's hair that smells like bread" (7). What starts with a seemingly childish and capricious description of humble human matter becomes, subtly and unobtrusively, a lyrical tribute to familial love. Both stories elevate the childish and comment on the way that the humblest objects can reveal elemental truths and experiences. After we read "Las uñas" and "Hairs" together, I provide students with the following creative writing prompt: "Choose a specific part of your body as the subject of your own short prose poem, employing personification and metonymy (so that the part represents the whole)." This exercise has proved particularly moving in the prison workshop setting, since it works to disrupt and question the negative effects of incarceration on women's relationships with their bodies.

The next topic we explore is one of encounters and dis-encounters in the Latin American city. Cisneros's poem "With Lorenzo at the Center of the Universe, El Zócalo, Mexico City" explicitly references Borges: "we said goodbye /

along two streets named after rivers. I / fumbled with the story of Borges and his Delia / When we meet again beside what river? / But this was no poem" (61–62). Her text refers to "Delia Elena San Marco," from *Dreamtigers*, whose text reads as follows:

> Nos despedimos en una de las esquinas del Once. . . . Un río de vehículos y de gente corría entre nosotros . . . cómo iba yo a saber que ese río era el triste Aqueronte, el insuperable. . . . Delia, algún día anudaremos ¿junto a qué río? este diálogo incierto y nos preguntaremos si alguna vez, en una ciudad que se perdía en una llanura, fuimos Borges y Delia. (*OC* 2: 282)
>
> We said goodbye at the corner of Eleventh. . . . A river of vehicles and people were flowing between us. . . . How was I to know that that river was Acheron the doleful, the insuperable? . . . Sometime, Delia, we will take up again—beside what river?—this uncertain dialogue, and we will ask each other if ever, in a city lost on a plain, we were Borges and Delia. (*Dreamtigers* 32)

Both authors' texts are written in the second person, directed to a love who is now absent—Delia who died before Borges saw her again, meaning he is speaking to her in the next world—hence his reference to the river Styx, where he will presumably see her again after death. Meanwhile, Cisneros's Lorenzo, still alive, is presumably a love from the past, never seen again. Both poems share philosophical concerns about time, eternity, and temporality. If Borges said that space is a function of time, love also in these poems appears rooted in that ephemeral space, a moment in time that dissolves into memory, which is also eternal.

Setting the stage for these two poems of love and loss is the vast transitional city. Mario Valdovinos writes that Borges narrates a "desencuentro" 'dis-encounter' in "Delia Elena San Marco," also speculating on the transitoriness of humanity and the ephemeral character of the faces that appear and disappear among the multitudes. The city itself becomes personified as an elusive lover: as Vicente Quirarte comments in *La ciudad como cuerpo* (*The City as Body*), any poem written to one of the great cities is one of unattainable love (30).

Borges's choice of location for "Delia Elena San Marco" is the Plaza del Once, one of Buenos Aires's oldest, busiest, most diverse, and most intensely commercialized quarters. Its name comes from the train station situated in its center. The station was in turn named for the date—*el once de Septiembre*, or the eleventh of September, 1852—on which the Estado de Buenos Aires (State of Buenos Aires) separated from the rest of Argentina for ten years ("Once"). The neighborhood was historically a center for Jewish migration; the Jews there worked as traders and producers of fabrics; additionally, the area has historically been a site of immigration from South Korea and Peru. The Corrales de Miserere, located in the barrio Once, was originally a farm, the site of the English invasions of 1806 and 1807, when the British were defeated in what became known as the Combate de Miserere (the Battle of Miserere). Finally, the plaza is the site of the mausoleum of Bernardino Rivadavia, the first president of Argentina. Borges's specification of the exact location of the encounter with Delia Elena San Marco at this historically significant plaza gives the prose poem a historically and politically charged tone; the love story becomes absorbed into the fabric of this history, and the account of two people and their parting takes on the quality of a moment in the city's past.

The location for Cisneros's poem, with its "streets named after rivers," is the Cuauhtémoc district; located south of the Centro Histórico (historic downtown) by Chapultepec Park and incorporating the impressive gold statue known as Ángel de la Independecia (Angel of Independence), including the historic Paseo de la Reforma, it features several streets named after rivers such as Río Nilo, Río Po, Río Senas, Río Amazonas, and so on. Here Cisneros cleverly links Mexico City's streetscape to the philosophical preoccupations of ephemerality and eternity that Borges raises in his poetry. The Zócalo referred to in the poem's title is the ancient city center of present-day Mexico City, which before the conquest was also the center of the Aztec capital of Tenochtitlán. Thus, it represents the continuity of the Aztec and colonial Spanish empires in contemporary Mexico.

"With Lorenzo at the Center of the Universe" is characterized by duality, like "Delia Elena San Marco": first there is the dualism and separation, marked by tension, of the two characters and then the division between the present—the now—and the eternal. Cisneros marks this divide, in different places in the poem, by mentioning the pre-Hispanic and the sacred dimensions of the ancient Zócalo and elsewhere by describing mundane material details of contemporary life, which she divides into the further dualism of night and day. Questions to discuss with students when reading Cisneros's poem include the following: How does she describe the Zócalo and its overlapping dimensions? How does she describe Lorenzo, and how does the relationship between the narrator and Lorenzo parallel the relationship between Borges's narrator and Delia? Depending on student answers, I often mention that in Cisneros's poem the male character becomes a cipher for more universal ruminations on eternity, temporality, and space and time in the city.

Later in the poem, the narrator admits that parts of the story might be fantasy: "I forget what's real. / I mix up the details of what happened / with what I witnessed inside my / universe" (Cisneros, "With Lorenzo" 62). This statement also raises questions of perception and reality: Berkeleyan idealism recognizes no other reality than mental processes.[7] By positing the Zócalo as the center of the universe and insisting on the primacy of mental processes and the negation of time, Cisneros illustrates a narrator attempting to realign her identity with Mexico. When the male love object refuses to allow himself to be appropriated for this purpose, the narrator appears to make the shift for herself, asserting her independent belonging to the city and its history: "See / this Zócalo? Remember me" (63).

After we read and analyze the connections between "Delia Elena San Marcos" and "With Lorenzo at the Center of the Universe," I ask students to write about an encounter or dis-encounter they remember experiencing, setting it against the backdrop of a richly described urban landscape. In the workshop I led in the Mérida CERESO, Yeni Marisol Solís wrote a remarkable piece called "Camino a la iglesia" ("The Walk to Church"), in which she describes her search for her absent mother and the hypocritical discrimination she experienced at the hands of other churchgoers for her shabby clothes and empty belly. Meanwhile, continuing the theme of family abandonment so common in carceral stories, Shirley Ventura Tun described meeting her father for the first time in a public park at the age of fifteen in her short essay "El encuentro" ("The Encounter").[8]

The topic of criminalization or exclusion of those who are seen as social others and of historically marginalized groups is an important one, as resonant today as it has been at any time in the postcolonial era. For a last assignment, I often assign Borges's story "The House of Asterion" (*CF* 220–22). We first talk about the story of the Minotaur (Asterion) from Greek mythology, his status as an outsider, a hybrid (half man, half bull), and his confinement in Minos's labyrinth. After reading "The House of Asterion," I ask how Borges rewrites Asterion; students often remark on his loneliness and sense of isolation. Alongside this story, I assign Cisneros's poem "It Occurs to Me I Am the Creative/Destructive Goddess Coatlicue." We discuss and draw on student knowledge of Coatlicue, the snake-skirted Aztec goddess who gave birth to the moon and stars and mothered Huitzilopochtli, the god of the sun and war. We talk about how Catholic priests demonized this powerful goddess during the Spanish conquest and ordered veneration instead of the Virgin of Guadalupe, who embodies the qualities of *marianismo* (maternity, submission, virginity, and other traits traditionally expected of women in Christian societies). After we read both stories, I ask students to write about a "monster" from the "monster's" perspective. (First I ask them to name some monsters: examples provided by my students in Southern California often include La Llorona, El Cucui, Bigfoot, etc.) Because of the social marginalization and ostracization of people in prison, particularly of women of color, this assignment has also produced powerful student work. In the workshop in the Mérida CERESO, Yesli Dayanili Pech wrote a fascinating story about a Huay Chivo (a half-goat, half-human character from Mayan mythology) who is ostracized in his pueblo for practicing sorcery and stealing chickens and is ultimately burned to death in his hut by his own brother. As the writer and activist Lope Ávila pointed out after reading the story, the punishment here is too harsh for the Huay Chivo's crimes, and so the story provides subtle commentary on the way people of indigenous descent and other marginalized groups are disproportionately penalized in the justice system.

Reading Borges alongside Cisneros allows students to reflect on a powerful constellation of themes. Both writers challenge fixed notions of individual personality and of time, and both, to paraphrase bell hooks, bring the margins to the center. Perhaps most importantly, when read together, these two authors demonstrate the way writers discover techniques and themes in other writers and employ them in service to their own literary inventions. In "Poetry" Borges notes that "en latín las palabras *inventar* y *descubrir* son sinónimas. . . . Cuando yo escribo algo, tengo la sensación que ese algo preexiste" 'In Latin the word for *to invent* and *to discover* is the same. . . . When I write something, I have the sensation that it existed before' (*OC* 3: 397; *Seven Nights* 80). Just as Cisneros made a discovery in Borges, I encourage students to look for those writers who inspire their own sense of beauty and to allow what Borges calls "el encuentro del lector con el libro" 'the encounter of the reader with the book' (*OC* 3: 397; *Seven Nights* 80) to nurture their own creativity, in our workshop and beyond.

NOTES

I wish to gratefully acknowledge the support I received for this essay from the Mellon Foundation and the Prison Education Program at the University of California, Los Angeles, and to thank Dr. Hector Calderón. My gratitude and affection also go out to the students whose writings and comments shaped these reflections.

1. Any discussion of Borges within a social justice framework requires an acknowledgment of his regrettable attitude of espoused approval toward the dictatorship of Jorge Videla, which perpetrated a state-sponsored campaign of violence against Argentine citizens (thirty thousand dead or disappeared), one of the largest-scale human rights abuses in the recent history of the Americas. On this subject, I draw a clear distinction between his writerly persona and his public persona and view him as a man whose literary creations stand completely at odds with the philosophies of political dictatorship. Although his public persona remains deservedly tarnished by any association with Videla, his literary works remain worthy of celebration and preservation.

2. Thich Nhat Hanh defines *interbeing* as the principle that "I am, therefore you are. You are, therefore I am" (87). A further elaboration of these terms and more of Borges's reflections on Buddhism can be found in "Buddhism" (*Seven Nights* 58–75) and *Qué es el budismo* (*What Is Buddhism*; Borges and Jurado). Borges's famous refutations of time and of Western individualism—"Nueva refutación del tiempo" ("A New Refutation of Time"; *OC* 2: 121–33; *SNF* 317–32) and "La nadería de la personalidad" ("The Nothingness of Personality"; *Inquisiciones* [Debolsillo] 81–90; *SNF* 3–9)—also draw on Buddhist principles.

3. This love of English literature descended from the Haslam family. Fanny Haslam's father, Edward Young Haslam, edited one of the first English-language journals in Argentina, *The Southern Cross*.

4. In *Heroes on Horseback: A Life and Times of the Last Gaucho Caudillos*, John Charles Chasteen describes what he calls "the last generation of real gauchos" (whom he places in the late nineteenth century) as racially and culturally mixed: "black, indigenous, white, and anywhere in between. They wore headbands to hold back their long hair, and, in lieu of pants, the Guaranó chiripá, a long woolen loin cloth secured around the waist by a very broad belt, and most carried their foot-long blades thrust diagonally under that belt at the small of their backs. Some still knew the Indian language, Guaraní, spoken by most of the first gauchos" (10).

5. Borges famously consulted encyclopedias for information on a wide variety of subjects. He also adopted a pseudoscientific tone to lend a credible tone to his fictions and to question the meaning of truth.

6. Borges's and Cisneros's concepts of cyclical time stem in large measure from Buddhist philosophy.

7. See Borges's "Nueva refutación del tiempo" ("A New Refutation of Time"; *OC* 2: 121–33; *SNF* 317–32) for a full exploration of Berkeleyan idealism.

8. The full text of both essays was published in Spanish in the anthology that developed out of the workshop, *Nos contamos a través de los muros* (*We Tell Our Stories through These Walls*): see Harris.

The Underlying Thread: Teaching "The House of Asterion"

Stephanie Contreras and Aldo Mendoza

As someone who famously defended monsters as nothing but "una combinación de elementos de seres reales" 'a combination of elements taken from real creatures' (Borges, *Manual* 2; Borges and Guerrero, Foreword xii), Jorge Luis Borges leaves readers of "La casa de Asterión" ("The House of Asterion") with a rather perplexing and uncanny representation of the Minotaur, the Cretan subterranean beast that stalks the corridors of its labyrinth, thereby yielding a momentary pause in the reader's immediate judgment of the case for the purported monster, Asterion. By combining the Minotaur's perspective; the voice of the presumed historical hero, Theseus; and an unsettling footnote left by an editor, the narrative demands an active and patient reader willing to analyze, question, and doubt the presentation of the truth. Given the rich complexity of this text, this essay offers instructors structured activities to guide students in the reading, comprehension, and discussion of the short story: a warm-up activity using George Frederic Watts's painting *The Minotaur* that primes students with an introduction to Borges's inspiration for the story and the myth and themes that guided its creation; graphic organizers and *YouTube* videos to help students understand the plot and tone; methods to analyze the paratextual content and recognize the narratological techniques that obfuscate the dialogue of the text; and discussion questions to evoke higher-order thinking skills and debate in the classroom as students consider the complexities and consequences of constructing, reconstructing, writing, and rewriting myths. Throughout this essay we address how this text can be taught in translation or in Spanish, with Spanish-language learners or with heritage and native speakers of Spanish.

Borges explicitly defended *The Aleph* as an extension of the fantastic genre (Hurley x). "The House of Asterion" is an influential text in this collection that can be used not only to explore the framework of the fantastic genre, the role of narratology, and literary genre studies but also as an introduction to numerous nonfiction genres, such as the essay and the *testimonio*. Because the text encourages students to question the relationship between literature and reality and its representation, in this case the construction and role of myths, the story can be used to raise students' awareness of the ways language, narrative, and testimony are manipulated, framed, and presented and represented.

Gods and monsters have often served a powerful purpose in literature (particularly fiction), allowing readers to digest and make sense of the horrors of the natural world. In *The Science of Monsters*, Matt Kaplan explains that in Greek mythology, the human-bull hybrid, which is often envisioned in a subterranean exile and bellowing with a force capable of shaking the earth, is understood today by Cretans as an attempt to rationalize unknown occurrences of earthquakes in Crete and the destruction and barren lands that followed this great seismic activity. Consequently, Kaplan captures the relationship between science and myths and their evolution as tools used to understand the world and reality.[1] Therein lies one of the greatest challenges of teaching Borges's text: how to guide students through the nuances of fiction and their interpretation of it. Borges, as an intellectual and storyteller obsessed with obscuring and exploring the depths of reality, was no newcomer to this objective and relied heavily on the development of a fantastic genre in order to push readers to question the creative process of all texts and the assumed line between fiction and reality (Duncan 8–9).

Borges indicates in the afterword of *The Aleph* that he found himself entranced with Watts's canvas painting *The Minotaur* (*OC* 1: 1071; *CF* 287). For this reason, as an introduction to the myth and its protagonist, we present students with the source of the inspiration. Prior to assigning the text, students participate in a five-minute warm-up activity in which they analyze the painting and its title and point out the apparent themes intended by the artist. The Minotaur, which is positioned *profil perdu* ("lost profile"), exposes primarily his brawny back and side; he rests his chest on the ramparts of the labyrinth and looks out to the sea, awaiting the fourteen Athenian sacrifices represented by the white sail of a ship on the left. What seems to be a relaxed disposition in fact proves to be riddled by tension, his left hand clutching a small bird. At first glance, students tend to note brown, yellow, and blue hues and the contrast between human and nonhuman, violence and peace, and so forth. Additionally, students can be asked to comment on the parts of the painting that sparked their interest or raised a question. Through this analysis of the painting, they begin to anticipate the paradoxical articulations of Asterion that permeate Borges's story. Although Borges is careful to conceal the identity of the narrator until the last line of the text, it is helpful to explain Asterion given that there is an explicit reference to the character in the title.

If time permits, we supplement this warm-up by having students read aloud two brief references to the Minotaur in Borges's *Seven Nights* and *The Book of Imaginary Beings*. The former is an anecdote that explains Borges's childhood fear of the Minotaur as he came upon a depiction of the labyrinth of Crete and imagined the beast escaping from the illustration and into his reality (*OC* 3: 369; *Seven Nights* 33). The latter is a concise historical explanation of the Minotaur's origin story and nobility (Borges, *Manual* 33–34; Borges and Guerrero, *Book* [Hurley] 132–33), which can be used to complement the story's epigraph. (Note that in this selection the Minotaur is not referred to as Asterion.) Another possibility would be to use the activity to conclude the conversation by having students compare Borges's varying presentations of the protagonist.

Understanding the Monsters of Our Making: Taking a Closer Look at the Paratext

Prior to assigning the text, we review some of the vocabulary pertinent to the analysis of the story's paratext, specifically *title*, *epigraph*, *afterword*, *footnote*, and *dedication*. For homework, students are asked to read the full text and detect these components. The following class, students are given six minutes to discuss in groups the importance of each component. For example, what does the title reveal about the story? Through the title, Borges humanizes the Minotaur by using his name, which connects him with his Cretan royal ancestry despite his banishment. In the English translations, most translators have opted for the translation "The House of Asterion" as opposed to "Asterius's House." This latter translation would capture the original name of the Minotaur as found in the third book of the *Apollodorus*, which is cited in the epigraph: "Y la reina dio a luz un hijo que se llamó Asterión. Apolodoro: Biblioteca, III, I" 'And the queen gave birth to a son named Asterion. Apollodorus, *Library*, Ill:i' (*OC* 1: 1019; *CF* 220). The translation "Asterius's House" would also emphasize the Minotaur as the owner of the house. Furthermore, students should focus on the intentional usage of "house," favored by Asterion throughout the narrative, rather than "prison," which he dismisses as an "especie ridícula" 'absurd tale' by his detractors (*OC* 1: 1019; *CF* 220).

When discussing the origin and importance of *The Bibliotheca*, also referred to as *The Library*, of pseudo-Apollodorus, which is cited in the epigraph, it is of upmost importance to identify this text as a fundamental insight into Greek mythology, one that was written by an unknown author and that serves as the story's primary source. According to James G. Frazer, the original text states, "And she gave birth to Asterius, who was called the Minotaur" (Apollodorus 305). By comparing Frazer's translation to the epigraph found in Borges's story, we see how the story's editor has taken liberties with the translation to highlight the royal lineage of the queen and to incorporate the usage of "son" and "Asterius" (or "Asterion") in order to humanize the creature. The importance of stressing Asterion's shared royal ancestry and name, in effect the social and cultural hierarchy of which he is deprived, will reappear throughout the text.

As is the case with many of Borges's stories, the art is in the details. Borges claimed to be someone who often began his own reading of a text with the footnotes, and he expected his reader not to gloss over the fine print. As famously noted by Gérard Genette and Marie Maclean, Borges understood the paratext as a vestibule into the text that offers the reader "an undecided zone" to consider their next step, be it to enter the text or turn back (261). Whereas footnotes are typically intended to provide relevant and true information, in Borges's writing, they are used to obscure the traditional limitations of fiction and urge the reader to question the motives of its writer.

In the three-page retelling of the legend, the one and only footnote pertains to the third sentence of the story. The note appears in parentheses, directly after the word "infinito" 'infinite': "Es verdad que no salgo de mi casa, pero también es verdad que sus puertas (cuyo número es infinito) están abiertas" 'It is true that I never leave my house, but it is also true that its doors (whose number is infinite) stand open night and day to men and also to animals' (*OC* 1: 1019; *CF* 220). At this point, the reader has already been introduced to a first-person narrator who provides a defense against accusations of arrogance, misanthropy, and insanity. To ignore the footnote would be to overlook another sign of a manipulated narrative voice; the editor-writer-transcriber filters, creates, and recreates Asterion's narrative by emphasizing his own voice in parenthesis, "(whose number is infinite)," and again in the footnote: "El original dice *catorce*, pero sobran motivos para inferir que, en boca de Asterión, ese adjetivo numeral vale por *infinitos*" 'The original reads "fourteen," but there is more than enough cause to conclude that when spoken by Asterion that number stands for "infinite"' (1: 1019n1; 220n1). An intrusive narrator, consistent with the narrators in Borges's other stories, makes his presence known; this narrator is behind and in full control of the "I" who offers his testimony and brings attention to Asterion's inability to conceptualize the infinite. This narrator appears to be omniscient within the context of the narrative and casts doubt on Asterion's memory and ability to transmit his version of the truth. Later in the text, there are other corrections of the number fourteen as infinite in brackets (1: 1020; 221). This is a curious change given that the original myth states that there were fourteen sacrifices sent to the Minotaur, yet Asterion claims there are nine. The concept of the infinite and, of course, the labyrinth are recurring themes in Borges's work. As such, they serve as a valuable reminder of the edited nature of the Minotaur's testimony; the narrator breaks the traditional limits and distance between literature and reality and disrupts the understanding between the narrator and the reader. Thus, we guide the discussion of the text with questions such as the following: Can this editor be trusted? How much of Asterion's monologue is indeed Asterion's? The footnote along with the parenthetical commentary in italics, brackets, and parentheses, all considered to be Borgesian trademarks, obfuscate Asterion's voice by confusing the literary distance between the narrator, editor, and reader and causing the real reader to doubt the historical reality of what transpired and how it is presented. As the real readers of the text, we are prompted to question the framing of the text and to reflect on how these details unsettle the reader and produce a sense of hesitation not only about the veracity of the account but also about the author's creative process.

Analysis of the Story

Much of the richness of this text is found in its intricate narrative levels, which contribute to Asterion's polyphonic (dialogic) construction. To understand the complexity of narrative levels within the text and how these levels are arranged and filtered, it is particularly helpful to introduce some elements of narratology, specifically the following mediators of narrative fiction: implied author, implied reader, (reliable and unreliable) narrator, and narratee.

The shifts between first-person narration and third-person narration disrupt the reader's understanding of the protagonist and the narrator and the points of view presented. We review with students the first sentence of the text, which presumably presents Asterion in the first person and refutes the defamation of his character. We discuss how the narrator's authority becomes unreliable when enough information is provided to the actual reader to cast doubt on the interpretation of the events and the protagonist or concern over the values shared by the reader and the narrator. At this point, students should be made aware of the relevance of a focalizer—in other words, how the events of the story are brought into focus and presented through the representation of Asterion, although not necessarily by him. It is only at the end of the text that the narratee, the implied reader, is explicitly identified as Ariadne. By identifying her as the implied reader, the text springs readers into another diegetic level. Cynthia Duncan echoes the work of Wolfgang Iser and notes that this hypothetical reader commonly appears in fantastic fiction in order to "act like an anchor to ground the work of a specific time, place and mindset" and to model for the actual reader an appropriate response in the situation (77). If we follow Duncan's premise and take a closer look at the character of Ariadne in the text, despite her being the key driver of Theseus's success, her inclusion is implicit until the end of the story. In other words, she only comes about if the reader refers to the myth as indicated in the epigraph and once the real reader reaches the end of the story. She is evoked in the ending as the implied listener but offers no reaction to Theseus's claim to triumph. Our editor has concluded the story with no model for the actual reader. So where does this leave the real reader?

Students should also be given time to consider what Asterion, if this even is Asterion, reveals about himself, his space, and others and how it differs from the perception of others. In this version of the myth, Asterion is an animal that describes his life, his space, his philosophy, and his relationship (or lack thereof) with his surroundings. He is filled with feelings of loneliness and depression while also reluctant to recognize such feelings. Execution presents itself as an escape, a punishment, and redemption all at once. His character is full of paradoxes: he is at once misanthropic and longing for human connection, weak and powerful, ignorant and knowledgeable, fearsome and charming, and imprisoned yet liberated. What happens when we read the text not through a critical lens but rather through an emotional lens? How do we react to the testimony?

Given these incongruities, it may happen that many students possess fragments of knowledge but are unable to organize them in a coherent way. A good option to remedy this problem is the implementation of a graphic organizer. It is well known that students store and retrieve learned information from their schemata. While there are different types of graphic organizers, we as instructors must know what we are trying to obtain from the student and accordingly choose the organizer that best achieves this goal. When we refer to schemata activation, we are touching on the creation of a bridge between old knowledge and new notions. Graphic organizers facilitate the connection between new and old information.

In the first graphic organizer activity (table 1), students work individually, highlighting selections from the text that convey different tones, such as pessimism, optimism, sarcasm, irony, objectivity, and others. They must then choose one tone and fill in the organizer. In the left-hand column, students select passages from the text that convey the particular tone, in this case pessimism. In the right-hand column, they describe how the passage helps reinforce that tone. It is important

Table 1. Sample of a completed organizer

Title: "The House of Asterion"	Tone: Pessimism
"Anyone who wishes to enter may do so. Here, no womanly splendors, no palatial ostentation shall be found, but only calm and solitude" (*CF* 220).	Asterion describes his austere life, which is void of luxuries and company.
"I have never grasped for long the difference between one letter and another. A certain generous impatience has prevented me from learning to read. Sometimes I regret that, because the nights and the days are long" (*CF* 221).	Asterion uses the verb "regret" to convey a feeling of sorrow or displeasure for not being able to read in the evening and during long days.
"I do not know how many there have been, but I do know that one of them predicted as he died that someday my redeemer would come. Since then, there has been no pain for me in solitude, because I know that my redeemer lives, and in the end he will rise and stand above the dust" (*CF* 221–22).	The Minotaur indicates that he longs for his savior to free him from the suffering that has been imposed upon him because of his confinement.

to ask students to justify their selections. After this stage and depending on the remaining time in the class, students discuss their selections in groups.

Thereafter, we transition to an activity with a fish-shaped graphic organizer to explore the causes and effects of a problem (fig. 1).[2] We ask students, through brainstorming, to identify the causes that generate the problem. We do provide the problem as well as the effects shown on the fish, while the student places the causes on the spines of the skeleton. Students use the fish-bone organizer to identify the causes that build the tone and to define the effects that the author exposes in the story.

This activity facilitates the discourse analysis of the story. It is easy to adapt to literary works, political speeches, propaganda, and other types of sources, regardless of whether the format is audio or text. If the level of the class is advanced, we usually ask students to complete this activity individually in order to promote debate among students; each student must defend their position. If the level is less advanced, we ask students to complete the activity in groups of up to four. Upon completion, each group presents its findings to the rest of the class.

Philosophical Connections

Knowledge of the thematic axes of Borges's various works provides the reader with a starting point that leads to an intertextual search. When one decides to enter the world of this author, one never knows where the labyrinths will lead. Prior to tackling the text, some students appreciate familiarizing themselves with the recurring

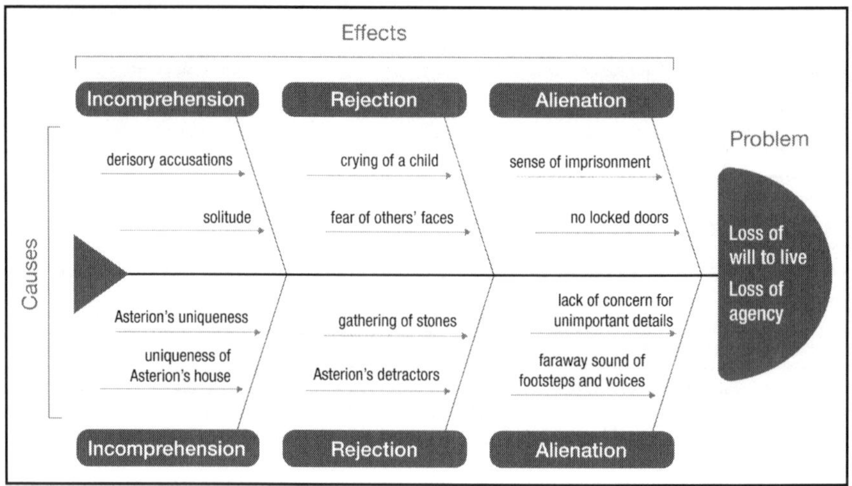

Figure 1. Sample of a fish-bone organizer

themes of Borges's literature in order to reach the highest level of analysis. In other cases, students enjoy being taken on the different paths that the author so skillfully proposes. Many of Borges's works seek to expose the incomprehensible reality to which we are subject, such as the concept of infinity. Another axis is the challenge of the physical world, as in "Tlön, Uqbar, Orbis Tertus." Borges also plays with the blurring of linear time and string theory as a means of understanding the different infinite possibilities.[3] Exposing oneself to themes such as these before plunging into the author's world ensures an effective reading in terms of content analysis. Key references to infinity, materialism, and linguistics can be observed in "The House of Asterion." These themes are also present in "The Garden of Forking Paths," "Funes the Memorious," and "The Other Duel," to mention a few. For this reason, we ask students to read three fragments written by other authors that carry similar ideas to those that Borges communicates through Asterion: the human condition, materialism, agency, time, and other ideas that are relevant to class topics. This also encourages students to improve their level of intertextual analysis. Given that we teach this course in Spanish, we provide the following selections in Spanish and clarify any parts that may be difficult for students to understand. Then we ask students to analyze Borges's story and detect connections to the recurrent topics. The following is an example of the activity:

> Read statements A, B, and C and connect them with Borges's story. Underline the corresponding parts of the story and justify your selection.
>
> A) "La teoría de cuerdas tiene un gancho tremendo. Te transporta a un mundo de 11 dimensiones, universos paralelos, y partículas formadas por cuerdecitas casi invisibles vibrando a diferentes frecuencias. Además, te

dice que no se trata de analogías sino de la estructura más profunda de la realidad, y que ésta podría ser la teoría final que unificará por fin a toda la física" 'Superstring theory has a great appeal. It transports you to a world of eleven dimensions, parallel universes, and particles formed by tiny nearly invisible strings vibrating at different frequencies. Additionally, it states that these are not analogies but rather the deepest structure of reality, suggesting that this could be the final theory that ultimately unifies all of physics' (Estupinya; our trans.).

B) "Speech [logos] is a powerful lord, which by means of the finest and most invisible body effects the divinest works: it can stop fear and banish grief and create joy and nurture pity. . . . Sacred incantations sung with words are bearers of pleasure and banishers of pain, for, merging with opinion in the soul, the power of the incantation is wont to beguile it and alter it by witchcraft" (Sprague 52).

C) "Vivimos en un mundo donde la cultura del consumismo y la indiferencia ante la difícil situación de los pobres y su sufrimiento se ha vuelto generalizado. Las personas son valoradas por lo que poseen en lugar de quiénes son y qué valores albergan para el mejoramiento de la humanidad. En resumen, el materialismo se ha convertido en una fuerza poderosa que influye en cómo algunas personas planifican sus vidas y persiguen sus metas y logros para el único beneficio y satisfacción de sí mismos" 'We live in a world where the culture of consumerism and indifference to the plight of the poor and their suffering has become pervasive. People are valued for what they possess rather than who they are and what values they hold for the betterment of humanity. In short, materialism has become a powerful force that influences how some people plan their lives and pursue their goals and achievements for the sole benefit and satisfaction of themselves' (Ghadirian; our trans.).

These kinds of exercises help develop students' ability to reach a higher level of analysis, considering the intertextuality that encourages an active reader to read between the lines. We recommend that after this activity, teachers encourage students to read more works by Borges. Students will feel more confident when they approach other works by the same author.

What do we know of the past? Is it all simply written in the present? Although what we know of Theseus comes from several sources, Greta Hawes focuses on Plutarch's contribution to the biography of this mythical figure. In her analysis, she notes that the task of historians is "to extract something of history from the mass of stories" (3). In other words, the Greeks were able to access the historiography of their past to a certain point; in order to access a distant past, they needed to refer to poetic accounts. In many ways, Borges highlights this conundrum to his readers and challenges them to extract something of history from the multiple accounts compiled in his story.

In teaching Borgesian literature, we ask students to engage in reading to question their subject position and reformulate accepted notions of truth and about reality. We ask them to interrogate the role of as well as the relationship between the reader, the writer, and the text. This effort necessitates patience and time, a reading that may prove frustrating and fruitless at first, but if presented thoughtfully, it can provide an underlying thread to the center of almost every text. As Duncan argues, "[O]ur understanding of the real shifts over time and from place to place" (5); what was once a Minotaur's bellows of hunger, today we might understand as earthquakes. What does this tell us about the role of myths, of stories, across the ages? What does this tell us about Borges's telling and retelling of myths? What is the purpose of the myth, the story, that he offers us? What do we gain by giving our monsters a name?

NOTES

1. Kaplan summarizes this hypothesis in a TED-Ed video available on *YouTube* (Kaplan, "Scientific Origins").

2. For more information on this type of organizer, which is one of the cause-and-effect diagrams created by Kaoru Ishikawa to study production, see Ishikawa's *Guide to Quality Control* (19–28).

3. Borges recurrently employs the concept of infinite possibilities—for instance, when addressing the notion of infinite doors or asserting that the number fourteen is equivalent to infinity. Additionally, the author's exploration of infinite realities becomes evident when Asterion states, "[T]ambién he meditado sobre la casa. Todas las partes de la casa están muchas veces, cualquier lugar es otro lugar. No hay un aljibe, un patio, un abrevadero, un pesebre; son catorce [infinitos] los pesebres, abrevaderos, patios, aljibes" 'I have also meditated on the house. All parts of the house are repeated many times, any place is another place. There is no one pool, courtyard, drinking trough, manger; the mangers, drinking troughs, courtyards, and pools are fourteen (infinite) in number' (*OC* 1: 1020; *CF* 221).

From Argentina to North America: A Tale of Two Souths

Jeffrey P. Thompson and Manuel Chinchilla

This essay details how we built an interdisciplinary course around the figure of the labyrinth and the fiction of Jorge Luis Borges while also describing how we brought together seemingly disconnected works and realities to bear on the idea of "the South" in the Argentine and American imaginaries. Our course was titled Reading the Labyrinth and was taught as part of the Interdisciplinary Humanities Program at Sewanee: The University of the South. The program focused on bringing together faculty members from multiple departments in order to model for students interdisciplinary teaching and learning. The program has been in place for over three decades and focuses on close reading and on cross-cultural comprehension, which gives instructors the unique freedom to explore new types of texts and new ways of learning. Our main objective was to introduce students to the fictional worlds and narrative styles of Borges while connecting those worlds and styles with current works and pressing issues. It was in this spirit that we paired short stories by Borges with innovative and recent works that spoke about the southern region of the United States.

Borges, Labyrinths, and the Humanities

In contrast with most departments or programs at Sewanee, the Interdisciplinary Humanities Program takes a collaborative approach in the construction of syllabi and highlights overlapping research and textual analysis across different departments. Taught by an interdisciplinary team—in our case, a team made up of faculty members in Spanish, art history, and mathematics—we consider common texts but approach them from our own disciplinary perspective, which allows students to observe both distinctions and commonalities between our methods. In general, the program features plenary lectures, classroom discussion, and breakout seminars for in-depth analysis.

Because the program builds on a tradition of interdisciplinary collaboration within the humanities, this curricular foundation set the stage for Reading the Labyrinth, allowing us to make intentional connections between Borges's short stories, the novel, and the podcast form. As such, the section of the course linked to the construct of "the South"—what it meant in the Argentine context and what it could mean when taught at a North American university—incorporated Borges's stories as guides for analyzing contemporary works about the southeastern portion of the United States: Brian Reed's podcast *S-Town* and Colson Whitehead's novel *The Underground Railroad*.

Lineages and Freedom

A comparison of Borges's "The South" (*CF* 174–79) and Whitehead's *The Underground Railroad* allowed students to think critically about Borges's writing by contrasting Juan Dahlmann's nostalgia with Cora's progressive yet never-ending story of escape and emancipation. The contrast between these two time-travelers—Dahlmann, who chooses the glory of a past golden age and the honorable death it affords, and Cora, who journeys through variable futures for survival and freedom—led to a critique of national history and belonging, giving us new avenues to relate both texts to the pasts they represent. Our aim was to instill in students a sense of history and geography not limited to the recounting of verifiable facts. Through readings, class discussion, and writing assignments, we worked together to highlight the ways in which fiction, in its creation of virtual landscapes and timescapes, enables us to delve into the darker side of national histories, their founding violence, and the utopian alternatives produced by those existing on their margins.

Our pedagogical approach took up matters that have been the object of ample theoretical discussion regarding Borges's writing and its ambiguous canonical standing, at once inside and outside the Western canon, as well as its use in discussions about radical politics. While Borges can be given the label of a cosmopolitan writer celebrated by cultural and academic circles in Europe and in the United States, including him in a great-books or humanities program elicits different responses from students and colleagues not familiar with his work. For many, he is an other who comes from outside the Western tradition and whose inclusion needs to be justified.

As a Latin American writer who wrote about the Argentine nation through fantastic and speculative fiction, but who at the same time produced a cosmopolitan writing able to transcend borders and incorporate diverse cultural traditions, Borges occupies an ambiguous space within the literary establishment. The Nobel laureate Mario Vargas Llosa, in a much quoted essay that circulated in the late 1980s, described Borges's work as liberating: "Before Borges, it seemed a piece of foolhardiness, or self-delusion for one of us to pursue universal culture as a European or North American might" (1326). For Vargas Llosa, Borges's use of foreign traditions allowed him to avoid the developmentalist trap that would make Latin American writing an imitator of European models, opting instead for an autonomous, free-flowing relationship with a diversity of traditions. Although Borges established literary freedom for Latin American writers, his representation of minorities, according to Vargas Llosa, often favored a Eurocentric view: "The black, the Indian, the primitive often appear in his stories as inferiors, wallowing in a state of barbarism" (1333). But for us, it was precisely this lack of resolution existing in literature's dark side that constituted fertile ground for discussing and comparing Borges's story and Whitehead's novel.

The problem of how to teach Borges's politics and works has to do with their difficult insertion into North American academic discourse, since they are resistant to the very representational categories and identity politics that surround curricular debates. Patrick Dove has outlined academia's dichotomous reaction to Borges as either a Eurocentric writer of conservative politics and nationalist views or a universal creator who is the epitome of artistic freedom. For Dove, neither of these avenues is able to contend with Borges's work, which he understands as a writing that "calls for an infinite and interminable reading," because it posits through content and form the very instability of identity ("Cultural Margins" 44). Such theoretical sensibility informed our teaching of Borges within the humanities, as we developed ways of relating his works to current discussions verging on diversity, racism, and nationalism. Our discussions produced a rereading of Borges that was also a critique of the national and Creole ideology found in stories like "The South," allowing us, too, to surpass the superficial assumption of a Latin American writer always being in defiance of tradition and conservatism.

At the same time, we did not want to dismiss Borges because of his dissimilarity with other Latin American figures and works (e.g., Rigoberta Menchú and her *testimonio*) that had entered the rarified air of humanities and great-books programs as relegated others finally acquiring visibility within academe. Therefore, it was important not only to instruct students on the particular racial makeup and colonialist history of Latin America in general and Argentina in particular but also to point them toward that conjectural and identity-resistant aspect of Borges's writing that permits it to converse with other works in productive and innovative ways.

Our lectures on "The South" established an understanding of the text as a commentary on the foundational violence of the Argentine nation, its mythical characters (the gaucho, the Pampa), and the Creole identity that Dahlmann adopts in order to be swept away from a modern, multiethnic Argentina. Beatriz Sarlo's well-known analysis of the short story as responding to the anxieties of the time and to Dahlmann's desire for belonging—his need to become more Argentine than he already feels through the reenactment of a national gauchoesque fantasy—points to an allegorical reading of the text centered on cultural, racial, and ethnic hybridity. While Sarlo believes the text to be a conveyor of conflicts depicting hybrid belongings that cannot be resolved, she also acknowledges the great freedom granted to Dahlmann, who "has constructed his fate through making small choices among all the possibilities offered to him by his dual origin" (*Jorge Luis Borges* [2006] 46). This freedom to choose a destiny between "the contrary pulls from his two lineages" (174) was the main narrative device we focused on to connect the protagonists and plots of "The South" and *The Underground Railroad*.

It is worth noting that scholarship on Borges has indeed paid attention to how his writing partakes in discussions about racial and ethnic identity, albeit from a different standpoint and style than the more accepted genres for such topics in the Latin American canon. Above all, Borges avoids a moment of identification that would solve the problem of the subject's identity and representation. Even when they, like Dahlmann, are attracted by a nostalgic vision of history, Borges's subjects are always open to interpretation, the same way their destinies are left in suspense with only hints to possible outcomes. Diemo Landgraf's reading of "The South," clearly expanding on Sarlo's work, focuses on Dahlmann's "identity conflict" and its reference to a postmodern sensibility that sees identity as constructed. Landgraf's conclusion is that the national allegory embedded in "The South," and in other stories like it, is a weak one that does not result in a positive national identity but that speaks of "potential conflicts inherent in hybrid identities and in identity constructions" (179). A similar dynamic is at play in Whitehead's reimagining of the Underground Railroad, the network of agents and safe houses that helped enslaved people escape the South during the nineteenth century. But what was a system of codes to covertly refer to such escape routes becomes in Whitehead's novel a machine that travels through the historical underground of the American territory.

Like Dahlmann, although certainly from a more disadvantaged position, Cora is the offspring of migration and violence. At the beginning of *The Underground Railroad*, we find her trying to decide between the two paths set forth by her grandmother Ajarry, who decided to make Georgia and the Randall Plantation her home, and her mother, Mabel, who Cora and all other characters in the novel believe has escaped to the North. Cora finally decides to follow Mabel's example, much like Dahlmann chooses the dangerous past of his military grandfather. But Cora's escape is not to the past, not a trip to a land and time of origins, but to an unrehearsed society. Her dream is a future one, a search for an unknown country yet to come. That is why Cora exists in an opposite framework where the idea of a nostalgic past is made impossible. Such idealization is available only through the fragile claim to the land established by her grandmother Ajarry, who tends a small plot of land on the plantation as her way of building a home there. (This is of course an inversion of Dahlmann's case; Dahlmann's trip back in time is to reclaim the Flores' country house.) Once Ajarry dies and Cora is unable to fend off other enslaved people who covet her inheritance, Cora becomes an outcast and soon after decides to escape. So students could delve into these ideas, we designed essay prompts that allowed them to think about the works in relation to their own lives. The essays for the unit on *The Underground Railroad* asked students to compare Cora's and Dahlmann's decisions regarding their lineages, and they also had the option to speak about their own ancestry. The essays worked well because they appealed to a narrative of family and belonging that students could easily incorporate into their own reflection. Many students spoke about histories of migration and heritage, seeing the importance they had in their own identity and family history.

Both plots employ the train as an anachronistic element signaling entrance into a fantastic arrangement of time and space. But Cora's time-traveling experience functions as a metaphor of what the country could be rather than what it has been. The many stops on Cora's route to freedom—the modern city in South Carolina that affords jobs to free people of color while exploiting them for medical research, the nightmarish scenario of lynching as pastime in North

Carolina, and the utopian community of the Valentine farm—are all rehearsals for a society that may at any turn find the key to a better social arrangement, to justice and equality, or one that fails and falls back on the violence of its foundation. But the movement is forward and toward life. Unlike Dahlmann, Cora wishes for survival at all costs, not for a worthy death. What we proposed in our classroom was an investigation into how each work envisioned national belonging from the point of view of their protagonists, both of whom are struggling to claim a version of the nation that would welcome them. In our class, the endings of the short story and the novel were the focus of comparative reflection. While Dahlmann goes out of the *pulpería* (a grocery store that also functions as a pub) to meet a worthy death, Cora, after escaping the fire at the Valentine farm and finally defeating Ridgeway, the bounty hunter hired to return her to the plantation, finds herself lost and destitute. If Dahlmann's destiny is sealed by the gift from the mythical gaucho who throws him the knife as a gateway to his destiny, in *The Underground Railroad* past and future are intertwined in the figure of Ollie. After reaching the end of the Underground Railroad and coming up to the surface, Cora runs into a caravan of migrants going west. This is of course a remaking of the American nation, its second mythology: the West as promised land. Ollie is a black man who has a symbol branded on his neck, a sign that he was once enslaved, and is also a link to Sybil, Cora's friend at the Valentine farm who was subjected to a similar horse brand by her master. After accepting Ollie's invitation to join his group, Cora muses on his life and motives, her thoughts also being the last words in the novel: "she wondered where he escaped from, how bad it was, and how far he traveled before he put it behind him" (Whitehead 306). When we reached the end of the novel, many students, like most readers, were surprised by the revelation of Mabel's death and the book's ending, and our discussion about Whitehead's decisions turned again to American history and nationalism. Many students were able to see how the novel, while not painting a rosy picture of America as the so-called promised land, did think of it as a space for the endless search for liberty by the likes of Cora and Ollie. For students, the novel's conclusion restated the myriad possibilities open to the American future, one in which marginal figures are able to belong and start anew. In contrast with Dahlmann's dream of returning to the past, Cora's journey was toward a nation yet to be made, but both Borges's and Whitehead's characters grapple with the violent origins of all nations.

Narratives of Revelation

The podcast *S-Town* was an attractive text to compare to Borges's work because it blurs the boundaries between media studies and comparative literature while presenting unique challenges for teaching and learning. Serial podcasts are a paradox, a new art form steeped in nostalgia. They combine the early-twentieth-century radio drama—and even recall the nineteenth-century serialized novel—with the portable and personalized digital device, their content resembling long-form investigative journalism found in magazines, and yet their form is intimate, their hosts and interview subjects "in your ear," seemingly talking only to you (Said and Silbey 104). Lectures on true crime, nonfiction novels like Truman Capote's *In Cold Blood*, and some brief excerpts from Orson Welles's *Mercury Theatre on the Air* (www.mercurytheatre.info) were helpful in establishing *S-Town* as part of a longer literary and cultural tradition. We also drew on students' own experiences of these cultural forms, true-crime documentaries on *Netflix*, and other formats they had experienced before taking the class.

In *S-Town*, the reporter Brian Reed travels to Alabama to investigate an alleged murder but, in turn, stumbles across the infinitely more complicated story of the horologist John B. McLemore, who resembles a Borgesian character, full of encyclopedic knowledge and intellectual hobbies like alchemy and labyrinth building, and who professes a love-hate relationship with his hometown in the rural American South. *S-Town* begins by focusing on allegations of corruption made by John B. (as he was known to friends) in the small, rural town of Woodstock, Alabama, about an hour outside Birmingham. Specifically, John B. alleges a murder cover-up—there are rumors that a member of a local wealthy family has gotten away with killing someone because of his family name and position in the community. John B.'s eccentric life is revealed early—he's a clockmaker who lives with his mother, who perhaps suffers from dementia, on a sprawling wooded farm that also hosts an intricate hedge maze. He makes clear that he has called and emailed the offices of *This American Life* multiple times about a murder in the "shit town" where he lives (Reed 4:02). His tenacity eventually piques Reed's interest. But by the second episode, listeners realize that the story is not what they were expecting and quickly discover that this show will take them on some shocking twists and turns. As such, the podcast abandons the true-crime format and the murder-mystery trope and instead becomes a multilayered story that is profound enough to meditate on mortality, provide insights into the tragedies that befall people who have to hide their true selves, and even offer a fascinating look at modern masculinity—a rare glimpse of southern men displaying their vulnerabilities with tenderness. First intrigued by a murder, listeners end up being fascinated instead by John B. and the entire cast. Every time we think we're encountering a stereotype within the narrative, the person says something that reveals them as more nuanced than we might have ever imagined, challenging our own assumptions about men, rural life, the working class, and the LGBTQ community.

We used two methods to help students extract meaning from their experience of the podcast. The first was to listen to one another and discuss our initial reactions to the story in seminar breakout groups. The second, more productive method was to convene a series of panels where students were selected at the start of class from the class roll. To be selected at random on any given panel day added an element of excitement to the process but also motivated all students to be prepared. Discussion prompts were distributed to everyone a day or two before the panel so that students could remind themselves about key issues in the narrative or aspects of the podcast's format. Chosen panelists spoke first, and their initial answers—and often their questions about *S-Town*—sparked a unique dialogue across the class as a whole. With their peers as guides, students tackled questions such as, Why does the rhetoric of the podcast work so well? How is the story encountered through voices and sounds? How do the strategies of the podcast deepen our understanding of the characters whose real lives are on display? What are the psychological or philosophical underpinnings that define these characters? Students gained confidence in their own analytical skills by recognizing how music and the soundtrack conditioned them to view the subjects of the podcast as though they were fictional characters. While the techniques of voice-over and personal interviews deepened our understanding of the people involved, students immediately recognized that the story was taking them on a labyrinthian journey that was compiled for dramatic flow after the events were recorded. Because *S-Town* is serialized, it contains cliff-hangers and is highly bingeable. It also elicits audience participation through conjectures and interpretations and employs intimate and personal delivery mechanisms that undermine omniscient authority, which serves to render a more authentic story. While *S-Town* initially casts Reed as an investigative journalist, he soon becomes a participant in the story, both reacting to events in the moment on tape and clearly editing those events later to heighten the riveting moments of high drama that string his audience along. It is one thing to know that this story exists about the small town of Woodstock, Alabama; it's another thing to experience the layered, labyrinthian narrative through the format of Reed's podcast, which is replete with music, sound effects, and overlapping voices.

In both the lecture and the seminar, we asked students not only to reflect on the themes of identity, masculinity, and sexuality that play out in the story of John B. but also to consider the narrative strategies and technologies of the podcast. A key point of emphasis for us was connecting these strategies to our understanding of Borges. In particular, "The Garden of Forking Paths" (*CF* 119–28) and "Funes, His Memory" (131–37) provided a lens for discussing themes of racism and memory in *S-Town* and enabled an aesthetic narrative comparison of how the podcast—manipulating the listener through music, sound effects, and its episodic structure—embellished real lives as fictions.

Our lecture material and discussion sections on "The Garden of Forking Paths" were tied to Borges's description of Yu Tsun, who, as a Chinese spy working for Germany during the First World War, exists in a liminal space between worlds. It was important for us to set up parallels for students between the story Dr. Stephen Albert tells about the character Ts'ui Pên, Yu Tsun's grandfather, and his abandoned novel and labyrinth, on the one hand, and John B.'s futile attempts to write and organize reams of data on climate change while also building and maintaining a labyrinth, on the other. In their essays and in seminars, students recognized that for John B., as for Ts'ui Pên, the writing itself was the labyrinth. Ts'ui Pên's abandoned novel could have many possible resolutions, several possible conclusions. A productive argument could be made that the same holds true for John B.'s legacy. One can read the podcast as following several of these threads after John B.'s suicide. Even so, the parallels between Borges and *S-Town* in this case were quite clear and helped us unpack the layers of narrative storytelling in both the podcast and the short story.

The question of race and prejudice in the story, especially Yu Tsun's desire to spy on behalf of his German handlers in order to prove himself worthy in the eyes of those who would discount him, was, as in the case of Dahlmann's identity in "The South," complex. Questions around identity in the case of Yu Tsun and John B. were never static but always in flux, and our writing and discussion prompts pushed students to question a number of their own assumptions about personal identity. With only minimal guidance from us, students recognized the conflict inherent in hybrid identities in their essays and in their answers to questions posed in the final exam.

Dr. Albert's story within a story was also a path toward greater understanding of Reed's role as podcast producer and host. We asked students to consider the similarities and differences between Dr. Albert and Reed as characters: How do they insert themselves into a drama that is already in progress? How do the different cultures and crime come together in these stories? What is significant about the coupling of crime stories with philosophical and intellectual discussions?

Students tended to accept the drama of the podcast, allowing themselves to enjoy the immersive experience of the music and soundtrack uncritically. As teachers, it was important to let students have that experience. Slowly, we worked to pull back the curtains, so to speak, by having students break down the elements of each technique used by Reed and his production team in order to understand how the podcast gained our confidence and created empathy for John B. In many ways, having a character like Ireneo Funes as part of earlier lectures and seminar discussions provided a model for how the retelling of past events can be unpacked. The narrator in "Funes, His Memory" treats his subject not only like a curiosity but also with a great deal of sympathy. The narrator recalls meeting Funes in 1884, when the narrator's father took him to Fray Bentos, Uruguay. The narrator and his cousin Bernardo are riding horses when they come across a young boy—Funes. Bernardo asks Funes for the time, and without consulting a clock or even the position of the sun, Funes responds with the correct time down to the minute. John B.'s vocation as a clockmaker made the links to Funes explicit; moreover, his encyclopedic rehearsal of facts related to progressive politics and the global climate crisis were eccentricities that read as particularly Borgesian. We constructed exam prompts that asked students to discuss how revelations such as those in "Funes, His Memory" and *S-Town* shape content and characters as well as how they persuade the reader to see the story in a certain way. Did they feel manipulated by the way information was presented, or did they feel in control once more was revealed? Did it really matter to them to find themselves in the hands of a creator who cunningly guided them through the work? The class was evenly split on these questions. Some students felt manipulated in a negative way or thought the podcast exploited its subjects. Others were happy to play along and admired the way the podcast format created a compelling narrative out of the lives lived in a small town in Alabama. Our aim was to use Borges's writing and Reed's production styles to analyze how art can reveal hidden realities (colonialist histories, racism, prejudice) and also, if analyzed with enough care and attention, something about the manner and style in which we as consumers of narratives are taken in by the power of narrators and characters.

Adapting the works of Borges to the humanities curriculum and placing them in dialogue with contemporary American works that speak about timely and important matters proved to us that diversifying the curriculum has as much to do with including previously ignored voices as with actively finding ways to reinvigorate their engagement with different cultures and across regional boundaries. The two Souths we spoke of presented not only many differences but also many mutually illuminating similarities that enriched discussions about history, identity, and artistic representation. It is important for us that Latin American cultural production, which is actively consumed and researched in the United States, also be part of broader interdisciplinary programs and that its contributions to the university as a place of learning be as diverse as possible. We hope to have made a strong case not only for including Borges's work in such curricula but also for studying his works in comparison with works that engage with new questions about race, identity, and the construct of "the South."

Vertigo, *Repens*, and *Repositio*: Introducing Students to Borges's Literary Games

Kimberly A. Nance

Teaching Jorge Luis Borges's stories as a form of play is not only a pedagogical strategy to engage students but also a matter of faithfulness to the texts. In his classic *Les jeux et les hommes* (*Man, Play and Games*), Roger Caillois sets forth a taxonomy of varieties of play: competition, chance, simulation, and vertigo. The play of Borges's stories belongs to this last category. Numerous critics have pointed to the characteristic uncertainty and slippages of the fantastic as a genre, from Harry Belevan's "vacillation" to Tzvetan Todorov's "evanescence" to Marcel Brion's direct "vertigo." Not only are Borges's texts rife with dizzying literary moves, they often contain explicit signposts to direct readers toward vertigo. It is no accident that Borges's stories, mostly written in the 1930s and 1940s, found their most receptive audience in the 1960s, a decade indelibly associated with hallucinogenic play. Jean-Luc Godard invoked Borges's work in his films *The Rifleman* and *Alphaville*, as did Bernardo Bertolucci in *The Spider's Stratagem*. By 1970, a copy of a Borges story collection would appear in Nicholas Roeg's film *Performance*, starring a young Mick Jagger. Rereading Caillois by the light of the video screen, the digital game theorists Maaike Lauwaert, Joseph Wachelder, and Johan van der Walle propose that the fundamental attraction of all games stems from a dynamic balance between two factors that they term *repens* and *repositio*. *Repens* "appeals to the player's desire to discover, explore and get to know the surprises a game has in store and to make progress by learning from these surprises" (89). *Repositio*, in contrast, is marked by opportunities "to retry, return, replay and repeat a certain action while getting better at it with every try" (89). These contemporary game theorists also describe striking parallels between designing successful video games and fostering the constellation of curiosity, attention, persistence, and confidence that enables and motivates learning in other contexts. Their research sheds light on how the internal structures of a game serve to heighten its cognitive and emotional rewards.

The work of Lauwaert and colleagues on learning and game design offers a useful corrective to a torrent of simplistic gamification of pedagogy in which task completion is tracked and rewarded with points. On the contrary, these researchers argue, the most compelling games, the ones to which players devote increasingly large shares of their waking hours, are not about points at all but rather about complex and difficult projects with unpredictable challenges. In these games, work comes to generate its own reward. In the case of Borges's stories, that reward is literary vertigo. In *Teaching Literature in the Languages*, I applied those principles to course design and class activities (Nance). This essay translates the implications of vertigo, *repens*, and *repositio* into practices specific to the teaching of Borges's stories, demonstrating how teachers can begin to enable all students to experience the sense of literary play and pleasure that makes those notoriously complex stories so compelling to expert readers—the ones who know how to play the game. The focus here is on the introductory stage, a critical moment for student engagement.

The process of introducing students to Borges's hyperliterary play begins by recognizing the barriers that bar their entry, the gaps between students' current knowledge, skills, and expectations and the ones they need in order to join this game. Do students possess the essential tools—for instance, the vocabulary and cultural references associated with a particular story? If not, they will need to be equipped before they begin to read so that everyone can play this literary game. Otherwise, most of the class will be relegated to spectatorship as the teacher executes a series of virtuoso moves. Beyond the basic equipment for reading, many students also need specific instructions on how to read a literary text, especially if that reading takes place in a second language. Beginning and intermediate language classes typically treat stories as springboards for conversation practice. Students have learned that the goals of reading are to recount the plot, describe the characters, and then relate the issues raised by the text to their own experience. If we expect them to play differently in a literature class, it is only fair to make it clear that the rules are about to change.[1]

Most teachers, of course, do provide pre-reading assignments and explicit instructions on how to read literature. Nevertheless, those conditions are not yet sufficient to enable students' entry into Borges's literary games. Students can be linguistically and culturally competent to read a given story and dutifully follow general instructions on how to read literature yet still be left out of Borges's game—indeed, left unaware that there is a vertiginous game going on. Even for the most conscientious students, the ones accustomed to reading, rereading, and researching the references of a literary story until they "get it," the forking paths of Borges's stories may lead only to frustration at their inability to suss out "the real story."[2] The problem here is that there is no singular real story to be found. As Cynthia Duncan writes, "[T]he slippery nature of the fantastic is part of what defines it as a genre" (3). Students on a competitive quest to finally understand every reference in a Borges story are likewise bound to lose—and not just because the writer is such a formidable opponent. Even if a hypothetical perfect reader could track down every last reference, those references would never add up to a winning solution. In their efforts to confront Borges, students keep losing because they are trying to play the wrong games.

Teaching students that the experience of readerly vertigo is a feature of Borges's literary game, not a failure, has a powerful effect on their experience of reading. The confusion that students find so frustrating when they think reading Borges is an unwinnable competitive game takes on a different valence when they learn that this is not a quest for the one true plot or a dogged hunt for all the literary references but rather the pursuit of the pleasure of vertigo. What follows is a description of a vertigo-based introduction to the literary games of Borges, one that gives all students a chance to experience the pleasure and sense of success that motivate further play.

This interactive orientation, a series of visual images and text slides interspersed with micro-lectures of a minute or two, and discussion—some of it in small groups, some of it whole-class—takes place in the classroom before students are ever assigned to read a Borges story.[3] The slide deck opens with a question: "What sort of pleasure do all these activities have in common?"[4] A series of photographic images scrolls past: a child holding out her arms as she spins in place; another child whose feet lift off the ground as he is spun around by an adult who holds his hands; and finally, a shot of riders on a giant roller-coaster in an amusement park. The answer, students recognize, is dizziness—the physical ecstasy of vertigo that Mary and Herbert Knapp identify as one of the most basic forms of human play (54). We talk for a moment about the vertigo-inducing activities that students enjoyed as children. The next slide sequence notes that many adults also find vertigo pleasurable, seeking it through physical movement and dance, at amusement parks, and through chemical means such as drugs and alcohol. Physical vertigo, a slide explains, is believed to be produced when the brain receives contradictory signals from the senses. For instance, our eyes may be telling us one thing about the position of our body while the vestibular structure of the inner ear, the organ of proprioception, tells us another. The inability to reconcile those signals is experienced as disorientation and dizziness (Moskvitch). Although in circumstances such as illness vertigo is unpleasant, in other settings it may be experienced as profoundly pleasurable.

But why are we talking about vertigo in a literature class? The next slide takes note that certain kinds of stories can produce a literary form of vertigo. How does that work? Stories, I tell students, contain internal instructions on how they should be read. "Not only that," another slide adds, "all of you probably learned to spot those instructions even before you learned to read, when other people told you stories or read to you. As very small children, you already knew that 'once upon a time . . .' signaled the start of one sort of story and 'yesterday, on my way home . . .' quite another. What kinds of expectations did each opening set up?" These are questions that all students can answer.[5]

Borges and some other writers, I tell students, take advantage of your ability to recognize those internal cues by embedding contradictory instructions within a single story, in effect disorienting readers and producing a sort of literary vertigo. "We've already mentioned some of the characteristics of fairy tales and 'anecdotes from my day' stories," reads the next slide, "here are some other kinds of stories: detective, supernatural, fantasy, truth is stranger than fiction, hallucinations, and dream sequences." Each genre is assigned to one group of students, who receive a copy of the first page of a typical story from that genre to help get them started. On a slide are questions for the group to answer: "How do readers recognize this kind of story? Once readers recognize this kind of story, what do they expect? In other words, what are the text's internal instructions for how we are supposed to read it?" After a few minutes, each group presents their answers.

After each group has had their chance to report their clues as to story type, I ask the class to take a step back, to group those clues into categories. I prompt, for instance, "Several groups reported that clues might take the form of formulaic lines or character types. What are some other categories?" If necessary, I ask leading questions until the list includes language (familiar styles or formulaic lines), plot features (patterns of events, characteristic lines of development), nature of events (realistic, impossible, coincidental), nature of characters, explicit categorizations (book covers and blurbs, marketing materials), and the writer's reputation (e.g., "a Stephen King novel").

I then ask another question, this time rhetorical. How might a writer use readers' ability to recognize different types of stories to figuratively spin those readers round and disorient them? In other words, how might a writer use readers' own familiarity with stories to create a state of uncertainty in which readers are unsure as to which kind of story they are reading? Most ordinary stories, I point out, either remain in one category throughout (the ghost story stays a ghost story) or else shift category definitively at a single point. For instance, the narrator might suddenly wake up (supernatural to dream sequence), or what people thought was a ghost might turn out to be mist from a leak in a steam pipe (supernatural to realist). Borges, however, does something more complicated. He embeds indicators of multiple genres of stories throughout, within a single narrative. There is never a definitive change from one genre to another. In fact, just when the reader thinks there might have been, they are directed back to the genre they thought had been abandoned. Those multiple twists and lack of firm ground induce a sensation of literary vertigo. Borges also deploys other strategies designed to strip readers of secure points of reference, preventing them from determining once and for all what is really happening in the story.

Each of these unmooring moves is illustrated by more slides with photographs. For instance, Borges often includes details that suggest that the narrator's perceptions may be limited or distorted (e.g., a narrator with a high fever may be subject to vivid dreams or hallucinations). Key events of the story may take place in isolated settings, where there are no other witnesses to corroborate the narrator's perceptions. As Todorov notes, subtle clues, such as phrases that at first appear to be merely figurative, may begin to accumulate, coming together to support a supernatural reading (56). A slide displaying the classic yellow sign denoting a slippery road, a car with squiggly lines behind it, introduces a microlecture on what Belevan terms "deslices textuales" (slippery spots in the text), ambiguous and polysemic phrases that open the door to the possibility that something else is happening beyond the story's literal events (33). I ask students to return to their groups, challenging them to spot points of possible slippage from literal to supernatural in three passages from "El Sur" ("The South"), the Borges story that I will be assigning for homework:

> Nadie ignora que el Sur empieza del otro lado de Rivadavia. Dahlmann solía repetir que ello no es una convención y que quien atraviesa esa calle entra en un mundo más antiguo y más firme. (*OC* 1: 916)
>
> Everyone knows that the South begins on the other side of Avenida Rivadavia. Dahlmann had often said that that was no mere saying, that by crossing Rivadavia one entered an older and more stable world. (*CF* 176)
>
> [P]ensó, mientras alisaba el negro pelaje, que aquel contacto era ilusorio y que estaban como separados por un cristal, porque el hombre vive en el tiempo, en la sucesión, y el mágico animal, en la actualidad, en la eternidad del instante. (*OC* 1: 916)
>
> [He] thought, while he stroked the cat's black fur, that this contact was illusory, that he and the cat were separated as though by a pane of glass, because man lives in time, in successiveness, while the magical animal lives in the present, in the eternity of the instant. (*CF* 176)
>
> Mañana me despertaré en la estancia, pensaba, y era como si a un tiempo fuera dos hombres: el que avanzaba por el día . . . y el otro, encarcelado en un sanatorio. (*OC* 1: 917)
>
> *Tomorrow I will wake up at my ranch*, he thought, and it was as though he were two men at once: the man gliding along . . . and the other man, imprisoned in a sanatorium. (*CF* 176–77)

The next slide reminds students that this type of story is not an ordinary one-time genre shift. Instead, a reader's experience of a single paragraph might look like this:

> [*Reads the first paragraph*]
>
> OK, I recognize this type of story—looks like an account of a person who has an accident and ends up in the hospital. It seems serious. I'm wondering whether or not he will recover.
>
> [*Reads another paragraph*]
>
> But no, this part looks a little eerie. Maybe it's some kind of supernatural story.
>
> [*Reads a few more lines*]
>
> OK, now it looks like the realist hospital experience again. That eerie part must have been a metaphor or something.

[*Reads another paragraph*]

Hmm. The details here could still fit the hospital plot, but they could also work in a supernatural plot.

This disorienting experience continues throughout the story. Owing to constant redirection from evidence for each genre and ambiguous details that might support both genres, the reader can never be certain what is really happening.

Finally, as if all these ambiguities and suggestions were not enough to cause readerly vertigo, Borges sometimes inserts explicit instructions on how to play the game of reading, a technique video gamers might call "cheat codes." In his prologue to *Artificios* (*Artifices*), later collected in *Ficciones*, Borges advises readers that regarding "'El Sur,' que es acaso mi mejor cuento, básteme prevenir que es posible leerlo como directa narración de hechos novelescos y también de otro modo" '"The South," which may be my best story, I shall tell the reader only that it is possible to read it both as a forthright narration of novelistic events and in quite another way, as well' (*OC* 1: 877; *CF* 129). You can read a Borges story a hundred times, I conclude, and you will never find a singular plot, because the text is expressly designed to keep that from happening.

Why would a writer do such a thing? This micro-lecture is illustrated by a photograph of Borges as a young man, closer to the age of most of my students than he is in the portraits of a distinguished gentleman nearing the end of a long life, as he is represented in most anthologies. Judging from Borges's biographies and autobiographies, this form of vertiginous literary play is the invention of a younger man who wrote because he was bored. A prodigious and passionate reader from the age of four, Borges found fascinating the stylistic and structural markers that distinguished one type of narrative from another (Rodríguez Monegal 78). From childhood he experimented with writing in a wide array of genres, including encyclopedia articles, memoirs, literary homages, logical proofs, histories, detective stories, biblical parables, and origin myths, to name only a few. After building, both individually and in collaboration with his friend Adolfo Bioy Casares, with whom he wrote under the joint pseudonym Honorio Bustos Domecq, all the narrative structures following the standard generic instructions, he essentially took them all apart and used their literary building blocks as moveable playing pieces in a new and intricate literary game (Nance, "Borges" 23).

The last slide sequence illustrates some artistic analogues of Borges's vertigo-inducing writing: the art of M. C. Escher, the balancing toy in which a tiny metal figure of a clown or acrobat perpetually teeters on one foot, and the topological curiosity known as a Möbius strip, in which an ordinary strip of paper is joined together with a twist that renders it demonstrably single-sided. Each group of students is asked to comment on the possible similarities between one of those items and what they have learned so far about Borges's literary techniques.[6]

Finally, students are sent home to complete their first assignment, one of Borges's short stories, in order to apply what they have learned and return to report on the literary play they discover in the text. At this point many students do start to chase down references from "El Sur," not because they were assigned to but out of curiosity as to whether the book Dahlmann is reading, the *Thousand and One Nights*, might be one of those slippery spots. The next day, small-group and class discussion questions focused on concepts from those introductory slides enable everyone to join in. Because of the attractions of *repens* and *repositio*, it is important not to leave the study of Borges after a single story. For a game to be truly pleasurable, students need time to experience the sense of mastery and confidence of *repositio*, not only the effort and struggle of *repens*. As Lauwaert and colleagues insist, it is the dynamic balance of the two in the "cycle of repeated time" that makes a game truly enjoyable and "arouses desire" to play it again (102). Assigning several Borges stories in a row affords students a further chance to experience literary play as a source of pleasure. Even more productive, and surprising to students, is the occasional assignment to simply reread a previous assignment after the discussion, which allows students to see what else they notice that they might have missed on the first reading. Because the fantastic does not rest on a single plot, it is largely resistant to spoilers. Instead, rereading continues to hold out the promise of new discoveries in the form of intertextual and cultural references and literary techniques. Unlike the first reading, the reading of *repens*, the *repositio* of rereading affords newer readers a taste of what it is like to play the game as an expert, to meet challenges with the benefit of experience and knowledge. Students also report that spotting how the vertigo was produced makes them feel accomplished, a pleasure akin to the attraction of Penn and Teller's television series *Fool Us*, in which the magicians watch other performers and attempt to discover the mechanism behind their illusions.

Reframing Borges's works as a form of literary play and taking care to equip all students to experience the sophisticated and fundamental pleasure of succumbing to literary vertigo and then to analyze it has had significant positive effects on their performance in the classroom. Students' essays in papers and exams, including independent analyses of works that we did not read or discuss in class, offer further evidence of pedagogical efficacy. Even better, in every class some students, including ones who profess never to have been very interested in literature, have reported talking to someone else outside class—a roommate or friend—about Borges and his stories. Not only are students beginning to join in Borges's literary game and experience the pleasure of vertigo, some of them are recruiting other players.

NOTES

1. For more on the process of identifying these gaps and strategies for addressing them, see Nance, *Teaching* 77–98.

2. As Joanna Wolfe notes, "For many students, the simple statement that complexity is a primary value in literary and cultural analysis can come as a major revelation. . . . The awareness that illuminating complexity is often the goal of textual analysis—and,

moreover, that complexity is established primarily through arguments of definition—can occasion a major shift in perspective for such students" (405–06). "By teaching students how to discover complexity in texts," she argues, "we can help them discover multiple ways of enjoying and engaging with them" (406).

3. The timing here is crucial. Students need to be prepared to play before they are sent home with an assignment. Turning over this same information only after the students have tried and mostly failed does not increase their confidence or motivation to read.

4. I teach literature courses entirely in Spanish; the text from slides and contents of micro-lectures are provided here in English translation. For images, see Nance, "Literary Play."

5. This introductory stage keeps the use of technical literary terms to a bare minimum. They will be introduced later in the course unit. As I explain in *Teaching Literature in the Languages*, "The decision to approach literature first through ordinary experience offered all students important news of themselves as well as news of literature. It let them see that discussion in this class was not restricted to elite or exotic 'literature people.' Everyone was expected to talk and everyone was able to participate fully. There was no expectation that students would already know any specialized terms" (Nance, *Teaching* 81).

6. For an illustration of how to construct a Möbius strip and what happens when it is cut in half, see the video "Cutting a Möbius Strip."

The Material History of Borges's Works

Nora Benedict

Jorge Luis Borges's writings, filled with dizzying labyrinths, doubling mirrors, and boundless libraries, appeal not only to literary scholars but also to philosophers, cognitive scientists, and even political theorists. In the classroom, these diverse scholars rely on a number of tactics to explain Borges's texts, from the use of thought experiments and mathematical proofs to a consideration of historical events and linguistic tendencies. As a result, the number of approaches to teaching Borges appears endless. However, a commonly overlooked facet of Borges's work is the material evidence of its production and manufacture: What was his writing process? Where did he publish his most canonical fictions, and why? Using these types of questions as a point of departure, this essay considers how to teach Borges's works from a material perspective by focusing on the physical journey that his writings took from initial manuscript drafts to final published editions. In terms of the specifics, I describe the complex material histories of two of Borges's short stories from *El Aleph* (*The Aleph*)—"El muerto" ("The Dead Man") and "La casa de Asterión" ("The House of Asterion")—alongside a series of pedagogical strategies for introducing them to students. While these two short stories might not traditionally be taught in most courses, they provide a unique glimpse into Borges's working life and writing processes and are thus an important grouping for students to analyze.

Prior to addressing the physical features and attributes of Borges's works, I believe that students need to have a clear grasp of the texts themselves.[1] That is to say, before learning about Borges's compositional and publishing practices, students must first perform a meticulous close reading of the works. To that end, the strategies and suggestions that I present here are intended to deepen students' understanding of Borges's texts and should serve as a supplement to a more traditional literary analysis. In other words, I envision that the plans outlined below will be used for a second class on Borges's work, which would immediately follow an introductory session dedicated to the linguistic form and content of his writings, with special attention to his short stories "El muerto" and "La casa de Asterión."[2]

The Writing Process

Most students do not consider—or have not been asked to consider—the process through which authors conceive of and ultimately compose their works. This fact is not unique to students of Latin American literature. It is true for students who study any kind of literary text. As a result, it is imperative to discuss how authors composed their works—from drafts to fair copies—and to contextualize these practices in a pre-digital era, since most twenty-first-century students write their academic essays and creative fictions with the help of (online) word processors, which obscure the notion of multiple drafts. Scholars have learned a great deal about Borges's writing process in the past decade, in large part because of the acquisition of many of his manuscripts by various universities and cultural institutions.[3] In fact, Daniel Balderston's work in this area has been groundbreaking, and Balderston's most recent monograph, *How Borges Wrote*, emphasizes the importance of analyzing all stages of Borges's compositional practices in order to best understand his writings.[4] While a number of Borges's extant manuscripts are fair copies that most likely went directly to a printer or publisher, the vast majority of these known documents are filled with cross-outs, smudges, and Borges's miniscule handwriting, which can prove quite challenging to decipher. Highlighting these features and sharing images of these difficult-to-read manuscripts allows students to get a better sense of the time, effort, and energy that went into writing something as short as a three-page essay or fictional story. Comparing and contrasting these extant documents with the streamlined (digital) output of word processors also causes students to reflect on how a great deal of our modern-day writing practice is invisible to the naked eye.

Although the surviving manuscripts for both "El muerto" and "La casa de Asterión" must be viewed in situ at the Albert and Shirley Small Special Collections Library at the University of Virginia, Balderston and María Celeste Martín's recent volume of facsimiles of Borges's manuscripts provides students with access to images of these rare documents along with their typographic transcriptions (Borges, *Cuentos* 43–72).[5] With regard to their shared physical features, both manuscripts are relatively clean, clear copies with very few cross-outs or textual variants. What is more, both are composed on similar—if not identical—graph paper that has been hand-numbered. In terms of the specifics, the manuscript for "El muerto" is a thirteen-page document written on graph paper with black ink. There are a total of sixteen lines or words in the manuscript that have been completely obscured with either black or red ink. Throughout the first seven pages, the text is neatly written on every other line of the page, while the remaining six pages revert to single-spaced printing. It is also important to note that virtually all pages have been cut into smaller pieces, with the exception of pages 8 and 13, which include a full page of the graph paper. The fragmentary nature of this particular manuscript raises the question of what Borges might have wanted to hide in a more permanent way that went beyond a simple strike-through of the text. The manuscript for "La casa de Asterión" is an eight-page document written in dark blue ink on graph paper. (The final page has no number because the top margin has been sliced from the rest of the page.) Throughout the pages there are a total of eleven cross-outs in black ink. Unlike in "El muerto," several of these cross-outs consist of one single line drawn through a word or a series of words, which makes the underlying text completely legible. On the last page of this manuscript, Borges has signed his name. Like the manuscript for "El muerto," this fair copy of "La casa de Asterión" has been cut into smaller strips of paper.

Since most students have not had the opportunity to work with or analyze original manuscripts prior to this class, I first ask them to describe as fully as possible what they see in (the replica images of) these documents: Is the handwriting easy or hard to read? Can they identify different handwritings throughout the document, or just one? What is the paper like? What about the ink? Is there anything strange or unexpected about the manuscript? After gathering their opinions and feedback, I explain how fair copies of manuscripts like these two differ from other types of manuscripts. More specifically, I point out the fact that these types of documents tended to go straight to a printer or publisher and, for that reason, had to be extremely clean and legible to avoid confusion and the introduction of any type of error. As a foil, I then show them a series of different Borges manuscripts that he revised and emended over a series of years, with special attention to different manuscripts that pertain to the same essay, short story, or poem. For instance, apart from the examples that I draw on from "El muerto" and "La casa de Asterión," I also share images of several manuscripts from Borges's first collection of poetry, *Fervor de Buenos Aires* (*Fervor of Buenos Aires*), such as "Música patria" ("Homeland Music"), "Ciudad" ("City"), "Judería" ("Ghetto"; Borges, *Poemas* 31–35), and "Calle desconocida" ("Unknown Street"; Borges, *Poemas* 15–22). These manuscripts are especially revealing, since they contain not only emendations in Borges's hand from various decades but also unique illustrations by Borges himself. In this way, students gain a nuanced understanding not only of how to read, interpret, and interact with manuscripts more broadly but also of Borges's unique writing process.

Periodical Publications

Because I first introduce students to the concept of fair copy manuscripts, the transition to discussing the publication process of "El muerto" and "La casa de Asterión" is a seamless one. That is to say, I return to the function of these types of manuscripts, which were most often destined for a printer or publisher. Before detailing the specific venues in which Borges published these two short stories, I provide students with an overview of Borges's extensive work with periodicals during the 1930s and 1940s in Argentina. In particular, students learn about his early work in the 1920s for more avant-garde literary magazines such as *Proa*, *Prisma*, and *Martín Fierro*; his stable jobs in the 1930s at periodicals with large circulation, including *Crítica*'s literary supplement, the *Revista Multicolor de los Sábados* (*Multicolor Saturday Magazine*), and *El Hogar* (*The Home*); and his notable work with Victoria Ocampo's *Sur* (*South*) and the literary magazine *Los Anales de Buenos Aires* (*Annals of Buenos Aires*) throughout the 1930s and 1940s.[6] In fact, these latter two venues are where "La casa de Asterión" and "El muerto" were first published, respectively. *Sur* and *Los Anales de Buenos Aires* are freely available in a digital format online, which makes them particularly accessible for teaching.[7] After this general introduction to Borges's editorial jobs, we turn to the specific publications of "El muerto" and "La casa de Asterión." In particular, I point out several changes between the manuscript versions of these two texts and their printed counterparts in *Sur* and *Los Anales de Buenos Aires*. I then ask student to identify trends that they see across these changes: Are there any patterns? Are there more substantive (words, phrasings, etc.) or accidental (punctuation, capitalization, etc.) changes? I then share broader tendencies in Borges's writing process, such as his frequent changes in the order of words in a given phrase or the substitution of one word for another, all of which showcase his marked desire for precision.[8]

Differences among Published Editions

In the final part of this class, I turn to the publication of *El Aleph*, which included both "El muerto" and "La casa de Asterión." In addition to examining the unique physical features of different editions of this collection—two editions published by Editorial Losada, one in 1949 and one in 1952, and a 1957 edition published by Emecé Editores—I also introduce students to the two main publishing houses that produced them. In this way, students gain insight into Borges's writing process and develop new techniques for approaching his works. Similar to our discussions surrounding the diversity of periodicals that Borges worked with during the 1920s, 1930s, and 1940s, this section of the class showcases the diversity of publishers with whom Borges produced his books during this same time frame. I first provide students with a brief overview of the publishing industry during the first half of the twentieth century in Buenos Aires in order to highlight its newness and overall rate of expansion.[9] From there, I explain how Borges moved from self-publishing (*Fervor de Buenos Aires*) to working directly with numerous publishers. More specifically, I stress how he published works with a variety of publishers ranging from those that specialized in cheap, mass-produced paperbacks to those that were known for their expensive luxury editions.

In terms of the specifics, I briefly describe this variety in Borges's published books by contrasting his early collection of fiction, *Historia universal de la infamia* (1935; *A Universal History of Iniquity*), first published by Editorial TOR, a publisher that was known for its interest in monetary gain above all else and that produced extremely cheap books of very poor quality, with his collection of essays *Historia de la eternidad* (1936; *A History of Eternity*), first published by Viau y Zona, a luxury publisher known for its carefully crafted editions.[10] From these two works, students begin to discern how the physical features of a specific book can affect its overall reception (and sales). We then move to consider the specific case of *El Aleph* in a bit more detail. After introducing students to Editorial Losada and Emecé Editores, I ask them to discuss the cover images for Losada's first and second editions (the first published in 1949, the second in 1952): How do these covers compare to those of *Historia universal de la infamia* and *Historia de la eternidad*? How does the inclusion of drawings alter our perception of the work? Do we know anything about the artist or artists who created these illustrations? Why do we think that these covers include images? How are the drawings on the first and second editions different? In general terms, students tend to highlight the presence of two unique illustrations on Losada's covers, while Borges's earlier works contain mostly typographic elements on their covers. I share details about Attilio Rossi, a close friend of Borges's and the illustrator for much of Losada's cover art.[11] I also emphasize the fact that *El Aleph* forms part of a larger collection produced by Losada, the Colección Prosistas de España y América (Collection of Prose Writers from Spain and America) and how all the titles in this collection present similarly striking cover illustrations. I also draw students' attention to the differences in content between these two editions in order to show how each edition (and each copy of an edition, for that matter) can alter its contents and, as a result, our reading experience.[12]

I then explain how Borges's publishing practices shifted in the early 1950s such that he began to publish his works exclusively with Emecé Editores. Following a brief description of this publisher, we consider the physical and textual aspects of Emecé's first edition of *El Aleph* (1957), which was the first publication in their collection of Borges's *Obras completas* (*Complete Works*): In what ways is this volume different from those of Losada? What might account for these differences? Can we still read this specific edition as a stand-alone publication, or does it need to be evaluated within the larger context of Emecé's *Obras completas*? As in their previous comments, most students home in on the fact that this edition of *El Aleph* does not present any cover illustration and is quite stark, which reminds them of the covers of earlier editions such as *Historia de la eternidad*. I use these observations to return to my previous point about publishers' collections and series, such as Losada's, and how these groupings of books tend to convey a unified aesthetic. As a way of concluding this session, I ask students to share the format in which they read "El muerto" and "La casa de Asterión" for class that week. Because it is highly unlikely that any students accessed either short story in its original periodical or book form, I then ask how their interpretations of these texts might have been altered by their physical experiences of reading.

Broadly speaking, looking to Borges's methodical systems of literary production allows students to better understand the impact of his lesser-known working life on his writings as well as the intricate relationship between text and (physical) context. In addition to deepening students' knowledge of Borges's writing process and his involvement in the publishing industry in Argentina, the tools that students acquire during this particular session, especially the ability to engage with and evaluate manuscript material, can be applied to many other classes and fields of study and, as a result, will serve them well beyond their courses on Borges or Latin American literature.

NOTES

1. I have taught a version of the class that I describe here as part of an upper-level undergraduate survey of Latin American literature (1900 to the present). I also guest-taught portions of the class for a graduate-level survey of twentieth-century Spanish American literature. As a result, the pedagogical suggestions I provide can be utilized for both graduate and undergraduate courses.

2. For an introduction to Borges's writings, see Williamson, *Cambridge Companion*; and Balderston, *Out of Context*. For an introduction to the author's linguistic nuances, see Balderston, *How Borges Wrote*; and Fishburn and Hughes.

3. The largest public collection of Borges's manuscripts is housed at the University of Virginia. Institutions with smaller collections include the University of Texas, Austin; the University of Notre Dame; the University of Pittsburgh; and Michigan State University. For more details on all known Borges manuscripts, see Balderston's list of manuscripts (housed in both public and private collections), which can be accessed on the Borges Center website ("Other Resources").

4. Along with this impressive book, Balderston has published numerous articles on Borges's manuscripts ("Genética textual," "Anotación," "Las páginas del Haber," "Puntos suspensivos," "Biografías infames," "Senderos," "Descubrimientos secretos," "'Demasiado evanescente,'" "Palabras rechazadas: Borges," "Detalles circunstanciales," "Theory of Games," "Liminares," "Palabras rechazadas: Lectura," "'His Insect-Like Handwriting,'" "Los manuscritos").

5. Both print and electronic versions of this facsimile edition can be purchased on the Borges Center website. Along with this specific edition dedicated to Borges's short stories, Balderston and Martín edited facsimile editions of his essays and poetry, which are also available for purchase through the Borges Center website (Borges, *Ensayos* and *Poemas*). When viewed together, all three editions showcase the level of compositional diversity in Borges's manuscripts and serve as excellent teaching resources.

6. For more details about Borges's employment history in the publishing industry, see Benedict, *Borges*; Rodríguez Monegal; and Williamson, *Borges*.

7. The entire run of Ocampo's literary journal, *Sur* (1931–92), is available through the Biblioteca Nacional Mariano Moreno in Buenos Aires (catalogo.bn.gov.ar), and *Los Anales de Buenos Aires* has been fully digitized for the *Archivo Histórico de Revistas Argentinas* (www.ahira.com.ar/revistas/los-anales-de-buenos-aires/). Digital copies of *Prisma*, *Proa*, *Martín Fierro*, and the *Revista Multicolor de los Sábados* can also be found in this archive.

8. For more on Borges's writing process, see Balderston, *How Borges Wrote*; Balderston's numerous articles on Borges's manuscripts; and Benedict, "Digital Approaches."

9. De Diego's edited collection *Editores y políticas editoriales en Argentina, 1880–2000* and Sorá's *A History of Book Publishing in Contemporary Latin America* serve as a great introduction to this topic. For details on specific publishing firms that emerged in Buenos

Aires during the first half of the twentieth century, see Buonocore. For a review of how changes in the publishing industry affected Borges's writings, see Benedict, *Borges*.

10. The cover images of all the books that Borges wrote and edited from the 1930s to the 1950s are included as a part of the descriptive bibliography of the digital project *Mapping Borges in the Argentine Publishing Industry* (norabenedict.github.io/borges/index.html).

11. For more on the relationship between Borges and Rossi as well as Rossi's many artistic contributions to the Buenos Aires publishing industry, see Benedict, *Borges*.

12. Editorial Losada's second edition of *El Aleph* adds four short stories that are not present in the first edition: "Abenjacán el Bojarí, muerto en su laberinto" ("Ibn Hakam al-Bokhari, Murdered in His Labyrinth"), "Los dos reyes y los dos laberintos" ("The Two Kings and the Two Labyrinths"), "El hombre en el umbral" ("The Man on the Threshold"), and "La espera" ("The Wait").

Teaching Borges through His Manuscripts

Daniel Balderston

Students, and readers in general, may find reading Borges less intimidating if they can retrace his process of composition, especially since it reveals that he was exceedingly unsure of himself at many stages of his writing process. An increasing number of his manuscripts, including poems, stories, essays, and notes for courses and talks, are available in various forms (some originals in libraries, some facsimiles, some on the web). A fair number of these are available in annotated editions, so it is now possible to follow Borges's writing practice in some detail, from the occasional outline to first and second drafts to revisions he made in printed copies of some of his texts. These materials, and the scholarly work on them, help shed light on—at least in some cases—exactly what works Borges consulted while he was writing, his hesitations, his certainties, and the way each text evolved. This is not particularly easy given his tiny handwriting and somewhat idiosyncratic system of abbreviations, but the materials now available show that he conceived of his works as open, never finished, full of lacunae and enigmas to be puzzled out by the reader. In this essay I explain the usefulness of these materials for teaching Borges at the undergraduate and graduate levels, but first, of course, I explain how to access some of the materials that are available.

The first significant group of published Borges manuscripts was included by the author's nephew Miguel de Torre Borges in the book *Borges: Fotografías y manuscritos* (*Borges: Photographs and Manuscripts*) in 1987, with a slightly different edition, *Borges: Fotos y manuscritos*, published in 2005. In 2001 the first draft of the story "El Aleph" ("The Aleph"), which is held by the National Library of Spain, was published in a facsimile edition by Julio Ortega and Elena del Río Parra, an edition whose critical apparatus instructors may find deficient (Borges, *"El Aleph"*). In 2010 Michel Lafon published *Deux fictions* (*Two Fictions*), a facsimile edition of the second draft of "Tlön, Uqbar, Orbis Tertius" and of the first draft of "El Sur" ("The South"), both held by the Fondation Martin Bodmer in Geneva, with introductions and French translations of the manuscript material. Many more Borges manuscripts were published in appendixes to my book *How Borges Wrote* and later in three volumes of facsimiles I prepared with María Celeste Martín that included typographic transcriptions, introductions, and notes: *Poemas y prosas breves* (*Poems and Short Prose*), *Ensayos* (*Essays*), and *Cuentos* (*Short Stories*). For the volume *Ensayos*, Mariana Di Ció and I did a full critical edition of a hitherto unpublished manuscript (held by the University of Virginia), "La obra de Flaubert" ("Flaubert's Work"), with more than two hundred notes, in which we were able to identify almost all the editions that Borges consulted and to transcribe many of the relevant passages that he read while preparing a course on Flaubert in 1952. And there are bits and pieces of other manuscripts that have been published elsewhere, including a manuscript on

Buddhism that is held at the Academia Argentina de Letras, which was published by Alicia Jurado in *Borges, el budismo y yo* (*Borges, Buddhism, and I*). There is thus much more material available than there was a dozen years ago, and much of it can be found in reliable scholarly editions.

Variaciones Borges devoted a special issue to genetic approaches to Borges manuscripts, which includes essays by a variety of scholars in the United States, Mexico, Argentina, and elsewhere (Balderston, Special issue). There is now an emerging field devoted to the study of Borges manuscripts, with recent sessions at conferences of the Society for Textual Scholarship, the Instituto Internacional de Literatura Iberoamericana, and the MLA. For instance, a large-scale project is now underway with an international team of some twenty scholars to study the notebooks that Borges used when preparing classes and talks from 1949 to 1955, notebooks housed in libraries in Texas, Virginia, Pennsylvania, New York, and Michigan; the first results of this work were published in the October 2021 and November 2022 issues of *Variaciones Borges*. (For the moment we are unable to study some eleven notebooks that are privately held in Buenos Aires.) A list of known Borges manuscripts is available on the Borges Center website ("Manuscripts"), along with several ancillary materials that help the reader find ways to understand Borges's compositional process.

In this essay I give several examples of how the manuscript material can be used to open up Borges's texts in ways that students will find puzzling and engaging. I have done fuller studies of these materials, and information about many of these essays is available on the Borges Center website ("Criticism"). In addition, the "Manuscripts" section of the website includes links to various collections of Borges manuscripts, many of them in libraries in the United States, so students and teachers can consult original materials in public collections.

My first examples are of the ways in which the manuscripts reveal that Borges self-consciously described his own writing practice. For instance, the final footnote of "Pierre Menard, autor del *Quijote*" ("Pierre Menard, Author of the *Quixote*") includes a reference to Menard's manuscripts, written in "cuadernos cuadriculados," on graph paper, with "negras tachaduras," dark blots of ink to mark some cancellations; his "peculiares símbolos tipográficos," or peculiar typographic symbols (which in Borges's own case include hollow and solid squares, circles and triangles, as well as a variety of parentheses and brackets, Greek letters, astrological symbols, and even something that looks like a camera on a tripod); and his "letra de insecto," or insect-like handwriting (*OC* 1: 847n1; *CF* 95n3). All these features correspond to things frequently encountered in Borges's manuscripts, particularly in his first drafts. (In his second drafts he often copied his texts in a larger, neater hand for the printer, since he did not know how to type.) In "El jardín de senderos que se bifurcan" ("The Garden of Forking Paths"), the description that Stephen Albert gives of the chaotic manuscripts of Ts'ui Pên's unfinished novel corresponds to Borges's own practices, in which the pullulation of possibilities described in the story is played out in a lengthy passage in which Albert says that he and Yu Tsun coexist in many dimensions of time, sometimes as friends but at least once as enemies; the passage is lengthy in the story but much more so in the manuscript, as Borges works out the permutations and combinations of two selves multiplied in bifurcating time frames (Balderston, *How* 169–82). Just as Alfred Hitchcock famously included himself in his films, Borges makes cameo appearances in his stories (Hladík's esoteric publications in "El milagro secreto" ["The Secret Miracle"], Dahlmann's accident in "El Sur," the nearsighted journalist and anti-religious atheist of Jewish descent in "La muerte y la brújula" ["Death and the Compass"]). He appears under his own name in "Hombre de la esquina rosada" ("Man on Pink Corner"), "El Aleph," and the essay "La nadería de la personalidad" ("The Nothingness of Personality"). It is a wonderful puzzle to find the ways in which the published texts mirror the story of their own composition, with an emphasis on uncertainty, possibility, gaps, and fragmentation.

A first, and very complex, example of that is the manuscript of Borges's first original story, which is also his first (and most radical) exploration of the detective genre, "Hombre de la esquina rosada." First published in a supplement illustrated in full color of a mass-circulation daily newspaper, *Crítica*, in 1933 under the pseudonym "F. Bustos," the story begins with an ellipsis: ". . . A mí, tan luego, venir a hablarme de Francisco Madrano / hablarme de Francisco el Corralero, tan luego a mí. / hablarme de Francisco Real / hablarme del finado F. R." '. . . Imagine you bringing up Francisco Madrano / bringing up Francisco el Corralero that way, out of the clear blue sky. / bringing up Francisco Real / bringing up F. R., him dead and gone and all' (Balderston, *How* 298 [see also *OC* 1: 628]; trans. modified from *CF* 45).

The ellipsis indicates that the story begins in medias res, with certain details to be concealed: a few lines later Borges writes, "Arriba de tres veces no lo traté" 'I doubt if I crossed paths with the man more than three times' (Balderston, *How* 298 [see also *OC* 1: 628]; *CF* 45), and then proceeds to have his narrator tell of the first and third encounters, leaving the reader to infer the second one after finishing the story and then having to hunt down the moment (which is not narrated) of the knife fight between Francisco Real and the narrator (Balderston, *How* 77–90). The manuscript gives many other hints of how Borges sought to have a *compadrito*, a young thug, tell his story years later as an old man and of how hard he worked to represent the *compadrito*'s language. Years later, in the 1965 lectures on the tango, he describes how he sought to transmit the tone, intonation, and vocabulary of a friend who had recently died in the late 1920s, Nicolás Paredes, who had also been a friend of the Buenos Aires poet of working-class life Evaristo Carriego (*El tango* 134–35).

Another important detail to be gleaned from the manuscript (which is reproduced in part in Balderston, *How* 297–300) is that the front cover of the notebook used for the writing of this story, of the brand Lanceros Argentinos de 1910, was covered with a whole spiderweb of notes for the 1931 essay "La postulación de la realidad" ("The Postulation of Reality") and the 1932 essay "El arte narrativo y la magia" ("Narrative Art and Magic"), both subsequently included in the book *Discusión* in 1932. These essays are concerned with the ways in which ellipses and what Borges calls "circumstantial details" (*CF* 269) can leave gaps in a text that the reader has to work to fill in, precisely the task of the reader of his 1932 story (Balderston, *How* 63–72). Borges worked out the strategies for a strange variety of verisimilitude, in which the representation of reality is incomplete or blurred or interrupted, as he was getting ready to write his first original story. (Up to then he had written stories that were retellings of others' stories, as is indeed the case with the rest of the 1935 book *Historia universal de la infamia* [*Universal History of Iniquity*].)

Another feature of the manuscripts, particularly of first drafts, is that in some of them (more frequently in the drafts of essays but also in the stories of the final period before the blindness set in, 1949–53) Borges carefully notes down the author, sometimes the short title, and the page number of the works he consults in the process of composition. Some of these are self-quotations—he refers to his prior publications through references to the magazine and page number where he had published them—but much more frequently the notations in the left margin give a precise idea of the works he consulted, checking and rechecking his sources. Some of these marginal references reveal hidden quotations or secret references—to John Stuart Mill's *System of Logic* for the discussion of tautology in "El escritor argentino y la tradición" ("The Argentine Writer and Tradition"); to a hidden translation of a line from a Rudyard Kipling poem in "El hombre en el umbral" ("The Man on the Threshold"), in the first paragraph of which Borges says he will tell the story without interpolations from Kipling; to a complex series of hidden references in the last story written before he went blind, "El fin" ("The End"). Here is the passage in the manuscript that pertains to Kipling:

> Bioy Casares trajo de Londres un puñal / curioso puñal de de hoja triangular y empuñadura en forma de H; nuestro común amigo / viejo amigo James / amigo Christopher Dewey, del Consejo Británico, declaró que esa arma era hindú Dewey, del Consejo Británico, dijo que tales armas eran de uso común en el Indostán; ese dictamen lo alentó a mencionar que había residido / algunos años en aquel remoto país + hace muchos años, en aquel remoto país / recorrido, en sus mocedades / había trabajado en aquel país, entre las dos guerras. (*Ultra Auroram et Gangen*, recuerdo que dijo en latín, equivocando un verso de Juvenal.) De las anécdotas / las historias que esa noche contó, me atrevo a reconstruir la que sigue / la siguiente. Mi texto será fiel; líbreme Dios de la tentación de agregar / añadir invenciones circunstancionales / breves rasgos circunstanciales y de acentuar, con / exaltar, con / agravar con interpolaciones de Kipling, el color / cariz exótico de la historia. Este, por lo demás, tiene un sabor que es más antiguo, y más simple, que . . . + un antiguo y simple sabor que sería una lástima perder, acaso de las 1001 Noches.
>
> (Balderston, *How* 294 [see also *OC* 1: 1057])

> Bioy Casares brought back from London a knife / a curious knife with a triangular blade and an H-shaped hilt; our common friend / old friend James / friend Christopher Dewey, of the British Council, said that sort of weapon was in common use in Hindustan, between the two wars. That statement led him to mention that he had resided / a few years in that remote country + many years ago, in that remote country / had traveled, in his youth / had worked in that country, between the two wars. (*Ultra auroram et Gangen*, I recall him saying in Latin, misquoting a line from Juvenal.) Among the anecdotes / stories he told us that night, I shall be so bold as to reconstruct the one that follows / the following one. My text will be a faithful one; may God prevent me from inserting / adding circumstantial fabrications / small circumstantial details and heightening / enhancing / exacerbating the exotic color / lineaments of the tale with interpolations from Kipling. Besides, it has a more antique and more simple flavor about it that . . . + an antique, simple flavor about it that it would be a shame to lose—something of the *1001 Nights*. (trans. modified from *CF* 269)

"[O]ur common friend" Christopher Dewey is here revealed to be a fictional character (initially named James), while the dagger with a triangular hilt, supposedly bought by Adolfo Bioy Casares on one of his many trips to London, is clarified in the manuscript to be a reference to the article on "sword" in the eleventh edition of the *Encyclopædia Britannica*. The English friend's misquote from Juvenal (who wrote "usque," not "ultra") contains a precise reference ("124- usque Auroram et Gangen") to the correct reading of the Latin poet, and in Borges's copy of Juvenal's satires he noted down this very quotation years before (Rosato and Álvarez 210). And the expression "líbreme Dios" 'may God prevent me' will later be corrected to "líbreme Alá" 'may Allah prevent me' (*OC* 1: 1057; *CF* 269) to make clearer the debt that Borges has to his readings about British India, with an emphasis that is also in Kipling on Muslim culture in the subcontinent. These little details taken together construct a fictional representation of British India, one that the story that is about to be told will critique, by giving voice to an old Indian man who tells his version of events and delays (and ultimately defeats) the police work of Dewey, the young British official.

The interpolation from Kipling is noted in the manuscript as "B.r. Ballads 265" (Balderston, *How* 48), referring to an edition of the Anglo-Indian writer's *Barrack Room Ballads*, to the poem "Evarra and His Gods," and to the following lines:

> And chafe his brain, Evarra mowed alone,
> Rag-wrapped, among the cattle in the fields,
> Counting his fingers, jesting with the trees,
> And mocking at the mist, until his God
> Drove him to labor. (Kipling 265–66)

The description of the madman in the story, who is also the judge, includes the old man's description of him as one who "andaba desnudo por estas calles, o cubierto de harapos, contándose los dedos con el pulgar y haciendo mofa de los árboles" 'wandered these streets naked, or covered with rags, counting his fingers with his thumb and hurling gibes at the trees' (*OC* 1: 1059; *CF* 272), a translation (and rewriting) of the passage from the Kipling poem (Balderston, *How* 45–49).

With a little coaching, then, readers can glean possibilities and hidden references in Borges's texts. Borges wrote of Dante that his most notable feature as a poet was the "presición" 'precision' with which he imagined the characters and the situations in his poem (*Nueve ensayos dantescos* 88; my trans.); Borges leaves a trail of hints about where to look for his sources and about the ways in which he weaves secrets and possibilities into his texts. This is true of the stories but is much more obvious in the essays; it is also true of some of the poems, particularly those from the early 1950s (just before his increasing blindness prevented him from reading and writing). The introduction to Rosato and Álvarez's *Borges, libros y lecturas* (*Borges, Books, and Readings*) is helpful to make sense of Borges's system of notes and includes a key to frequently consulted editions like the eleventh edition of the *Encyclopædia Britannica* (see also Borges, *Ensayos*). The October 2021 issue of *Variaciones Borges* also includes a lot of information about abbreviations and about particular sections of some of the notebooks held in US libraries.

Another feature of the manuscripts that will be of interest to students is the ways in which Borges sets out a plethora of possibilities, usually without crossing any of them out, in the first drafts and how even the second drafts, sometimes thought of as fair copies, are rarely free of new changes and corrections. In the poem "A Francisco López Merino" ("To Francisco López Merino"), as many as fifteen alternatives are given to the two words chosen in the published versions of the poem (Balderston, *How* 131–40, 260–66), while in "Viejo hábito argentino" ("An Old Argentine Habit"), the 1946 manuscript that became the political essay "Nuestro pobre individualismo" (1946; "Our Poor Individualism") but that Borges continued to add to (and to note down the years in which he modified the manuscript, until 1955), contains a complex system of parentheses, plus signs, square and angle brackets, and various other things to mark alternatives at the level of the word (plus signs), the clause (often parentheses), and larger blocks of text (angle and square brackets). Sometimes entire paragraphs are marked with large numbers (they are marked as "1," "2," and "3" in the "Historia de la eternidad" ["A History of Eternity"] manuscript, for instance [Balderston, *How* 341–43]), and often the same loose pages or notebook will contain not just the initial drafts of a passage but clean copies, or at least later copies, of the same passage (this can be seen, for instance, in the manuscript of "La lotería en Babilonia" ["The Lottery in Babylon"] that is at the New York Public Library and that was published in *Cuentos*).

Using the available manuscript materials, students can be asked to do the following: to figure out what the sources are, including precise editions, page numbers, and passages; to determine the sequence of the drafts of a given passage (this is fun and challenging); and to infer from the manuscript materials what Borges's intentions were and his changes of direction as he wrote. I describe each of these pedagogical possibilities in some detail in what follows.

If we take as a model the critical edition of "La obra de Flaubert" that Mariana Di Ció and I did for *Ensayos*, it is often possible to determine from Borges's brief annotations in the left margin (usually just the surname of an author or a short title or abbreviation for the name of a book plus a page number) which edition he used. Readers who think of Borges's library as extensive and rare will often be surprised that he used cheap popular editions, such as Everyman's Library editions, for many consultations. The main encyclopedia he used was the eleventh edition of the *Encyclopædia Britannica*, while the Spanish language encyclopedia that he consulted on occasion was Montaner and Simón's *Diccionario enciclopédico hispano-americano* (*Spanish American Encyclopedic Dictionary*). His references to Jonathan Swift and William Blake, to give two examples, were to single-volume selections of their works, not to multivolume critical editions. It is useful to remember that Borges was a man of modest means, and the apartment that he shared with his mother on Calle Maipú in Buenos Aires had space for only about thirteen hundred books (though later, when he was blind and became the director of the National Library, his office there contained many more books, at least some of which were the ones he donated to the library before resigning in 1973, at the moment that Peronism was returning to power). Borges's friends, particularly Bioy Casares and Silvina Ocampo, had greater possibilities of acquiring books and lending them to him; on occasion they ordered them from other countries. Some of those annotated books are now being processed as part of a donation of some seventeen thousand books from the Bioy Casares and Ocampo personal libraries to the National Library. Some two thousand books are held at the Fundación Internacional Jorge Luis Borges in Buenos Aires, and a selection of their covers, frontispieces, and brief notes have been published in Fernando Flores Maio's *La biblioteca de Borges* (*Borges's Library*), although the book is far less complete than the title implies and not very informative about the contents of a library that is not yet open to the public.

Once a page number is found to refer to a particular edition, it is interesting to figure out from Borges's notes (sometimes as brief as "Carlyle once . . ." [Balderston, *How* 23]) which passage Borges was focusing on and what comes before and after that passage in the book in question. In the case I just mentioned, the edition in question is a selection of the essays by Oscar Wilde, in which Wilde (remarking on various biographies of English writers, particularly a biography of Samuel Taylor Coleridge) says that it would be interesting to imagine a life of Michelangelo that makes no reference to his artistic work (373); the anecdote that Wilde is referring to (which was subsequently published in books by James McNeill Whistler and E. R. and J. Pennell) shows that Carlyle was dead serious about this idea, not speaking in jest (as Wilde thought). This so-called jest becomes the beginning of Borges's essay on Willam Beckford's *Vathek*, so there is a lot to say about Borges's use of this source, one that he is accessing indirectly (Rosato and Álvarez 353; Balderston, *How* 24–27). (Wilde does not quote directly from the diary sources about Carlyle that were published later.) Similarly, Borges often uses articles from the *Encyclopædia Britannica* as initial sources for further research: he does this with the self-proclaimed first emperor of China, Shih Huang Ti (Shi Huang Di) at the beginning of "La muralla y los libros" ("The Wall and the Books"), the lead essay in the major collection of the essays of his central period, *Otras inquisiciones* (*Other Inquisitions*); he then gleans information from other sources and compares and contrasts them. With the manuscripts that have been published to date, it is a challenging but fascinating exercise to assign a page of a manuscript to a student or group of students and have them comment on the use of the sources, which often goes off in unexpected directions.

Another important exercise that can help students understand the rudiments of genetic criticism is to have them transcribe a page of a manuscript, or just a paragraph or stanza if a page is too much, and then to figure out the order in which Borges set out alternatives, made insertions (often in the left margin or upside-down at the top of the page), and made initial choices about which possibilities he preferred. In genetic criticism it is often said that to do this kind of work it is important to have a complete genetic dossier of a text, including *avant-textes* (preparatory notes, outlines, sketches), first drafts, second and subsequent drafts, fair copies, first printed versions, and versions that the author chooses to publish in books or compilations; in the case of Borges's manuscripts, many of these stages are crammed onto a single page, which once it is deciphered can be compared to the published versions. Given that Borges sets out alternatives with a variety of punctuation marks (including the parentheses and brackets mentioned earlier), it is possible to glean an order from what initially looks like chaos: he is setting down as many alternatives as possible, eventually choosing certain ones but leaving the rest as latent possibilities (as Stephen Albert explains in "El jardín de senderos que se bifurcan" [*OC* 1: 873; *CF* 126–27]).

It takes a while to get used to Borges's tiny handwriting, in which various letters can look almost the same (*n* and *u*, *e* and *a*) and in which the small *t* looks like a capital *T* (but the capital *T* is different, with serifs). Borges also has a very idiosyncratic system of abbreviations, not just for book titles but also for phrases of his own that he is rewriting, so it is important to learn to make educated guesses about what he is setting out. In some cases, second versions, fair copies, first published versions (almost always in newspapers and magazines), and versions in Borges's published books are also accessible, so it is possible to ascertain the stages of a project in some detail (including changes from first book versions to later ones).

A third avenue for student assignments—one that can be approached only once students have a firm understanding of Borges's sources (not only in his reading but also in his earlier writing) and compositional strategies—is an assessment of his intentions. Borges's writing often relies on suggestion and inference (as in the details of "Hombre de la esquina rosada" mentioned earlier), but a careful reader begins to have a sense of the man behind the texts—not only of what he says but also of what he implies. Genetic criticism has been important in illuminating the questions of authorial intention (once dismissed as irrelevant or impossible to know, as in William K. Wimsatt and Monroe Beardsley's famous essay). In Borges's case, the manuscripts in their many stages, and alternatives, and reorderings, and rewritings provide a wealth of material for the study of his intentions. I close with a brief but complex example.

In 1950, at the close of his essay on the emperor of China who ordered not only the building of the Great Wall but also the destruction of Chinese libraries that registered what was already a long written tradition, Borges imagines what the relationship might be between these simultaneous acts of creation and destruction. He suggests that it is impossible to know what that relationship signifies, but that it is fascinating to speculate about it, and runs through various hypotheses, none of which convince him completely. The essay concludes with a reflection on the ways in which "the aesthetic fact" (a term from Kant) or beauty suggest, but do not close off, possibilities:

> [Y]a Pater, en 1877, afirmó que todas las artes aspiran a la condición de la música, que no es otra cosa que forma. La música, los estados de felicidad, la mitología, las caras trabajadas por el tiempo, ciertos crepúsculos y ciertos lugares, quieren decirnos algo, o algo dijeron que no hubiéramos debido perder, o están por decir algo; esa inminencia de una revelación, que se no produce, es, quizá, el hecho estético. (*OC* 2: 14)

> [B]y 1877, Pater had already stated that all the arts aspire to the condition of music, which is nothing but form. Music, states of happiness, mythology, faces worn by time, certain twilights and certain places, all want to tell us something, or have told us something we shouldn't have lost [missed], or are about to tell us something: that imminence of a revelation as yet unproduced is, perhaps, the aesthetic fact. (*SNF* 346)

The manuscript shows that Borges worked hard to achieve the magic of this sentence:

[Y]a Pater, en 1877, afirmó que todas las artes aspiran a la condición de la
música, que no es otra cosa que forma. La música, la brusca felicidad, ~~las mitologías~~ la mitología,
las caras trabajadas
por el tiempo, ciertos crepúsculos y ciertos lugares, {<u>están por decir algo</u> o dijeron algo que no
hubiéramos
debido perder; esta inminencia de una revelación, que no se produce, es quizá el hecho estético. + quieren decirnos algo, o algo dijeron que no hubiéramos debido perder, o están por decir algo; esta
inminencia
de una revelación, que {nunca se cumple + no se produce} es quizá el hecho estético.}
de una revelación, que no se produce, es quizá el hecho estético.

(Balderston, *How* 143)

> [B]y 1877, Pater had already stated that all the arts aspire to the condition of
> music, which is nothing but form. Music, states of happiness, ~~mythologies~~ mythology, faces worn by
> time, certain twilights and certain places, {are about to tell us something or have told us something we shouldn't
> have lost; that imminence of a revelation as yet unproduced is, perhaps, the aesthetic fact. + want
> to tell us something, or have told us something we shouldn't have lost, or are about to tell us something; that imminence
> of a revelation {as yet fulfilled + as yet unproduced} is, perhaps, the aesthetic fact.}
> a revelation as yet unproduced is, perhaps, the aesthetic fact.
>
> (trans. modified from *SNF* 346)

Three years later, in a Cuaderno Mérito that is now at Michigan State University in the Stephen O. Murray and Keelung Hong Special Collections Library, Borges wrote the first draft of a story, "El fin" ("The End"), in which he proposed a sequel to the action of José Hernández's *La vuelta de Martín Fierro* (*Martín Fierro's Return*), one in which Fierro returns from the conversations with his sons (and Cruz's son) to have a knife fight with the younger brother of the Afro-Argentine man he had killed early in Hernández's earlier poem *El gaucho Martín Fierro* (*The Gaucho Martin Fierro*). Borges carefully reviewed the several editions and works of criticism he had at hand about the Hernández poems; noted down details from a famous study of the poems, Leopoldo Lugones's *El payador* (*The Gaucho Singer*); and consulted two novels of gaucho life, one by his late friend Ricardo Güiraldes (*Don Segundo Sombra*) and one by the Uruguayan husband of his cousin Esther Haedo, Enrique Amorim (*El paisano Aguilar* [*The Gaucho Aguilar*]). He sets out his version of a sequel to the Hernández poems, explores a number of alternatives, and reaches an ending, which he marks with the place of writing and a date, "Buenos Aires, 13 de setiembre de 1953" (Balderston, "Point" 19). Then, a few lines down in the same notebook, he sets out a version of the passage from "La muralla y los libros," now applied not to the "hecho estético" in general but to the experience of the Argentine plains:

> Hay una hora del atardecer
> de la tarde en que la llanura está por decir algo; nunca lo dice o acaso está diciéndolo siempre y no lo entendemos
> Tal vez lo dice infinitamente y no lo entendemos, o
> lo entendemos pero es intraducible como una música . . . Desde su catre,
>
> (Balderston, "Point" 19)

> There is an hour
> of the afternoon in which the plains are about to say something; they never say it or perhaps they are saying it always and we don't understand
> Perhaps they say it infinitely and we don't understand it, or
> we understand it but it is untranslatable like music . . . From his cot,
>
> (my trans.)

This passage will be incorporated into the published versions of the story, not at the very end (that is, not as it is in the notebook, just before the place and date) but earlier, at the beginning of the last paragraph of the story:

> Hay una hora de la tarde en que la llanura está por decir algo; nunca lo dice o tal vez lo dice infinitamente y no lo entendemos, o lo entendemos pero es intraducible como una música. . . . Desde su catre . . . (*OC* 1: 910)
>
> There is an hour just at evening when the plains seem on the verge of saying something they never do, or perhaps they do—eternally—though we don't understand it, or perhaps we do understand but what they say is as untranslatable as music. . . . From his cot . . . (*CF* 470)

What does he have in mind here? He is reflecting on his earlier essay, which was a reflection on some ideas from Benedetto Croce and Walter Pater (apropos of surmises he makes about the intentions of the self-proclaimed first emperor of China), but now is reworking that formulation to apply not to some distant region of the world that he had never visited but to the Argentine plains where his city is set and to the famous narrative poems that Lugones and Ricardo Rojas had claimed were national epics, foundations of a national tradition (and hallmarks of Argentine citizenship). What was distant is suddenly local, and what he undertook as a speculative reader of encyclopedias and reference works now refers to the most famous work of the national tradition in which he was working. The phrase from "La muralla y los libros" now suggests that the relation of the Argentine writer, or even more specifically the writer from Buenos Aires, to the land on which the city was built, and to the great plains that extend to the east, south, and north of that city, is one that is not fully knowable, certainly not in advance (so much for the idea of a national canon), one that is richer as suggestion than as affirmation. In the manuscript of "La muralla y los libros," the definition of the aesthetic fact is one that is the product of a process of intense rewriting; in "El fin," the presence of the endless plains is an invitation to the imagination. Borges has finished his story, but the subsequent insertion of the self-quotation leaves the meaning of it open, which is precisely what we can infer is Borges's intention: the manuscript material supplements, and complicates, what Joseph Conrad called the "the terrific suggestiveness of words" (65), a phrase that Borges had just rewritten (plagiarized?) in the defense of plagiarism, or of uncertainties about authorship, in his 1947 story "El inmortal" ("The Immortal"), which would become the lead story in the 1949 and 1952 editions of his collection *El Aleph*.

Imperial Cartographies in the Work of Borges

Adelaida López-Mejía

Jorge Luis Borges incorporates and transforms ancient Mediterranean, West Asian, and Central Asian history in some of his most celebrated stories. A passage in "Funes, His Memory" evokes Achaemenid Persia and Rome's enmity with Mithridates of Pontus; "The Lottery in Babylon" describes a peculiar Mesopotamia; some form of Greek competes with the language of Zoroastrian scripture in "The Circular Ruins"; "The Immortal" foregrounds Roman North Africa. Teaching these stories with attention to ancient history and to geography can take up to four weeks, especially if students are assigned brief passages by Greek and Roman historians and from Edward Gibbon. Borges read their work avidly. Most students need assistance in taming the array of place-names that stud Borges's fiction, and I recommend maps from Arthur Cotterell's *The Penguin Encyclopedia of Classical Civilizations* and *The Penguin Encyclopedia of Ancient Civilizations*; online maps are useful as well. The paper topics suggested here are not primarily cartographic in focus; the goal is for students to engage with Borges's erudition and his wily misrepresentations of the ancient world.

A good place to start is "Funes, His Memory," set in a time and place close to Borges's own: the Uruguayan town of Fray Bentos at the end of the nineteenth century. The place lies a few hours upriver from Buenos Aires, and Borges spent several summers there as a teenager ("Maps of Uruguay"; Williamson, *Borges* 34). In "Funes," the eponymous working-class protagonist, Ireneo Funes, lives in Fray Bentos. Paralyzed after being thrown by a horse, Funes asks a well-schooled narrator (named Borges) for a volume of Pliny's *Naturalis Historia* (*Natural History*). The story breaks with realism when Funes reads Pliny effortlessly after a day or two; the narrator knows more than a little Latin but still finds Pliny difficult (*CF* 133). Edwin Williamson discusses Borges's engagement with the study of Latin since the writer's teenage years in Geneva (*Borges*, 55–57, 200); the language stimulated a lifelong interest in imperial Rome.

Funes astonishes the narrator with a recitation of a passage from Pliny's *Naturalis Historia*; an ensuing conversation between the two characters lasts long into the Uruguayan night. Borges cites Pliny's original Latin, and an English translation of book 7, chapter 24, of *Naturalis Historia* should be read in class (e.g., H. Rackham's translation). A brief lecture on the encyclopedic scope of the *Naturalis Historia* can be helpful; after students become more familiar with Borges's fiction, some might choose to write on Borges's encyclopedic vision in the context of the Argentine writer's fondness for Pliny. Daniel Balderston's essay "Borges and the Universe of Culture" can be a good springboard.

In the passage chosen by Funes, Pliny lists various ancient kings and poets endowed with a privileged memory: Cyrus the Great, Mithridates, Simonides (*CF* 134; Pliny 7.24). A map of the empire founded by Cyrus can help the class imagine his successor's crossing of the Hellespont in 486 BCE ("Persian Empire"; "Aegean"; Herodotus 7.35–37). Xerxes's lashing of the sea, described by Herodotus in his *History*, takes minutes to read; Borges considered Herodotus's work on the wars between Greece and Persia indispensable to his own book collection ("Prologues" 512). Many students of Borges's generation were taught that the Persian invasion of Greece constituted a defining moment in Western civilization.

The passage chosen by Funes also mentions a Mithridates who "administraba la justicia en los veintidós idiomas de su imperio" 'metes out justice in the twenty-two languages of the kingdom over which he ruled' (*OC* 1: 881; *CF* 134; Pliny 7.24). Tradition identifies this polyglot as Mithridates Eupator of Pontus, whose fierce resistance to Rome's expansion in Asia Minor ended in suicide. Plutarch describes the tale in his life of Pompey (251–60). Pliny himself does not identify the polyglot king as Mithridates Eupator; Borges does. The *Naturalis Historia* also mentions Simonides (556–468 BCE) for that poet's invention of mnemonic techniques. Simonides is also remembered for his epigraph to Greeks who died battling the Persians at Thermopylae (Herodotus 7.228; "Ancient Greece"). In short, Funes's incantatory recitation of Pliny is not only a commentary on the faculty of memory but also a rumination on empire.

Intriguingly, Borges erases Pliny's account of individuals with prodigious memories who lost that gift after a physical accident (Pliny 7.24). Instead, Borges imagines the opposite: Funes's incapacitation grants him a memory capable of recording and retrieving any and every perception. Instructors should stress the ironic reversal in this adaptation of Pliny and ask the class to remain attentive to Borges's relentless irony.

Toward the end of "Funes," Borges forces his readers to reflect on Latin America's position in Western cultural hierarchies. While evoking the magnetism of imperial centers ancient and new, the narrator muses on Latin America's marginality: "Babilonia, Londres y Nueva York han abrumado con feroz esplendor la imaginación de los hombres; nadie, en sus torres populosas o en sus avenidas urgentes, ha sentido el calor y la presión de una realidad tan infatigable como la que día y noche convergía sobre el infeliz Ireneo, en su pobre arrabal sudamericano" 'Babylon, London, and New York dazzle mankind's imagination with their fierce splendor; no one in the populous towers or urgent avenues of those cities has felt the heat and pressure of a reality as inexhaustible as that which battered Ireneo, day and night, in his poor South American hinterland' (*OC* 1: 883; *CF* 137). I like to ask students to analyze the juxtaposition between "fierce splendor" and "poor . . . hinterland" and to discuss what might be meant by the "inexhaustible" "reality" of a sleepy Uruguayan town. New York and London are easily recognizable as imperial metropolises, but Babylon needs more introduction, especially before the class tackles Borges's "The Lottery in Babylon" (*CF* 101–06).

Distorted echoes of Babylon's history run through the story, and students appreciate learning how to identify them. The city's position on the shores of the Euphrates appears in ancient and modern maps of Mesopotamia and the Middle Eastern region known as the Fertile Crescent ("Ancient and Modern Maps"). A. K. Grayson's essay can pique interest in the city's culture of astrology and divination and can serve as material for a group oral report. Jews are an encrypted presence in Borges's text; students should know that in 589 BCE Neo-Babylonian armies captured Jerusalem, and many Jews were deported to the shores of the Euphrates ("Captivity"). In 539 BCE Cyrus the Great (whom students should remember from "Funes") allowed Babylon's Jews to return to Israel; many stayed behind. The city fell to Alexander the Great in 333 BCE; the Parthian Mithridates II reoccupied the area in 120 BCE ("Parthian and Sasanian Empires"). Under the Parthians and the Sasanians, renowned academies of Talmudic learning developed in the central Mesopotamian region known as Babylonia (Schiffman 220–23). In Spanish, "Babilonia" refers both to the area and to the city. Borges's story conflates the two.

The first paragraph of "The Lottery in Babylon" (*OC* 1: 852; *CF* 101) describes a fictive system of subjugation encoded by the first three letters of the Hebrew alphabet: men tattooed with the letter *aleph* wield power over men branded by the letter *beth*; these humiliate others marked with the letter *gimel*, who then subjugate the group of men bearing the sign of *aleph*. Borges may allude here to a different play of letters imagined in the *Sepher Yetsirah* (*Book of Formation*), the mystical Jewish treatise probably written in Babylonia sometime between the third and sixth century CE; the *Sepher Yetsirah* links divine combinations of letters to cosmic acts of creation (Scholem 75–77). Borges's lifelong interest in Jewish mysticism should be given class time, presented either through lecture or in a group oral report. (Jaime Alazraki ["Conversación"] and Edna Aizenberg ["'I'"] provide overviews of the topic.) Interpretations of "The Lottery in Babylon" as an allegory of the Holocaust or of any state that strips its citizens of agency are essential supplementary readings (Aizenberg, "'I'"; Dapía, "Borges").

Borges's nameless narrator makes no further reference to the Jews; instead, he reviews the (imaginary) history of a lottery in which drawings take place every sixty nights (*CF* 102). Ancient Babylonian mathematicians utilized a numerical base of sixty; Asger Aaboe's essay is a good resource for students interested in the mathematical achievements of Babylonian civilization. Although Borges's narrator affirms that "el pueblo de Babilonia es muy devoto de la lógica, y aun de la simetría" 'the people of Babylon are great admirers of logic, and even of symmetry' (*OC* 1: 853; *CF* 102), they are titillated by the thought of drawing lots imposing torture or penury. This calls for discussion of the pessimistic psychology of the story and its exploration of sadomasochism. Students should note the story's association of West Asia with irrationality.

Claiming that he knows "lo que ignoran los griegos: la incertidumbre" 'what the Greeks knew not—uncertainty' (*OC* 1: 852; *CF* 101), Borges's narrator sets Greek ideals of rational self-mastery against stereotypes of non-Greek excess. This opposition permeated Roman imperial ideology as much as it did that of classical Greece (Beard 205, 349–50). Historically, Babylon's legal code (developed by Hammurabi in 1792 BCE) fit the punishment (severely) to the crime; the lottery of Borges's story follows no such logic. Just as a lottery drawing can allot suffering (or pleasure), it can decree "que se arroje a las aguas del Éufrates un zafiro de Taprobana" 'that a sapphire from Taprobana be thrown into the waters of the Euphrates' (*OC* 1: 855; *CF* 105). Students wondering about Taprobana will find a brief reference in book 6, chapter 24, paragraph 22, of Pliny's *Naturalis Historia*: it was the name of the island now known as Sri Lanka, and its inhabitants, Pliny notes, were much too fond of luxury.

Borges knew his Babylonian history; in his story only those who are not enslaved participate in the lottery, once "iniciado en los misterios de Bel" 'initiated in the mysteries of Baal' (*OC* 1: 853; *CF* 103). Ancient Babylon was a society based on slave labor, and in the first millennium BCE its god Marduk was worshipped as Bel (Jacobsen 169). Yet Borges also presents a society subject to Roman administration: "Como todos los hombres de Babilonia, he sido procónsul; como todos, esclavo" 'Like all men in Babylon, I have been proconsul; like all, a slave' (*OC* 1: 852; *CF* 101). Proconsuls governed imperial Rome's provinces; there was no Babylon left by the time the emperor Trajan established his short-lived Mesopotamian province in 116 CE (Gibbon 31–55; "Roman Empire on the Death of Trajan"). By Pliny's time (23–79 CE), the city had been reduced to rubble (Pliny 6.30.121–22). The northern Mesopotamian province established by Septimius Severus (r. 193–211 CE) never controlled the area around Babylon (for an online map, see "Provincia Mesopotamia"). Babylonian proconsuls never existed, and Borges knew it.

His story defies temporal logic. When the narrator bemoans his separation "de Babilonia y de sus queridas costumbres" 'from Babylon and its beloved customs' (*OC* 1: 852; *CF* 101), readers might conclude that he is mourning the Babylon of astronomical science and cuneiform tablets, the legendary city of the first and second millennia BCE. But the shadow of Rome moves that narrator into the Common Era, especially after he cites a third-century CE biography of the Roman emperor Elagabalus (*CF* 105).

Aelius Lampridus, the fictitious author of the biography, is one of six apocryphal writers gathered under the title *Scriptores Historiae Augustae* (for an online version and commentary, see "Historia Augusta"). The life of Elagabalus is considered to be the most mendacious biography in the collection; its fanciful descriptions of Elagabalus's party favors and games of chance, paraphrased by Borges, merit a look (Aelius Lampridus 149; *CF* 105). Before Rome's soldiers acclaimed Elagabalus emperor in 218 CE, he officiated as the priest of a solar cult in Emesa, today's Homs ("Maps of Syria"; Gibbon 163–68). Borges's narrator attributes the emperor's love of bizarre games of chance to his origins in Asia Minor (*CF* 105). "The Lottery in Babylon" (and the pages on Elagabalus by Aelius Lampridus and Gibbon) are awash with stereotypes of West Asian excess and decadence.

The Scriptores Historiae Augustae actually invents some of its own sources ("Historia Augusta"). Borges's familiarity with Aelius Lampridus attests to the Argentine author's interest in Roman history and his mischievous love of false sources. A key example of Borges's own fabrication of sources is "The Approach to Al-Mutasim" (*CF* 82), a story-cum-essay presented as a book review of a nonexistent novel. Students intrigued by the theme of deceptive sources could explore their function and significance in "The Lottery in Babylon" and "The Approach to Al-Mutasim" (for good commentary on the latter, see Christ 109–10; Bell-Villada [1999] 73–75). Students wishing to focus solely on "The Lottery in Babylon" might analyze the story's references to Rome, to astronomy and astrology, or to the Jews.

Just as Borges garbles history in "The Lottery in Babylon," he etherealizes geography in "The Circular Ruins," a story with absolutely no place-names: the opening sentence has a man sailing downriver "del Sur. . . . [S]u patria era una de las infinitas aldeas que están aguas arriba, en el flanco violento de la montaña, donde el idioma zend no está contaminado de griego" 'from the South. . . . [H]is homeland was one of those infinite villages that lie up-river, on the violent flank of the mountainside, where the language of the Zend is not contaminated with Greek' (*OC* 1: 848; *CF* 96). The entry on the Zoroastrian scriptures of the Zend-Avesta in the 1911 *Encyclopædia Britannica* (always an important reference point for Borges) questions whether Zend was ever a spoken language (Geldner), not that this would deter Borges from making it one. Mac Williams argues that "The Circular Ruins" is set in Greek-controlled Seleucid Persia, but there was Greek interaction with Persians in Achaemenid Egypt as well. Herodotus remembers Achaemenid guards in the southern city of Elephantine (2.30; for the location of Elephantine, see "Pharaonic Egypt"). Although the Oxus River of ancient northeastern Iran flows northwest, there are no pyramids near its banks, which makes Borges's reference to "pirámides . . . aguas abajo" 'pyramids . . . downriver' (*OC* 1: 850; *CF* 99) a more plausible allusion to Egypt. The online map "The Sassanid Empire" shows both the Oxus and the Nile; upstream "on the violent mountainside" matches the Hindu Kush but could also refer to the mountains separating the Nile from the Red Sea (Herodotus 2.8).

Borges had a lifelong interest in Persia and by 1935 had read Sir Percy Sykes's two-volume *A History of Persia* (*CF* 64). Yet "The Circular Ruins" (1941) seems a closer evocation of Egypt than of ancient northeastern Iran. The phrase "infinitas aldeas que están aguas arriba" 'infinite villages that lie upriver' (*OC* 1: 848; *CF* 96) suggests a source impossible to reach; the source of the Nile was long inaccessible. The river of Borges's story is lined with "fango sagrado" 'sacred mud' (1: 848; 96); ancient Egyptians knew that their livelihood depended on silt left behind by the Nile's flooding. Herodotus refers to Egypt as "a gift of the river" (2.5), "a land of black soil" (2.12). The Greek historian closes his description of the Nile with a hearsay account of a city upstream "where the people were all sorcerers" (2.33). Perhaps Borges took his cue from Herodotus when he imagined a magician whose homeland lay somewhere upstream.

Williams and Jay Corwin correctly assert that the temple of the fire god in "The Circular Ruins" evokes Zoroastrian fire temples, but Zoroastrian practices in fifth-century Egypt were not an impossibility (Young 160). And ancient Egyptians, Herodotus reports, regarded "fire . . . as a living beast" (2.16). In Borges's story the statue of the fire god shifts from horse to tiger to bull (*CF* 99). In the entry on Egyptian religion in the 1911 *Britannica* (available online through college libraries), Borges would have found references to early, sometimes zoomorphic stone fetishes or statues worshipped in small shrines (Gardiner). The encyclopedia left an immeasurable impact on Borges's imagination (Bell-Villada [1999] 22; Balderston, "Borges" 176). It can provide students with further evidence arguing for an Egyptian subtext to "The Circular Ruins." A textual analysis of the rites and invocations practiced by the story's magician may also illumine the story in new ways. Differing interpretations of the geographic and cultural setting of the story provide good fodder for a class debate.

Among all of Borges's stories, "The Immortal" (*CF* 183–95) is the most cluttered with gentilics and place-names, the most intriguing in its use of narrators. Djelal Kadir's commentary is thorough and insightful (39–69). A map of ancient Greece is helpful for discussions of the first paragraph of "The Immortal": I find it best if students know from the outset that Homer's birthplace was Smyrna and his burial place Ios ("Aegean"; see also "Smyrna"). When reading "The Immortal," students benefit from creating a hand-drawn map-journal with annotations on the intersection between place-name and plot. Should the class become interested in theories of literary cartography, David Woodward's edited collection *Cartography in the European Renaissance* is a good place to begin.

Sections 1 through 5 of "The Immortal" are presented as a manuscript penned in English by a London bookseller named Joseph Cartaphilus; that manuscript's first-person Roman narrator has such a convincing presence that students may need reminding that a third-century CE Roman could not have written an English-language text. Marcus Flaminius Rufus begins as a legionary tribune (a high-ranking Roman soldier) during the reign of Diocletian (*CF* 183). Determined to shield his empire from its enemies, that emperor "fixed a line of camps from Egypt to the Persian dominions" (Gibbon 368). Students should look at Gibbon's description of Diocletian's wars in North Africa (368–72). Borges claimed that by the time he wrote "The Immortal," he had read the British historian's work twice ("Autobiographical Essay" 170). In "The Immortal," Marcus Flaminius Rufus remembers "guerras egipcias" 'Egyptian wars,' saw "Alejandría, debelada" 'Alexandria, subdued' and "mauritanos . . . vencidos" 'Mauretanians . . . defeated' (*OC* 1: 989; *CF* 183–84). Gibbon's vivid account of Diocletian's bonfire of alchemical books in Alexandria can flesh out Borges's terse allusions to third-century CE Roman Egypt.

Alexandria's position on the Mediterranean seaboard appears clearly in the map "Ptolemaic Egypt circa 235 BC." The city of Berenice is on that same map: Berenice Troglodytae lies on the southeastern coast of Egypt, facing the Red Sea, and Borges's narrator was once quartered there (*CF* 184). When the soldier is transferred from Berenice to "Tebas Hekatómpylos" 'hundred-gated Thebes' (*OC* 1: 989; *CF* 183), Borges has begun his coded transformation of a Roman's voice into Homer's. Another narrator eventually notes that Thebes Hekatompylos is a Greek city named in the *Iliad* (*CF* 193). Borges's Marcus Flaminius Rufus was in the Egyptian Thebes (for its location, see "Pharaonic Egypt"); there, a dying horseman inspires the legionary tribune to go west in search of a river "cuyas aguas dan la inmortalidad" 'whose waters grant immortality' (*OC* 1: 990; *CF* 184). At one point the Roman soldier meets "Flavio, procónsul de Getulia" 'Flavius, the Getulian proconsul' (1: 990; 184). There were no proconsuls in Gaetulia (Fishburn and Hughes 75); placing Roman proconsuls where there were none attests to Borges's spirit of play.

The online map "The Roman Empire under Augustus" can help students track Marcus Flaminius's movements across North Africa (in particular his crossing of territory inhabited by the Garamantes and Gaetulians). From the Egyptian Thebes he heads north to Arsinoe and then west toward Libya; it is unclear whether Borges was thinking of Arsinoe-Crocodopolis or the Arsinoe to the northwest of Alexandria: "partimos de Arsinoe y entramos en el abrasado desierto" 'we departed from Arsinoë and entered the ardent desert' (*OC* 1: 990; *CF* 184; see also "Ptolemaic Egypt"). The *Naturalis Historia* provides a guide to what follows.

Marcus Flaminius Rufus walks from the Nile to Tangier; Pliny's stereoscopic gaze in the *Naturalis Historia* moves from Tangier to Libya, across regions "spreading as far as the Garamantes and Augilae and the Cave-Dwellers" (5.8.43). Pliny's "Garamantes . . . live with their women promiscuously. The Augilae only worship *the powers of the lower world*" (5.8.45–46; emphasis added). Marcus Flaminius Rufus closely echoes Pliny: "Atravesamos el país de los trogloditas . . . ; el de *los garamantas, que tienen las mujeres en común* . . . el de *los augilas, que sólo veneran el Tártaro*" 'We crossed the land of the Troglodytes . . . ; that of *the Garamantas, whose women are held in common* . . . the land of *the Augiles, who worship only Tartarus*' (*OC* 1: 990; *CF* 184; emphasis added). Borges's soldier remembers "la montaña que dio nombre al Océano . . . en la cumbre habitan los sátiros" 'the mountain which gave its name to the Ocean . . . on its peaks live the Satyrs' (1: 990; 184–85). The word *Atlantic* derives from the name Atlas; for Pliny, Mount Atlas "is the subject of much the most marvellous stories of all the mountains in Africa . . . at night *this peak* . . . *swarms with* the wanton gambols of Goat-Pans and *Satyrs*" (5.1.5; emphasis added). Eventually the voice of Marcus Flaminius Rufus becomes that of a man who passes through Samarkand and reaches India (*CF* 193); so, too, did Alexander the Great (Samarkand lies slightly west of Bokhara: see "Alexander the Great's Asian Campaigns"). Allusions to empire crisscross the story.

The postscript to "The Immortal" introduces Nahum Cordovero, who "denuncia" 'denounces' Joseph Cartophilus's manuscript for its "interpolaciones de Plinio" 'interpolations from Pliny' (*OC* 1: 998; *CF* 195). In Ronald Christ's reading, part of Borges's intention was to trace how throughout history the words of one man can become the words of another and thus, according to Christ, the story invalidates "all accusations of plagiarism" (198). Whether Borges's reference to the story as a "bosquejo de una ética para inmortales" 'outline for an ethics for immortals' (*OC* 1: 1071; *CF* 287) has any relevance to questions of plagiarism can be a topic for discussion in class. Borges's acknowledgment of his own plagiarism is playful, yet there is an underlying seriousness to his choice of sources.

In book 5 of the *Naturalis Historia*, there are candid reflections on imperial cupidity: "luxury acts as an extremely great and powerful stimulus, inasmuch as forests are ransacked for ivory and citrus-wood and all the rocks of Gaetulia explored for the murex and for purple" (Pliny 5.1.12). Perhaps in Borges's fatalistic vision, empire constituted an inescapable aspect of human history. Notions of military valor had mattered to him since childhood ("Autobiographical Essay" 139–40). Borges was a lucid observer of the Second World War: the two empires of searing personal significance for him when he wrote the stories discussed here were Nazi Germany and England. He cast his lot with the latter, although not all of his fellow Argentines did. In a manuscript owned by the Harry Ransom Center at the University of Texas, Austin (dated 1941), Borges proposes Gibbon, Plutarch, and Tacitus as ideal readings for a desert island (Couyoumdji). A cautious comparison with J. R. R. Tolkien might interest US students: both writers turned to seemingly remote worlds as their own times took an increasingly nightmarish turn.

NOTE

This essay is dedicated to the memory of Angela Mejía de López, professor of ancient history at the Universidad Nacional de Colombia.

NOTES ON CONTRIBUTORS

Daniel Balderston is Andrew W. Mellon Professor of Modern Languages at the University of Pittsburgh, where he directs the Borges Center and edits the journal *Variaciones Borges*. His extensive work on Borges includes most recently *How Borges Wrote* (2018; French edition: *La méthode Borges* [2019]; Spanish edition: *El método Borges* [2022]); with María Celeste Martín, three facsimile editions of Borges manuscripts titled *Poemas y prosas breves* (2018; *Poems and Short Prose*), *Ensayos* (2019; *Essays*), and *Cuentos* (2020; *Short Stories*); and *Lo marginal es lo más bello: Borges en sus manuscritos* (2022; *The Marginal Is the Most Beautiful: Borges in His Manuscripts*).

Nora Benedict is assistant professor of Spanish and digital humanities in the Department of Romance Languages at the University of Georgia. Her research centers on twentieth-century Latin American literature, book history, and questions of access and maintenance surrounding both digital and print cultures. Her first monograph, *Borges and the Literary Marketplace* (2021), considers the marked presence of books, periodicals, and other print mediums in Jorge Luis Borges's life by analyzing the physical features of his publications.

Carol Mastrangelo Bové is teaching professor emerita in English at the University of Pittsburgh and professor emerita in French at Westminster College, Pennsylvania. She is the author of *Kristeva in America: Re-imagining the Exceptional* (2020), *Language and Politics in Kristeva: Literature, Art, Therapy* (2006), and many articles on twentieth- and twenty-first-century literature, film, and literary translation. She has also translated books and articles on psychoanalytic theory and criticism, including the work of Hélène Cixous, Serge Doubrovsky, Luce Irigaray, and Julia Kristeva. Her book *Colette and the Incest Taboo: That Most Disturbing of Drives* is forthcoming from Anthem Press, and her new translation of Colette's *La Maison de Claudine* will appear soon in Oxford University Press's World's Classics series.

Pablo Brescia is professor of Spanish at the University of South Florida, where he teaches courses on contemporary Latin American literature. He is the author of *Borges: Cinco especulaciones* (2015; *Borges: Five Speculative Essays*) and *Modelos y prácticas en el cuento hispanoamericano: Arreola, Borges, Cortázar* (2011; *Models and Practices in the Latin American Short Story: Arreola, Borges, Cortázar*). He has also edited critical anthologies on the McOndo literary movement and the Crack generation and on the Latin American short story sequence as well as collections on Borges, Julio Cortázar, and Sor Juana Inés de la Cruz.

Stephen Buttes is associate professor of Spanish at Purdue University, Fort Wayne. He writes about aesthetics and politics in Latin America. His research has appeared in a variety of academic journals, and his writing on teaching appeared in the edited volume *Quick Hits for Teaching with Digital Humanities* (2020). He is editor in chief and a founding editor of *FORMA: A Journal of Latin American Criticism and Theory* and is currently completing revisions on a book that analyzes poverty, aesthetic form, and politics in Latin America.

Manuel Chinchilla teaches Spanish language and culture at University School in Hunting Valley, Ohio. Previously, he was associate professor of Spanish and Italian at Sewanee: The University of the South. He has published academic work on contemporary literature and culture from Mexico, Central America, and Italy. His draft for an English translation of Jorge Medina García's *Cenizas en la memoria* (*Ashen Memories*) is complete and will include a critical apparatus and an interview with the author.

Stephanie Contreras is a lecturing fellow of Romance studies at Duke University, where she teaches Spanish language courses and coordinates the Elementary Spanish I level. Her fields of interest include Latin American testimonial literature and cultural memory. Additionally, she coleads a Duke Bass Connections research project, "¡Celebra mi herencia! A Spanish Reading Program."

Emron Esplin is professor of English at Brigham Young University, where he teaches courses in US literature, inter-American literary studies, and translation studies. He is coeditor, with Margarida Vale de Gato, of *Translated Poe* (2014) and *Anthologizing Poe* (2020). He edited the journal *Poe Studies: History, Theory, Interpretation* from 2018 to 2023, and he currently edits the journal's running feature "Newly Translated Poe Scholarship." He is the author of *Borges's Poe: The Influence and Reinvention of Edgar Allan Poe in Spanish America* (2016).

José Eduardo González is associate professor of Spanish and ethnic studies at the University of Nebraska, Lincoln. His research centers on twentieth- and twenty-first-century Latin American narratives and digital humanities approaches to literary history. He is the author of *Borges and the Politics of Form* and *Appropriating Theory: Angel Rama's Critical Work* and coeditor of *Primitivism and Identity in Latin America*, *New Trends in Contemporary Latin American Narrative*, and *Urban Spaces in Contemporary Latin American Literature*.

Audrey Harris Fernández teaches classes on Chicana/o and Latin American literature at the University of California, Los Angeles. Her writings have been published in *Variaciones Borges*, *Chasqui*, *Chiricú*, *Aztlán: A Journal of Chicano Studies*, the *Paris Review Daily*, and *Transmotion*. She is the translator, with Matthew Gleeson, of Amparo Dávila's *"The Houseguest" and Other Stories* (2018).

Kate Jenckes is professor of Spanish at the University of Michigan. She is the author of *Reading Borges after Benjamin: Allegory, Afterlife, and the Writing of History* (2007) and *Witnessing beyond the Human: Addressing the Alterity of the Other in Post-coup Chile and Argentina* (2017) and coeditor of a special issue of *The Yearbook of Comparative Literature* on Borges and Kafka (2017). She is currently working on several projects concerning the relationship between violence and aesthetics, including a book on Borges and the limits of sovereignty.

Adelaida López-Mejía is professor emerita of Spanish at Occidental College. She has published *Las dos caras de la escritura: Conversaciones con Ernesto Sábato, Umberto Eco, Susan Sontag, Mario Benedetti* (1989; *Two Faces of Writing: Conversations with Ernesto Sábato, Umberto Eco, Susan Sontag, Mario Benedetti*) and *Magia de tierra y agua* (1986; *Land and Water Magic*). Her articles on Latin American fiction have appeared in periodicals such as *MLN*, *Latin American Literary Review*, *Revista de Estudios Hispánicos*, *Revista Hispánica Moderna*, and *Bulletin of Hispanic Studies*.

Luciano Martínez is professor in the Department of Spanish at Swarthmore College. His research and teaching deal with contemporary Latin American literature with a focus on gender studies and literary theory. He is coauthor of *Miguel Briante: Genealogía de un olvido* (2001; *Miguel Briante: Genealogy of an Oblivion*) and the editor of two special issues of *Revista Iberoamericana: Los estudios lésbico-gays y queer latinoamericanos* (2008; *Latin American Lesbian-Gay and Queer Studies*) and *Escritoras latinoamericanas del siglo XXI* (2023; *Twenty-First-Century Latin American Women Writers*). Additionally, he has curated the collection *Pedro Lemebel, belleza indómita* (2022; *Pedro Lemebel, Untamed Beauty*).

Aldo Mendoza is assistant professor at the Defense Language Institute Foreign Language Center, where he creates and teaches courses on Latin American social movements, culture, and cryptologic linguistics. Previously, he was a Spanish enhancement coordinator for the National Cryptology School. He is also a former communication noncommissioned officer and performed active-duty assignments at Operation Iraqi Freedom V, Bagdad, Iraq.

Kimberly A. Nance is professor in the Department of Languages, Literatures, and Cultures at Illinois State University. She has published on the nature of the fantastic, folklore and ideologies of reading, and the influence of childhood reading on Borges's writing. Her most recent books are *Ethics of Witness in Global Testimonial Narratives* (2020) and *Teaching Literature in the Languages* (2010). She has chaired the executive committees of the MLA forums The Teaching of Literature and Teaching as a Profession.

Christian Reed teaches English and humanities in the upper school of Geffen Academy at UCLA. He has published on the writings of Herman Melville and the history of the Los Angeles Aqueduct.

Jeffrey P. Thompson is associate professor of art history in the Department of Art, Art History, and Visual Studies at Sewanee: The University of the South. His research and writing on post-minimalism and conceptual art of the 1960s and 1970s, in particular the work of Robert Smithson, Mel Bochner, and Gordon Matta-Clark, has appeared in *Art Journal*, *Art Bulletin*, and the exhibition catalogs *Moving Targets* and *New Installations*. His interest in film studies and media has led to book reviews and conference presentations on Weimar cinema and Hollywood in the 1970s.

Rhona Trauvitch is associate teaching professor at Florida International University, where she teaches courses in multicultural literature, speculative fiction, narrative theory, and popular culture. She is also the founding director of the university's Science and Fiction Lab. Her scholarship focuses on narratology, particularly in relation to science fiction and the intersections of science and storytelling. She is writing a book about the role of fictionality in conceptualizations of science.

Max Ubelaker Andrade is associate teaching professor in Latin American studies at the University of Massachusetts, Lowell. He is the author of *Borges beyond the Visible* (2019) and the translator of Néstor Ponce's *Disappearance without Absence* (2017). His writing has appeared in *Chasqui*, *Variaciones Borges*, *Cervantes*, *AGNI*, and Argentina's *La Nación*.

SURVEY PARTICIPANTS

Marvin L. Astrada, *New York University*
Daniel Balderston, *University of Pittsburgh*
Mayra Bottaro, *University of Oregon*
Carol Mastrangelo Bové, *University of Pittsburgh*
Pablo Brescia, *University of South Florida*
Stephen Buttes, *Purdue University, Fort Wayne*
Manuel Chinchilla, *University School, Hunting Valley, Ohio*
Jorgelina Corbatta, *Wayne State University*
Emron Esplin, *Brigham Young University*
Brian Gollnick, *University of Iowa*
Afruza Khanom, *Shahjalal University of Science and Technology*
Shirley Lua, *De La Salle University*
Linda S. Maier, *University of Alabama, Huntsville*
Luciano Martínez, *Swarthmore College*
Kimberly A. Nance, *Illinois State University*
Ricardo Pedroarias, *Loyola High School*
Christian Reed, *Geffen Academy at UCLA*
Ramón Saldívar, *Stanford University*
Francisco J. Solares-Larrave, *Northern Illinois University*
Henry Sussman, *Rutgers University*
Jeffrey P. Thompson, *Sewanee: The University of the South*
Rhona Trauvitch, *Florida International University*

WORKS CITED

Aaboe, Asger. "Babylonian Mathematics, Astrology, and Astronomy." *The Assyrian and Babylonian Empires and Other States of the Near East, from the Eighth to the Sixth Centuries BC*, edited by John Boardman et al., 2nd ed., Cambridge UP, 1991, pp. 276–90. Vol. 3, part 2 of *The Cambridge Ancient History*.

Accaria, Diane. "'A. W.' y 'D. W.': El gigantismo de Kane y la nueva narrativa de Jorge Luis Borges." *Imágenes*, vol. 2, no. 1, 1986, pp. 28–31.

"The Aegean." "Hellenic Civilization, 500–338 BC," by J. T. Hooker. Cotterell, *Penguin Encyclopedia of Classical Civilizations*, p. 46. Map.

Aelius Lampridus. "Antoninus Elagabalus." *Scriptores Historiae Augustae*, translated by David Magie, vol. 2, Harvard UP, 1967, pp. 105–77. Loeb Classical Library 140.

Aguilar, Gonzalo, and Emiliano Jelicié. *Borges va al cine*. Libraria, 2010.

Aizenberg, Edna. *The Aleph Weaver: Biblical, Kabbalistic and Judaic Elements in Borges*. Scripta Humanistica, 1984.

———. "'I, a Jew': Borges, Nazism, and the Shoah." *The Jewish Quarterly Review*, vol. 134, no. 3, 2014, pp. 339–53.

Alazraki, Jaime. *Borges and the Kabbalah*. Cambridge UP, 1988.

———. "Conversación con Borges sobre la Cábala." *Variaciones Borges*, no. 3, 1997, pp. 163–76.

———. *Jorge Luis Borges*. Columbia UP, 1971.

———. *La prosa narrativa de Jorge Luis Borges*. Gredos, 1968.

"Alexander the Great's Asian Campaigns." "The Hellenistic Age (336–321 BC)," by Frank Walbank. Cotterell, *Penguin Encyclopedia of Classical Civilizations*, p. 46. Map.

Allen, Esther. "Translation, Globalization, and English." *To Be Translated or Not to Be: PEN/IRL Report on the International Situation of Literary Translations*, edited by Allen, Institut Ramon Llull, 2007, pp. 17–33.

Almond, Ian. "Borges the Post-Orientalist: Images of Islam from the Edge of the West." *Modern Fiction Studies*, vol. 50, no. 2, 2004, pp. 435–59.

Alonso, Carlos J. "Borges y la teoría." *MLN*, vol. 120, no. 2, Mar. 2005, pp. 437–56. *Project Muse*, https://doi.org/10.1353/mln.2005.0078.

"Ancient and Modern Maps of Mesopotamia and the Fertile Crescent." *Mpoweruk .com*, www.mpoweruk.com/figs/Mesopotamia.htm. Accessed 5 Jan. 2024.

"Ancient Greece." "Archaic Greece," by J. T. Hooker. Cotterell, *Penguin Encyclopedia of Ancient Civilizations*, p. 216. Map.

Apollodorus. *The Library*. Translated by James G. Frazer, vol. 1 (books 1–3.9), Harvard UP, 2014.

Arias, Martín. Afterword. Borges, *Professor Borges*, pp. 253–57.

Arnold, Matthew. "The Study of Poetry." *The Essential Matthew Arnold*, edited by Lionel Trilling, Chato and Windus, 1969, pp. 299–331.

———. "The Translator's Tribunal." Robinson, pp. 250–55.

Les autres. Directed by Hugo Santiago, Ilos Films, 1974. *YouTube*, uploaded by Video Teca, 14 Aug. 2020, www.youtube.com/watch?v=k5EujfsScdk.

Ávila, Lope. Interview. Conducted by Audrey Harris Fernández, 20 July 2016.

Balderston, Daniel. "'Anotación al 23 de Agosto de 1944': Reflections on a Newly Acquired Manuscript." *Letras*, vol. 81, 2020, pp. 77–90.

———. "Biografías infames: Reflexiones sobre cuatro manuscritos de *Historia universal de la infamia*." *Variaciones Borges*, no. 42, 2016, pp. 217–31.

———. "Borges and the Universe of Culture." *Variaciones Borges*, no. 14, 2002, pp. 175–83.

———. "'Demasiado evanescente y extático': Reflexión sobre unas anotaciones de Borges en un ejemplar de las *Noches áticas* de Aulo Gellio." *Variaciones Borges*, no. 37, 2014, pp. 69–79.

———. "Descubrimientos secretos: Reflexiones en torno al manuscrito de 'Destino escandinavo' (1953)." *Lo que los archivos cuentan*, vol. 3, 2014, pp. 213–28.

———. "Detalles circunstanciales: Sobre dos borradores de 'El escritor argentino y la tradición.'" *La Biblioteca*, vol. 13, 2013, pp. 32–45.

———. "Genética textual a partir de fragmentos: Una página y media del manuscrito de 'Abenjacán el Bojarí, muerto en su laberinto' y otros enigmas." *El Hilo de la Fábula*, vol. 20, 2020, pp. 14–27.

———. "'His Insect-Like Handwriting': Marginalia and Commentaries on Borges and Menard." *Variaciones Borges*, no. 31, 2010, pp. 125–36.

———. *How Borges Wrote*. U of Virginia P, 2018.

———. "Liminares: Sobre el manuscrito de 'El hombre en el umbral.'" *Hispamérica*, vol. 41, no. 122, 2012, pp. 28–36.

———. *The Literary Universe of Jorge Luis Borges*. Greenwood, 1986.

———. "Los manuscritos de Borges: 'Imaginar una realidad más compleja.'" *Variaciones Borges*, no. 28, 2009, pp. 15–26.

———. *Out of Context: Historical Reference and the Representation of Reality in Borges*. Duke UP, 1993.

———. "Las páginas del Haber de un cuaderno de contabilidad, marca Caravela: Las copias en limpio de los cuentos de Borges de 1939 a 1941." *La Palabra*, vol. 38, 2020, pp. 21–32.

———. "Palabras rechazadas: Borges y la tachadura." *Revista Iberoamericana*, vol. 80, no. 246, 2014, pp. 81–93.

———. "Palabras rechazadas: Lectura de los manuscritos de un poema de Borges." *Palabra y Persona*, vol. 6, nos. 10–11, 2011, pp. 9–19.

———. "Point and Counterpoint: On the Manuscript of 'El fin' (1953)." *Variaciones Borges*, no. 51, 2021, pp. 3–24.

———. *El precursor velado: R. L. Stevenson en la obra de Borges*. Sudamericana, 1985.

———. "Puntos suspensivos: Sobre el manuscrito de 'Hombre de la esquina rosada.'" *Cuarenta Naipes*, vol. 24, no. 1, 2019, pp. 260–74.

———. "Senderos que se bifurcan: Dos manuscritos de un cuento de Borges." *Cuadernos LIRICO*, vol. 12, 2015, https://doi.org/10.4000/lirico.1992.

———, editor. Special issue of *Variaciones Borges*. No. 38, 2014.

———. "The Theory of Games and Genetic Criticism: On the Manuscript of 'La lotería en Babilonia.'" *Variaciones Borges*, no. 36, 2013, pp. 155–65.

Barnes, Richard. "The Other Borges." *The Wilson Quarterly*, vol. 21, no. 3, summer 1997, pp. 93–96.

Beard, Mary. *SPQR: A History of Ancient Rome*. Norton Liveright, 2015.

Belevan, Harry. *Teoría de lo fantástico*. Anagrama, 1976.

Bell-Villada, Gene H. *Borges and His Fiction: A Guide to His Mind and Art*. U of Texas P, 1981.

———. *Borges and His Fiction: A Guide to His Mind and Art*. Revised ed., U of Texas P, 1999.

Benedict, Nora C. *Borges and the Literary Marketplace: How Editorial Practices Shaped Cosmopolitan Reading*. Yale UP, 2021.

———. "Digital Approaches to the Archive: Multispectral Imaging and the Recovery of Borges's Writing Process in 'El muerto' and 'La casa de Asterión.'" *Variaciones Borges*, no. 45, 2018, pp. 153–69.

Berkeley, George. *A Treatise concerning the Principles of Human Knowledge*. 1710. *Project Gutenberg*, Dec. 2023, www.gutenberg.org/files/4723/4723-h/4723-h.htm.

Bernstein, Richard. "*Collected Fictions*: Savoring a Blend of Borges Imaginings." *The New York Times Book Review*, 9 Sept. 1998. *The New York Times Web Archive*, archive.nytimes.com/www.nytimes.com/books/98/09/06/daily/borges-book-review.html.

———. "*Selected Nonfictions*: Borges' Worlds of Reality and Invention." *The New York Times Book Review*, 6 Oct. 1999. *The New York Times Web Archive*, archive.nytimes.com/www.nytimes.com/library/books/100699borges-book-review.html.

Berrenechea, Ana María. *La expresión de la irrealidad en la obra de Jorge Luis Borges*. El Colegio de México, 1957.

Betancort, Sonia. *Oriente no es una pieza de museo*. Ediciones Universidad Salamanca, 2018.

Beverley, John. *Latinamericanism after 9/11*. Duke UP, 2011.

Bloom, Harold. *How to Read and Why*. Fourth Estate, 2001.

———. *The Western Canon: The Books and School of the Ages*. Harcourt Brace, 1994.

Boldy, Steven. *A Companion to Jorge Luis Borges*. Tamesis, 2009.

"Borges." *Listening Booth*, Harvard Library, library.harvard.edu/sites/default/files/static/poetry/listeningbooth/poets/borges.html. Accessed 5 Jan. 2024.

Borges, Jorge Luis. *El Aleph*. Editorial Losada, 1949.

———. *El Aleph*. Editorial Losada, 1952.

———. *El Aleph*. Emecé Editores, 1957.

———. "The Aleph." Translated by Norman Thomas di Giovanni and Borges. Borges, *"The Aleph,"* pp. 15–30.

———. "The Aleph." Translated by Andrew Hurley. Borges, *Collected Fictions*, pp. 274–86.

———. "The Aleph." Translated by Anthony Kerrigan. *A Personal Anthology*, edited by Kerrigan, Grove Press, 1967, pp. 138–54.

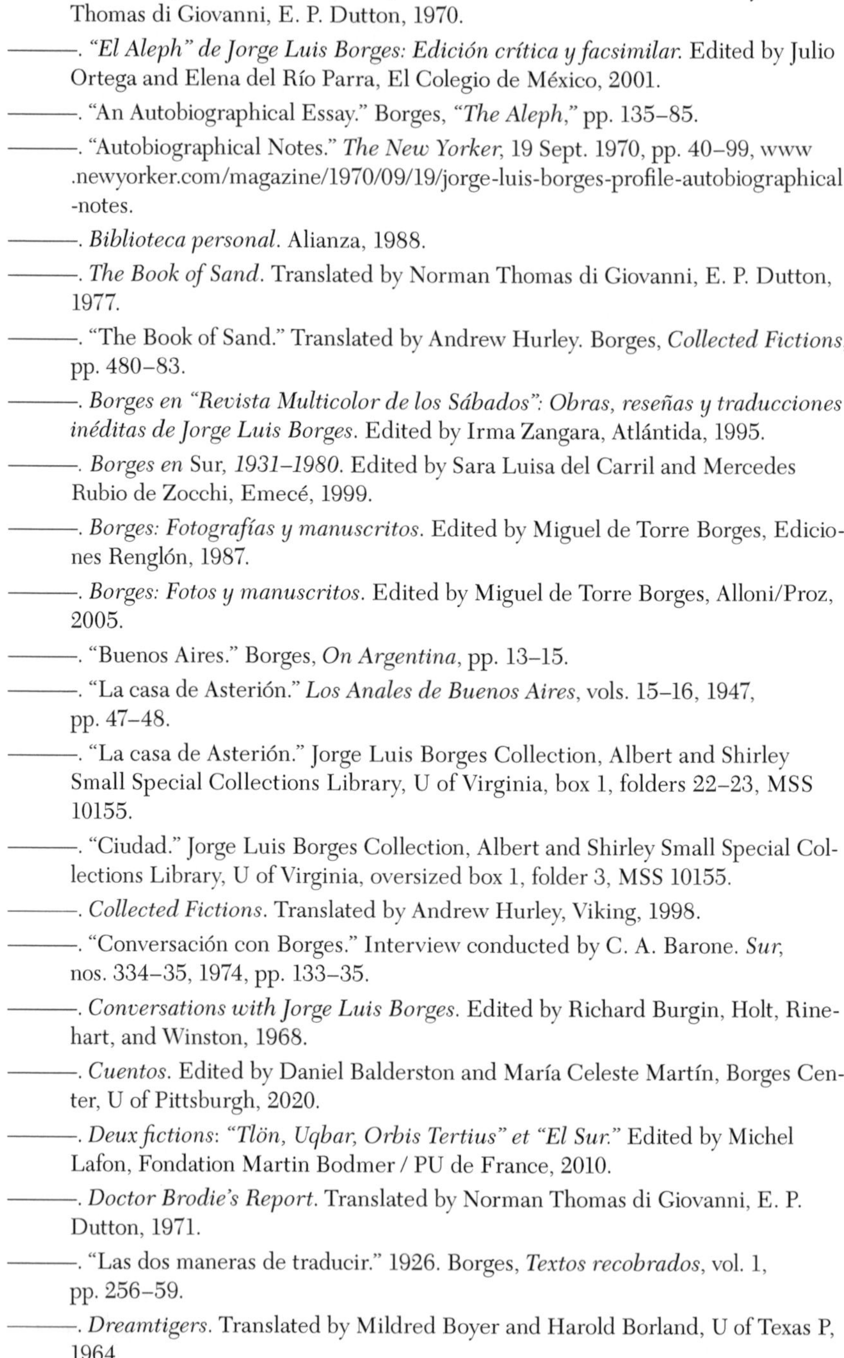

———. *"The Aleph" and Other Stories, 1933–1969*. Edited and translated by Norman Thomas di Giovanni, E. P. Dutton, 1970.

———. *"El Aleph" de Jorge Luis Borges: Edición crítica y facsimilar.* Edited by Julio Ortega and Elena del Río Parra, El Colegio de México, 2001.

———. "An Autobiographical Essay." Borges, *"The Aleph,"* pp. 135–85.

———. "Autobiographical Notes." *The New Yorker*, 19 Sept. 1970, pp. 40–99, www.newyorker.com/magazine/1970/09/19/jorge-luis-borges-profile-autobiographical-notes.

———. *Biblioteca personal*. Alianza, 1988.

———. *The Book of Sand*. Translated by Norman Thomas di Giovanni, E. P. Dutton, 1977.

———. "The Book of Sand." Translated by Andrew Hurley. Borges, *Collected Fictions*, pp. 480–83.

———. *Borges en "Revista Multicolor de los Sábados": Obras, reseñas y traducciones inéditas de Jorge Luis Borges*. Edited by Irma Zangara, Atlántida, 1995.

———. *Borges en* Sur, *1931–1980*. Edited by Sara Luisa del Carril and Mercedes Rubio de Zocchi, Emecé, 1999.

———. *Borges: Fotografías y manuscritos*. Edited by Miguel de Torre Borges, Ediciones Renglón, 1987.

———. *Borges: Fotos y manuscritos*. Edited by Miguel de Torre Borges, Alloni/Proz, 2005.

———. "Buenos Aires." Borges, *On Argentina*, pp. 13–15.

———. "La casa de Asterión." *Los Anales de Buenos Aires*, vols. 15–16, 1947, pp. 47–48.

———. "La casa de Asterión." Jorge Luis Borges Collection, Albert and Shirley Small Special Collections Library, U of Virginia, box 1, folders 22–23, MSS 10155.

———. "Ciudad." Jorge Luis Borges Collection, Albert and Shirley Small Special Collections Library, U of Virginia, oversized box 1, folder 3, MSS 10155.

———. *Collected Fictions*. Translated by Andrew Hurley, Viking, 1998.

———. "Conversación con Borges." Interview conducted by C. A. Barone. *Sur*, nos. 334–35, 1974, pp. 133–35.

———. *Conversations with Jorge Luis Borges*. Edited by Richard Burgin, Holt, Rinehart, and Winston, 1968.

———. *Cuentos*. Edited by Daniel Balderston and María Celeste Martín, Borges Center, U of Pittsburgh, 2020.

———. *Deux fictions*: *"Tlön, Uqbar, Orbis Tertius" et "El Sur."* Edited by Michel Lafon, Fondation Martin Bodmer / PU de France, 2010.

———. *Doctor Brodie's Report*. Translated by Norman Thomas di Giovanni, E. P. Dutton, 1971.

———. "Las dos maneras de traducir." 1926. Borges, *Textos recobrados*, vol. 1, pp. 256–59.

———. *Dreamtigers*. Translated by Mildred Boyer and Harold Borland, U of Texas P, 1964.

———. *Ensayos*. Edited by Daniel Balderston and María Celeste Martín, Borges Center, U of Pittsburgh, 2019.

———. *Evaristo Carriego: A Book about Old-Time Buenos Aires*. Translated by Norman Thomas di Giovanni, E. P. Dutton, 1984.

———. *Ficciones*. Edited by Anthony Kerrigan, Grove Press, 1994.

———. "The Garden of Forking Paths." Translated by Anthony Boucher. *Ellery Queen's Mystery Magazine*, vol. 12, no. 57, 1948, pp. 101–10.

———. "The Garden of Forking Paths." Translated by Andrew Hurley. Borges, *Collected Fictions*, pp. 119–28.

———. "The Garden of Forking Paths." Translated by Helen Temple and Ruthven Todd. *Ficciones*, by Borges, edited by Anthony Kerrigan, Grove Press, 1962, pp. 89–101.

———. "The Garden of Forking Paths." Translated by Donald A. Yates. Borges, *Labyrinths*, pp. 19–29.

———. "The Gospel according to Mark." Translated by Andrew Hurley. Borges, *Collected Fictions*, pp. 397–401.

———. "The Homeric Versions." Translated by Eliot Weinberger. Borges, *Selected Non-fictions*, pp. 69–74.

———. *El idioma de los argentinos*. Seix Barral, 1994.

———. *In Praise of Darkness*. Translated by Norman Thomas di Giovanni, E. P. Dutton, 1974.

———. *Inquisiciones*. Seix Barral, 1994.

———. *Inquisiciones / Otras Inquisiciones*. Debolsillo, 2013.

———. *Labyrinths: Selected Stories and Other Writings*. Edited by Donald A. Yates and James E. Irby, New Directions Publishing, 1962.

———. *Manual de zoología fantástica*. Fondo de Cultura Económica, 1957.

———. "Místicos del Islam." Jorge Luis Borges Collection, Harry Ransom Center, U of Texas, Austin, MS-0453, container 1.13.

———. "El muerto." Jorge Luis Borges Collection, Albert and Shirley Small Special Collections Library, U of Virginia, box 1, folder 21, MSS 10155.

———. "El muerto." *Sur*, vol. 145, 1946, pp. 42–48.

———. "Música patria." Jorge Luis Borges Collection, Albert and Shirley Small Special Collections Library, U of Virginia, box 1, folder 1, MSS 10155.

———. *Nueve ensayos dantescos*. Espasa-Calpe, 1982.

———. *Obras completas*. Emecé, 1996. 4 vols.

———. *Obras completas: Edición crítica*. Edited by Rolando Costa Picazo and Irma Zangara, Emecé, 2009. 3 vols.

———. *On Argentina*. Edited by Suzanne Jill Levine and Alfred Mac Adam, Penguin Books, 2010.

———. "On William Beckford's *Vathek*." Translated by Eliot Weinberger. Borges, *Selected Non-fictions*, pp. 236–39.

———. *Other Inquisitions, 1937–1952*. Translated by Ruth L. C. Simms, U of Texas P, 1964.

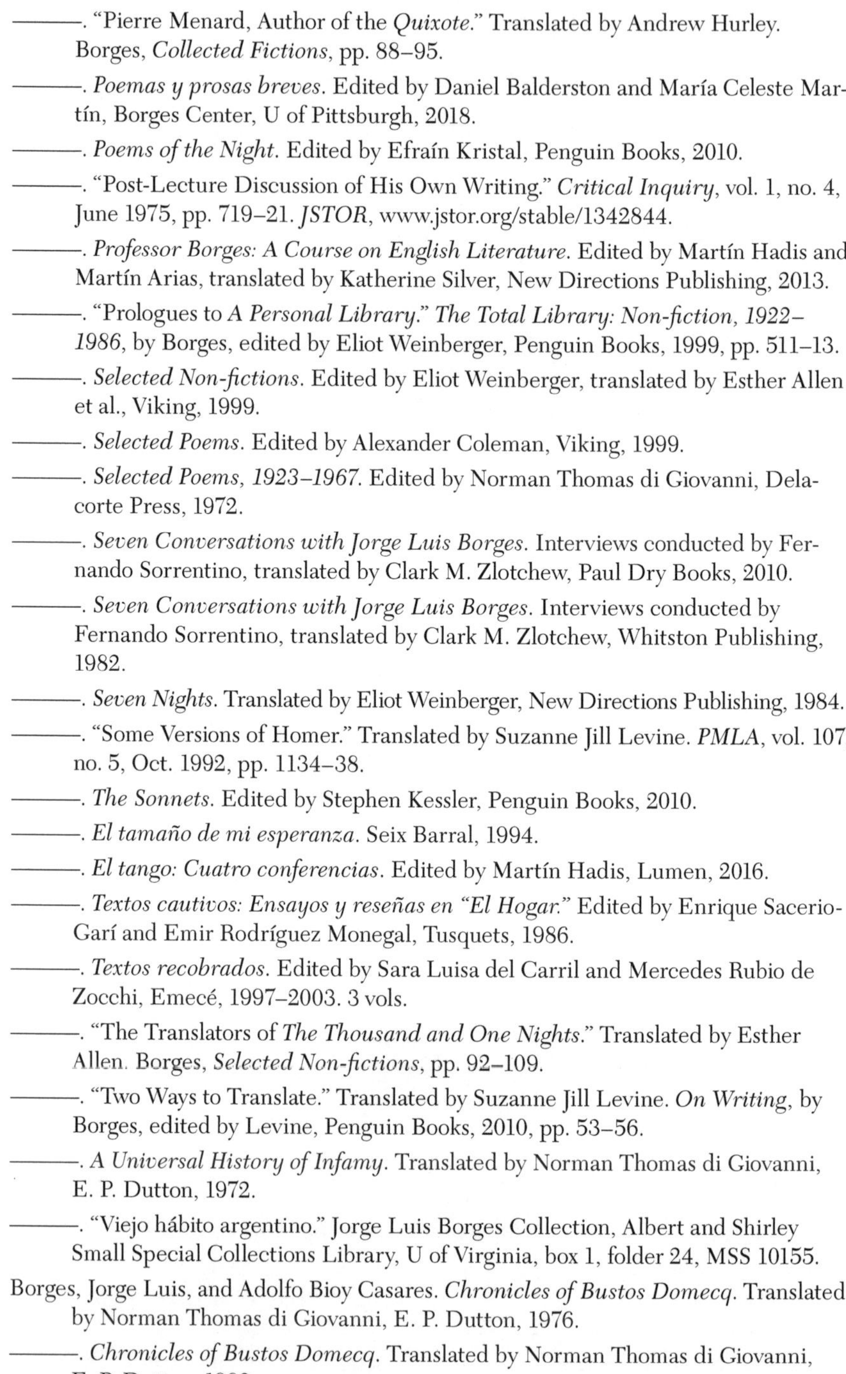

———. "Pierre Menard, Author of the *Quixote*." Translated by Andrew Hurley. Borges, *Collected Fictions*, pp. 88–95.

———. *Poemas y prosas breves*. Edited by Daniel Balderston and María Celeste Martín, Borges Center, U of Pittsburgh, 2018.

———. *Poems of the Night*. Edited by Efraín Kristal, Penguin Books, 2010.

———. "Post-Lecture Discussion of His Own Writing." *Critical Inquiry*, vol. 1, no. 4, June 1975, pp. 719–21. *JSTOR*, www.jstor.org/stable/1342844.

———. *Professor Borges: A Course on English Literature*. Edited by Martín Hadis and Martín Arias, translated by Katherine Silver, New Directions Publishing, 2013.

———. "Prologues to *A Personal Library*." *The Total Library: Non-fiction, 1922–1986*, by Borges, edited by Eliot Weinberger, Penguin Books, 1999, pp. 511–13.

———. *Selected Non-fictions*. Edited by Eliot Weinberger, translated by Esther Allen et al., Viking, 1999.

———. *Selected Poems*. Edited by Alexander Coleman, Viking, 1999.

———. *Selected Poems, 1923–1967*. Edited by Norman Thomas di Giovanni, Delacorte Press, 1972.

———. *Seven Conversations with Jorge Luis Borges*. Interviews conducted by Fernando Sorrentino, translated by Clark M. Zlotchew, Paul Dry Books, 2010.

———. *Seven Conversations with Jorge Luis Borges*. Interviews conducted by Fernando Sorrentino, translated by Clark M. Zlotchew, Whitston Publishing, 1982.

———. *Seven Nights*. Translated by Eliot Weinberger, New Directions Publishing, 1984.

———. "Some Versions of Homer." Translated by Suzanne Jill Levine. *PMLA*, vol. 107, no. 5, Oct. 1992, pp. 1134–38.

———. *The Sonnets*. Edited by Stephen Kessler, Penguin Books, 2010.

———. *El tamaño de mi esperanza*. Seix Barral, 1994.

———. *El tango: Cuatro conferencias*. Edited by Martín Hadis, Lumen, 2016.

———. *Textos cautivos: Ensayos y reseñas en "El Hogar."* Edited by Enrique Sacerio-Garí and Emir Rodríguez Monegal, Tusquets, 1986.

———. *Textos recobrados*. Edited by Sara Luisa del Carril and Mercedes Rubio de Zocchi, Emecé, 1997–2003. 3 vols.

———. "The Translators of *The Thousand and One Nights*." Translated by Esther Allen. Borges, *Selected Non-fictions*, pp. 92–109.

———. "Two Ways to Translate." Translated by Suzanne Jill Levine. *On Writing*, by Borges, edited by Levine, Penguin Books, 2010, pp. 53–56.

———. *A Universal History of Infamy*. Translated by Norman Thomas di Giovanni, E. P. Dutton, 1972.

———. "Viejo hábito argentino." Jorge Luis Borges Collection, Albert and Shirley Small Special Collections Library, U of Virginia, box 1, folder 24, MSS 10155.

Borges, Jorge Luis, and Adolfo Bioy Casares. *Chronicles of Bustos Domecq*. Translated by Norman Thomas di Giovanni, E. P. Dutton, 1976.

———. *Chronicles of Bustos Domecq*. Translated by Norman Thomas di Giovanni, E. P. Dutton, 1982.

———. *Crónicas de Bustos Domecq*. Losada, 1968.

———. *Dos fantasías memorables*. Edicom, 1971.

———. *Un modelo para la muerte*. Edicom, 1970.

———. *Nuevos cuentos de Bustos Domecq*. Ediciones Librería La Ciudad, 1977.

———. *Seis problemas para don Isidro Parodi*. Sur, 1964.

———. *Six Problems for Don Isidro Parodi*. Translated by Norman Thomas di Giovanni, E. P. Dutton, 1981.

Borges, Jorge Luis, and Betina Edelberg. *Leopoldo Lugones*. Pleamar, 1965.

Borges, Jorge Luis, and Margarita Guerrero. *The Book of Imaginary Beings*. Translated by Norman Thomas di Giovanni, E. P. Dutton, 1969.

———. *The Book of Imaginary Beings*. Translated by Andrew Hurley, illustrated by Peter Sís, Penguin Books, 2005.

———. Foreword to the first edition. Borges and Guerrero, *Book* [Hurley], pp. xi–xiii.

———. *El libro de los seres imaginarios*. Kier, 1967.

———. *El Martín Fierro*. Emecé, 1979.

Borges, Jorge Luis, and Delia Ingenieros. *Antiguas literaturas germánicas*. Fondo de Cultura Económica, 1965.

Borges, Jorge Luis, and Alicia Jurado. *Qué es el budismo*. Alianza, 2000.

Borges, Jorge Luis, and María Kodama. *Atlas*. Emecé, 2009.

———. *Atlas*. Translated by Anthony Kerrigan, E. P. Dutton, 1985.

———. *Breve antología anglosajona*. La ciudad, 1978.

Borges, Jorge Luis, and Luisa Mercedes Levinson. *La hermana de Eloísa*. Centro Editores, 2009.

Borges, Jorge Luis, and María Esther Vázquez. *Introducción a la literatura inglesa*. Alianza, 2005.

———. *Literatura germánicas medievales*. Falbo, 1966.

Borges, Jorge Luis, et al. *Obras completas en colaboración*. Emecé, 1979.

———. *Obras completas en colaboración*. Emecé, 1991.

"Borges y la Universidad." *Variaciones Borges*, no. 1, 1996, pp. 141–44. *JSTOR*, www.jstor.org/stable/24879599.

Brescia, Pablo. "El cine como precursor: Von Sternberg y Borges." *Espacios de Crítica y Producción*, no. 17, 1995, pp. 64–70.

———. "Citizen Borges." *La Colmena*, no. 24, 1999, pp. 13–24.

———. "Máquinas de ficción: Borges, la literatura y el cine." *CELEHIS*, vol. 19, no. 21, 2010, pp. 145–63, fh.mdp.edu.ar/revistas/index.php/celehis/article/view/792/813.

Brion, Marcel. *Art fantastique*. A. Michel, 1961.

Brodski, Bella. "'She Was Unable Not to Think': Borges's 'Emma Zunz' and the Female Subject." *MLN*, vol. 100, no. 2, 1985, pp. 330–47.

Brook, Taylor. *El jardín de senderos que se bifurcan*. *YouTube*, uploaded by Taylor Brook, 29 Mar. 2013, www.youtube.com/watch?v=4oLvTqOICTM.

Brooks, Peter. "An Ethics of Reading?" *Diversity and Democracy*, vol. 20, no. 1, winter 2017, pp. 22–23.

Browne, Thomas. Religio Medici, Hydriotaphia, *and the* Letter to a Friend. 1869. *Project Gutenberg*, 11 Nov. 2019, www.gutenberg.org/files/586/586-h/586-h.htm.

Buonocore, Domingo. *Libreros, editores e impresores de Buenos Aires: Esbozo para una historia del libro argentino*. Bowker Editores, 1974.

Burton, Isabel. Introduction. I. Burton, *Lady Burton's Edition*, pp. 1–21.

———. *Lady Burton's Edition of Her Husband's* Arabian Nights. Vol. 1, prepared by Justin Huntly McCarthy, Waterlow and Sons, 1886.

———. Preface. I. Burton, *Lady Burton's Edition*, pp. v–vi.

Burton, Richard Francis, translator. Introduction. *The Book of the Thousand Nights and a Night*, vol. 1, translated by Burton, 1885. *Project Gutenberg*, www.gutenberg.org/cache/epub/3435/pg3435.html.

———. "The Translator's Foreword." *The Book of the Thousand Nights and a Night*, vol. 1, translated by Burton, 1885. *Project Gutenberg*, www.gutenberg.org/cache/epub/3435/pg3435.html.

Butler, Rex. *Borges' Short Stories: A Reader's Guide*. Continuum, 2010.

Cacique Bandeira. Directed by Héctor Olivera, Aries Cinematográfica Argentina, 1975.

Caillois, Roger. *Les jeux et les hommes*. Gallimard, 1958.

Capote, Truman. *In Cold Blood: A True Account of a Multiple Murder and Its Consequences*. New American Library, 1965.

"The Captivity of Judah." *Bible History*, 2023, www.bible-history.com/map_babylonian_captivity/. Map.

Caxton, William, translator. "Of the Foxe and of the Storke." 1484. *Aesopica: Aesop's Fables in English, Latin and Greek*, mythfolklore.net/aesopica/caxton/213.htm.

Cervantes, Miguel de. *Don Quixote*. Translated by Edith Grossman, Ecco, 2003.

Chapman, George, translator. "The First Book of Homer's Iliads." *The Iliads of Homer*, translated by Chapman, 1611. *Project Gutenberg*, www.gutenberg.org/files/51355/51355-0.txt.

———. "To the Reader." *The Iliads of Homer*, translated by Chapman, 1611. *Project Gutenberg*, www.gutenberg.org/files/51355/51355-0.txt.

Chasteen, John Charles. *Heroes on Horseback: A Life and Times of the Last Gaucho Caudillos*. U of New Mexico P, 1995.

Christ, Ronald. *The Narrow Act: Borges' Art of Allusion*. New York UP, 1969.

Cisneros, Sandra. *A House of My Own*. Alfred A. Knopf, 2015.

———. *The House on Mango Street*. 25th anniversary ed., Vintage Books, 2009.

———. "It Occurs to Me I Am the Creative/Destructive Goddess Coatlicue." *The Massachusetts Review*, vol. 36, no. 4, 1995, p. 599.

———. "Letter to My Readers." *Sandra Cisneros*, 26 Apr. 2011, www.sandracisneros.com/2011_0426-1.

———. "With Lorenzo at the Center of the Universe, El Zócalo, Mexico City." *Loose Woman*, by Cisneros, Alfred A. Knopf, 1994, pp. 60–63.

Citizen Kane. Directed by Orson Welles, RKO Radio Pictures, 1941.

Conrad, Joseph. *The Heart of Darkness*. W. W. Norton, 2008.

"Consubstantial, *Adj.*" *Oxford English Dictionary*, Oxford UP, 2023, www.oed.com/dictionary/consubstantial_adj.

"Consustancial." *Real Academia Española*, 2023, dle.rae.es/consustancial.

Cook, Albert. *The Meaning of Fiction*. Wayne State UP, 1960.

Corbett, Eustace K. "The History of the Mosque of Amr at Old Cairo." *Journal of the Royal Asiatic Society of Great Britain and Ireland*, vol. 22, no. 4, 1890, pp. 759–800.

Corwin, Jay. "Borges, the Magi and Persian Histories." *Variaciones Borges*, no. 41, 2016, pp. 27–39.

Costa, René de. *Humor in Borges*. Wayne State UP, 2000.

Cotterell, Arthur, editor. *The Penguin Encyclopedia of Ancient Civilizations*. Penguin Books, 1988.

———, editor. *The Penguin Encyclopedia of Classical Civilizations*. Viking, 1993.

Couture, Mark. "Empty Words: Vanity in the Writings of Jorge Luis Borges." *Romance Notes*, vol. 39, no. 3, spring 1999, pp. 265–71.

Couyoumdji, Francisca Folch. "Jorge Luis Borges Muses on His Desert Island Book Selections." *Ransom Center Magazine*, 8 Feb. 2011, sites.utexas.edu/ransomcentermagazine/2011/02/08/jorge-luis-borges-muses-on-his-desert-island-book-selections/.

Cozarinsky, Edgardo. *Borges in/and/on Film*. Translated by Gloria Waldman and Ronald Christ, Lumen Books, 1988.

———. *Borges y el cine*. Sur, 1974.

"Criticism." *Borges Center*, U of Pittsburgh, 2010–19, www.borges.pitt.edu/criticism.

Currie, Mark. Introduction. Currie, *Metafiction*, pp. 1–18.

———, editor. *Metafiction*. Routledge, 2016.

"Cutting a Möbius Strip in Half (and More): Animated Topology." *YouTube*, uploaded by Think Twice, 11 Sept. 2017, www.youtube.com/watch?v=XlQOipIVFPk.

Damrosch, David. "World Literature and Figure and Ground." Heise, pp. 134–40.

Dapía, Silvia G. "Borges, Social Order and Human Action." *Variaciones Borges*, no. 36, 2013, pp. 125–53.

———. *Jorge Luis Borges, Post-analytic Philosophy, and Representation*. Routledge, 2016.

de Diego, José Luis, editor. *Editores y políticas editoriales en Argentina, 1880–2000*. Fondo de Cultura Económica, 2014.

de la Fuente, Ariel. *Borges, Desire, and Sex*. Oxford UP, 2019.

Deleuze, Gilles, and Félix Guattari. *A Thousand Plateaus: Capitalism and Schizophrenia*. Translated by Brian Massumi, U of Minnesota P, 1987.

Dell'Aria, Annie. "The Scaffolded Research Paper." *Art History Teaching Resources*, 4 June 2016, arthistoryteachingresources.org/2016/06/the-scaffolded-research-paper.

Derrida, Jacques. *Monolingualism of the Other; or, The Prosthesis of Origin*. Translated by Patrick Mensah, Stanford UP, 1998.

———. "Des tours de Babel." Translated by Joseph Graham. *Acts of Religion*, edited by Gil Anidjar, Routledge, 2002, pp. 104–34.

Devlin, Marcia, and Gayani Samarawickrema. "The Criteria of Effective Teaching in a Changing Higher Education Context." *Higher Education Research and Development*, vol. 29, no. 2, 2010, pp. 111–24.

Dewey, John. "Education in Relation to Form." *Pragmatism, Education, Democracy*, edited by Larry A. Hickman and Thomas M. Alexander, Indiana UP, 1998, pp. 274–77. Vol. 1 of *The Essential Dewey*.

Días de odio. Directed by Leopoldo Torre Nilson, Sociedad Independiente Filmadora Argentina, 1954. *YouTube*, uploaded by CINEAR, 26 May 2014, www.youtube.com/watch?v=DnzSMB4-1h4.

Dove, Patrick. *The Catastrophe of Modernity: Tragedy and the Nation in Latin American Literature*. Bucknell UP, 2004.

———. "Cultural Margins in Borges: Mimesis, Autobiography and Catastrophe." *Revista Canadiense de Estudios Hispánicos*, vol. 23, no. 1, 1998, pp. 41–60.

Duncan, Cynthia K. *Unraveling the Real: The Fantastic in Spanish-American Ficciones*. Temple UP, 2010.

Dyer, Geoff. "In Borges, a Surfeit of Riches." *SFGATE*, 18 Apr. 1999, www.sfgate.com/books/article/In-Borges-a-Surfeit-of-Riches-Poetry-2935797.php.

Ebor, Donald. "Preface to the New English Bible." *The New English Bible*, Oxford UP / Cambridge UP, 1970, pp. v–vii.

Eco, Umberto. "Overinterpreting Texts." *Interpretation and Overinterpretation*, edited by Stefan Collini, Cambridge UP, 1992, pp. 45–66.

Emmerich, Karen. "Difference at the 'Origin,' Instability at the 'Source': Translation as Translingual Editing." *Literary Translation and the Making of Originals*, by Emmerich, Bloomsbury, 2017, pp. 1–36.

Esplin, Emron. *Borges's Poe: The Influence and Reinvention of Edgar Allan Poe in Spanish America*. U of Georgia P, 2016.

Estupinya, Pere. "Teoría de cuerdas: ¡A por ella!" *El País*, 1 July 2008, blogs.elpais.com/apuntes-cientificos-mit/2008/07/teor%C3%ADa-de-cuerdas-a-por-ella.html.

Fernández, Macedonio. *The Museum of Eterna's Novel (The First Good Novel)*. Translated by Margaret Schwartz, Open Letter, 2010.

———. *Teorías*. Corregidor, 1974.

Fiddian, Robin. "Borges on Location: Duplicitous Narration and Historical Truths in 'Tema del traidor y del héroe.'" *The Modern Language Review*, vol. 105, no. 3, 2010, pp. 743–60. *JSTOR*, jstor.org/stable/25698806.

———, editor. *Jorge Luis Borges in Context*. Oxford UP, 2020.

———. *Postcolonial Borges: Argument and Artistry*. Oxford UP, 2017.

Finney, Gail. "The Reign of the Amoeba: Further Thoughts about the Future of Comparative Literature." Heise, pp. 19–23.

Fishburn, Evelyn. "Borges and Buddhism." Fiddian, *Jorge Luis Borges*, pp. 211–18.

Fishburn, Evelyn, and Psiche Hughes. *A Dictionary of Borges*. Revised ed., Duckworth, 1990.

Flood, Finbarr B. "Between Cult and Culture: Bamiyan, Islamic Iconoclasm, and the Museum." *Art Bulletin*, vol. 84, no. 4, 2002, pp. 641–59.

Flores Maio, Fernando. *La biblioteca de Borges*. Paripé, 2018.

"Frank Stella: A Retrospective." *Whitney Museum of American Art*, 2024, whitney.org/exhibitions/frank-stella.

Fried, Michael. "Shape as Form: Frank Stella's *Irregular Polygons*." *Art and Objecthood: Essays and Reviews*, by Fried, U of Chicago P, 1998, pp. 77–99.

Froehlich, Heather. "Corpus Analysis with AntConc." *Programming Historian*, 19 June 2015, https://doi.org/10.46430/phen0043.

García Morales, Alfonso. "Jorge Luis Borges, autor del *Martín Fierro*." *Variaciones Borges*, no. 10, 2000, pp. 29–63.

Gardiner, Alan Henderson. "Egypt: Ancient Religion." *The Encyclopædia Britannica*, edited by Hugh Chisholm, 11th ed., vol. 9, Encyclopædia Britannica, 1910, pp. 48–57.

Gasquet, Alex. *Oriente al Sur: El orientalismo literario argentino de Esteban Echeverría a Roberto Arlt*. Eudeba, 2007.

Geldner, Karl Friedrich. "Zend-Avesta." *The Encyclopædia Britannica*, edited by Hugh Chisholm, 11th ed., vol. 28, Encyclopædia Britannica, 1910, pp. 967–69.

Genette, Gérard, and Marie Maclean. "Introduction to the Paratext." *New Literary History*, vol. 22, no. 2, 1991, pp. 261–72. *JSTOR*, https://doi.org/10.2307/469037.

Ghadirian, Abdu'l-Missagh. "El materialismo: Una distracción de nuestras vidas espirituales." *BahaiTeachings.org*, 13 Jan. 2019, bahaiteachings.org/es/el-materialismo-una-distraccion-de-nuestras-vidas-espirituales/.

Gibbon, Edward. *The Decline and Fall of the Roman Empire*. Vol. 1, Penguin Books, 2004.

Gonzalez, Evelyn S. "The Book That Gave Us Shakespeare." *FIU News*, 29 Jan. 2016, newsarchives.fiu.edu/2016/01/the-folio-that-gave-us-shakespeare.

González, José Eduardo. *Borges and the Politics of Form*. Garland, 1998.

Gonzalez, Mike, and Marianella Yanes. *Tango: Sex and Rhythm of the City*. U of Texas P, 2015.

González Echevarría, Roberto. "Man without a Life." *The New York Times Book Review*, 31 Aug. 1997. *The New York Times Web Archive*, archive.nytimes.com/www.nytimes.com/books/97/08/31/reviews/970831.31gonz01.html.

Gracia, Jorge. *Painting Borges: Philosophy Interpreting Art Interpreting Literature*. State U of New York P, 2012.

Grayson, A. K. "Babylonia." Cotterell, *Penguin Encyclopedia of Ancient Civilizations*, pp. 89–101.

Griffin, Clive. "Philosophy and Fiction." Williamson, *Cambridge Companion*, pp. 5–15.

Haddawy, Husain, translator. *The Arabian Nights*. Edited by Muhsin Mahdi, W. W. Norton, 1990.

———. Introduction. Haddawy, *Arabian Nights*, pp. vii–xv.

———, translator. Prologue. Haddawy, *Arabian Nights*, pp. 3–16.

Harris, Audrey, editor. *Nos contamos a través de los muros*. Catarsis, 2016.

Hart, David Bentley. Introduction. *The New Testament: A Translation*, translated by Hart, Yale UP, 2017, pp. xiii–xxxv.

Hart, Stephen M., editor. *The Cambridge Companion to Latin American Poetry.* Cambridge UP, 2018.

Hawes, Greta. *Rationalizing Myth in Antiquity.* Oxford UP, 2014, https://doi.org/10.1093/acprof:oso/9780199672776.001.0001.

Heise, Ursula J., editor. *Futures of Comparative Literature: ACLA State of the Discipline Report.* Routledge, 2017.

Herodotus. *The History.* Translated by David Grene, U of Chicago P, 1987.

Hillis, Ken, et al. *Google and the Culture of Search.* Routledge, 2013.

"Historia Augusta." *Livius.org*, 1995–2023, www.livius.org/sources/content/historia-augusta.

Hombre de la esquina rosada. Directed by René Mugica, Argentina Sono Film, 1962. *YouTube*, uploaded by Ger Luc, 13 July 2017, www.youtube.com/watch?v=FFW4flxgZtM.

hooks, bell. *Feminist Theory: From Margins to Center.* South End Press, 1984.

Hurley, Andrew. Introduction. *"The Aleph" and Other Stories*, by Jorge Luis Borges, translated by Hurley, Penguin Books, 2000, pp. vii–xiii.

Ibrakhimovna, Khamraeva Gulchekhra. "Benefits of Implementations of Pre-, While and Post Reading Activities in Language Learning." *International Scientific Journal Internauka*, vol. 3, no. 4, 2016, pp. 45–46.

The Immortal. Directed by Ewan Jones Morris, 2007. *YouTube*, uploaded by Zen Pylon, 14 June 2011, www.youtube.com/watch?v=C9IK6DLlP3s.

Interstellar. Directed by Christopher Nolan, Paramount Pictures, 2014.

Invasión. Directed by Hugo Santiago, Proartel, 1969. *YouTube*, uploaded by Billionaire Mayor, 13 Jan. 2017, www.youtube.com/watch?v=TkZp39MEDGA.

Irby, James E., translator. "The Library of Babel." Borges, *Labyrinths*, pp. 51–58.

———. *The Structure of the Stories of Jorge Luis Borges.* 1962. U of Michigan, PhD dissertation.

Isaacson, José. *Macedonio Fernández, sus ideas políticas y estéticas.* Editorial de Belgrano, 1981.

Ishikawa, Kaoru. *Guide to Quality Control.* Asian Productivity Organization, 1976.

Jacobsen, Thorkild. "Mesopotamian Religion." Cotterell, *Penguin Encyclopedia of Ancient Civilizations*, pp. 164–71.

James, Daniel. "Peron and the People." Nouzeilles and Montaldo, pp. 273–95.

Jenckes, Kate. *Reading Borges after Benjamin: Allegory, Afterlife, and the Writing of History.* State U of New York P, 2007.

———. "Walls, Towers, Books: Borges, Kafka, and the Limits of the Proper." *The Yearbook of Comparative Literature*, vol. 63, 2017, pp. 2–21.

Johnson, David E. *Kant's Dog: On Borges, Philosophy and the Time of Translation.* State U of New York P, 2012.

"Jorge Luis Borges Google Doodle." *YouTube*, uploaded by Google Doodle Videos, 23 Aug. 2011, www.youtube.com/watch?v=RFcFWkeEEbE.

"Jorge Luis Borges: Siete Noches." *YouTube*, uploaded by Griss, 2 June 2014, www.youtube.com/playlist?list=PL3LHRqpp-eTdk1SzHkKep_J7NPiUN5dnf.

Jullien, Dominique. *Borges, Buddhism and World Literature: A Morphology of Renunciation Tales*. Palgrave Macmillan, 2019.

Jurado, Alicia. *Borges, el budismo y yo*. Academia Argentina de Letras, 2011.

Kadir, Djelal. *Questing Fictions: Latin America's Family Romance*. U of Minnesota P, 1986.

Kadir, Djelal, and Ursula K. Heise, editors. *The Longman Anthology of World Literature*. Vol. F, 2nd ed., Pearson, 2009.

Kafka, Franz. *The Complete Stories*. Edited by Nahum N. Glatzer, translated by Willa Muir et al., Schocken Books, 1971.

———. "On Building the Chinese Wall." Translated by Willa Muir and Edwin Muir. Kafka, *Complete Stories*, pp. 235–48.

———. "The Trees." Translated by Willa Muir and Edwin Muir. Kafka, *Complete Stories*, p. 382.

Kaplan, Matt. *The Science of Monsters*. Scribner, 2012.

———. "The Scientific Origins of the Minotaur." *YouTube*, uploaded by TED-Ed, 20 July 2015, www.youtube.com/watch?v=2aoIs-5zqoI&vl=en.

Kazin, Alfred. "Meeting Borges." *The New York Times Book Review*, 2 May 1971. *The New York Times Web Archive*, archive.nytimes.com/www.nytimes.com/books/97/08/31/reviews/borges-meeting.html.

Kipling, Rudyard. "Evarra and His Gods." Barrack-Room Ballads *and* The Story of the Gadsbys, by Kipling, A. L. Burt, 1909, pp. 265–66.

Kleege, Georgina. "Blind Imagination: Pictures into Words." *Southwest Review*, vol. 93, no. 2, 2008, pp. 227–39.

———. *More Than Meets the Eye: What Blindness Brings to Art*. Oxford UP, 2018.

Knapp, Mary, and Herbert Knapp. *One Potato, Two Potato: The Secret Education of American Children*. W. W. Norton, 1976.

Kristal, Efraín. *Invisible Work: Borges and Translation*. Vanderbilt UP, 2002.

———. "Jorge Luis Borges on War." *YouTube*, uploaded by University of California Television (UCTV), 13 Feb. 2016, www.youtube.com/watch?v=5P1-q7hokE8.

———. "Jorge Luis Borges's Literary Response to Anti-semitism and the Holocaust." *The Jewish Quarterly Review*, vol. 104, no. 3, summer 2014, pp. 354–61.

Landgraf, Diemo. "The Question of Identity in Borges's 'El Aleph' and 'El Sur.'" *Variaciones Borges*, no. 34, 2012, pp. 161–81.

Lane, Edward William. *An Account of the Manners and Customs of the Modern Egyptians*. London, 1871.

———, translator. Introduction. Lane, *Thousand and One Nights*, pp. 1–42.

———, translator. *The Thousand and One Nights*. Vol. 1, C. Knight, 1841.

———. "Translator's Preface." Lane, *Thousand and One Nights*, pp. vii–xxiii.

Lattimore, Richmond, translator. "Book 1." Lattimore, *Iliad*, pp. 59–75.

———, translator. *The Iliad of Homer*. U of Chicago P, 1962.

———. "A Note on the Translation." Lattimore, *Iliad*, p. 55.

Lauwaert, Maaike, et al. "Frustrating Desire: On *Repens* and *Repositio*; or, The Attractions and Distractions of Digital Games." *Theory, Culture and Society*, vol. 24, no. 1, 2007, pp. 89–108.

Lefevere, André. *Translating Literature: Practice and Theory in a Comparative Literature Context*. Modern Language Association of America, 1992.

Li, Charles. "Schopenhauer's Fictions." *Variaciones Borges*, no. 41, 2016, pp. 115–27.

Lombardo, Stanley, translator. "Book 1." Lombardo, *Iliad*, pp. 1–19.

———, translator. *Iliad*. By Homer, Hackett Publishing, 1997.

———. "Translator's Preface." Lombardo, *Iliad*, pp. ix–xv.

LoMonico, Michael. *The Shakespeare Book of Lists: The Ultimate Guide to the Bard, His Plays and How They've Been Interpreted (and Misinterpreted) through the Ages*. Bounty Books, 2006.

Louis, Annick. *Borges ante el fascismo*. Peter Lang, 2007.

———. "Instrucciones para buscar a Borges en la *Revista Multicolor de los Sábados*." *Variaciones Borges*, no. 5, 1998, pp. 246–64.

Luiselli, Valeria. *Tell Me How It Ends: An Essay in Forty Questions*. Coffee House Press, 2017.

Mac Adam, Alfred J. "Translation as Metaphor: Three Versions of Borges." *MLN*, vol. 90, no. 6, 1975, pp. 747–54.

Mack, Robert L. "Arabian Nights' Entertainments." Mack, *Arabian Nights' Entertainments*, pp. 1–17.

———, editor. *Arabian Nights' Entertainments*. Oxford UP, 1995.

———. Introduction. Mack, *Arabian Nights' Entertainments*, pp. ix–xxvi.

———. "Note on the Text." Mack, *Arabian Nights' Entertainments*, pp. xxv–xxvi.

Manguel, Alberto. *With Borges*. Telegram, 2006.

Manguel, Alberto, and Gianni Guadalupi. *The Dictionary of Imaginary Places*. Expanded ed., Harcourt Brace, 2000.

"Manuscripts." *Borges Center*, U of Pittsburgh, 2010–19, www.borges.pitt.edu/manuscripts.

"Maps of Syria." *WorldAtlas*, 2024, www.worldatlas.com/maps/syrian-arab-republic.

"Maps of Uruguay." *WorldAtlas*, 2024, www.worldatlas.com/maps/uruguay.

Marín, Marta. *Guía para docentes: Lengua 7°/8° E.G.B.* Aique, 1997.

Martín, Marina. "Borges via the Dialectics of Berkeley and Hume." *Variaciones Borges*, no. 9, 2000, pp. 147–62.

McMurray, George R. *Jorge Luis Borges*. Ungar, 1980.

McNeese, Tim. *Jorge Luis Borges*. Chelsea House, 2008.

Melville, Herman. *Moby-Dick*. Edited by Hershel Parker and Harrison Hayford, 2nd ed., W. W. Norton, 2002.

Mikics, David. *Slow Reading in a Hurried Age*. Harvard UP, 2013.

Mohanty, Satya. "Identity Politics." *The Encyclopedia of Literary and Cultural Theory*, edited by Michael Ryan, vol. 3, Wiley and Sons, 2011, pp. 1126–30.

Molloy, Sylvia. *Signs of Borges*. Translated by Oscar Montero, Duke UP, 1993.

Monterroso, Augusto. "The Dinosaur." Translated by Valeria Luiselli. *Lost Children Archive*, by Luiselli, Alfred A. Knopf, 2019, p. 382.

Moskvitch, Katia. "The Search for an Effective Cure for Motion Sickness." *BBC Future*, 17 Aug. 2015, www.bbc.com/future/article/20150814-the-search-for-an-effective-cure-for-motion-sickness.

Nance, Kimberly A. "Borges and Georgie: Childhood Reading, Adult Writing, and the Shape of the Latin American Fantastic." *Twice-Told Children's Tales: The Influence of Childhood Reading on Writing for Adults*, edited by Betty Greenway, Routledge, 2005, pp. 11–25.

———. "Literary Play in the Fantastic Short Stories of Jorge Luis Borges." *Zenodo*, 7 Mar. 2024, https://doi.org/10.5281/zenodo.10794814.

———. *Teaching Literature in the Languages*. Prentice-Hall, 2010.

Newman, Francis William, translator. "Book 1." *The Iliad of Homer*, translated by Newman, 1856. *Internet Archive*, archive.org/details/ iliadhomerfaith00newmgoog/page/n6/mode/2up.

———. Preface. *The Iliad of Homer*, translated by Newman, 1856. *Internet Archive*, archive.org/details/iliadhomerfaith00newmgoog/page/n6/mode/2up.

———. "The Unlearned Public Is the Rightful Judge of Taste." Robinson, pp. 256–58.

"Newspaper Blackout Poems." *Austin Kleon*, 2001–23, austinkleon.com/category/newspaper-blackout-poems/.

Nhat Hanh, Thich. *Being Peace*. Parallax Press, 2005.

"1911 *Encyclopædia Britannica*." *Wikisource*, 26 Feb. 2023, en.wikisource.org/wiki/1911_Encyclop%C3%A6dia_Britannica.

Nouzeilles, Gabriela, and Graciela Montaldo, editors. *The Argentina Reader: History, Culture, Politics*. Duke UP, 2002.

O'Grady, Thomas. "Richard Madden's War: Borges, Joyce, and the Labyrinth of History." *Joyce Studies Annual*, 2017, pp. 94–114.

"Once, el barrio que no figura en el mapa pero tiene libro propio." *Clarín*, 24 Mar. 2006, www.clarin.com/ediciones-anteriores/once-barrio-figura-mapa-libro-propio_0_BJtlU9HJCFg.html.

Los orilleros. Directed by Ricardo Luna, Cine Internacional de Argentina, 1975. *YouTube*, uploaded by Los Orilleros - Topic, 20 Feb. 2017, www.youtube.com/watch?v=4XYoyKzcy0g.

Ortega, Julio, et al. *"El Aleph" de Jorge Luis Borges*. El Colegio de México, 2008.

"Other Resources." *Borges Center*, U of Pittsburgh, 2010–19, www.borges.pitt.edu/other-resources.

Oubiña, David. "El espectador corto de vista: Borges y el cine." *Variaciones Borges*, no. 24, 2007, pp. 133–52.

Palma, Cristobal. "The Garden of Forking Paths / Beals Lyon Arquitectos." *Arch Daily*, 26 Mar. 2013, www.archdaily.com/350038/video-the-garden-of-forking-paths-beals-lyon-architects-by-cristobal-palma.

"The Parthian and Sasanian Empires." "The Parthians (247 BC–AD 226)," by E. J. Keall. Cotterell, *Penguin Encyclopedia of Classical Civilizations*, p. 165. Map.

"Perceive, V. (II.8.a)." *Oxford English Dictionary*, Oxford UP, Mar. 2024, https://doi.org/10.1093/OED/8940345481.

"Percibir." *Diccionario de la lengua española*, Real Academia Española, 2024, dle.rae.es/percibir.

"The Persian Empire of the Achaemenids on the Eve of the Invasion of Greece in 480 BC." "The Achaemenids," by T. Cuyler Young. Cotterell, *Penguin Encyclopedia of Classical Civilizations*, p. 151. Map.

Petersen, Alice. "Borges's 'Ulrike'—Signature of a Literary Life." *Studies in Short Fiction*, vol. 33, no. 3, 1996, pp. 325–32.

"Pharaonic Egypt." "Ancient Egypt," by Colin Walters. Cotterell, *Penguin Encyclopedia of Ancient Civilizations*, p. 2. Map.

Phené Spiers, Richard. "Mosque." *The Encyclopædia Britannica*, edited by Hugh Chisholm, 11th ed., vol. 18, Encyclopædia Britannica, 1910, pp. 899–901.

Pisani, Silvia. "Revelan que Borges tuvo una fugaz carrera como actor de cine." *La Nacion*, 8 May 2007, www.lanacion.com.ar/cultura/revelan-que-borges-tuvo-una-fugaz-carrera-como-actor-de-cine-nid906672/.

Pliny. *Naturalis Historia*. Translated by H. Rackham, vol. 2, Harvard UP, 1989. Loeb Classical Library 330.

Plutarch. *Roman Lives*. Translated by Robin Waterfield, Oxford UP, 1999.

Pontes Velasco, Rafael. "La influencia de Jorge Luis Borges en las películas de Christopher Nolan." *INTI*, nos. 87–88, 2018, pp. 187–97, digitalcommons.providence.edu/inti/vol1/iss87/15/.

Pope, Alexander, translator. "Book 1." *The Iliad*, by Homer, translated by Pope, 1720. *Project Gutenberg*, www.gutenberg.org/cache/epub/6130/pg6130-images.html.

———. "Pope's Preface to the *Iliad* of Homer." *The Iliad*, by Homer, translated by Pope, 1720. *Project Gutenberg*, www.gutenberg.org/cache/epub/6130/pg6130-images.html.

"Provincia Mesopotamia within the Roman Empire." *Wikipedia*, 8 Dec. 2023, en.wikipedia.org/wiki/Mesopotamia_(Roman_province). Map.

"Ptolemaic Egypt circa 235 BC." *Wikipedia*, 25 Dec. 2023, en.wikipedia.org/wiki/Ptolemaic_Kingdom. Map.

Puchner, Martin, et al., editors. *The Norton Anthology of World Literature*. Vol. F, 4th ed., W. W. Norton, 2018.

Pym, Anthony. *Exploring Translation Theories*. 2nd ed., Routledge, 2014.

———. "Pym on Equivalence contra Williams." *YouTube*, uploaded by Anthony Pym, 23 Nov. 2015, www.youtube.com/watch?v=wzPjn9i_230.

———. "Theories of Directional Equivalence in Translation." *YouTube*, uploaded by Anthony Pym, 23 Apr. 2012, www.youtube.com/watch?v=ZP9PcjIMkVU.

———. "Theories of Natural Equivalence in Translation." *YouTube*, uploaded by Anthony Pym, 23 Apr. 2012, www.youtube.com/watch?v=_G5oAMWfObI.

———. "What's Wrong with Equivalence? (Exploring Translation Theories)." *YouTube*, uploaded by Anthony Pym, 26 Sept. 2009, www.youtube.com/watch?v=cBZ1m1cAd6I.

Quirarte, Vicente. *La ciudad como cuerpo*. Biblioteca del ISSSTE, 1999.

Rancière, Jacques. *The Ignorant Schoolmaster: Five Lessons in Intellectual Emancipation.* Translated by Kristin Ross, Stanford UP, 1991.

Reed, Brian, host. "Chapter 1." *S-Town*, episode 1, Serial / This American Life, 28 Mar. 2017, stownpodcast.org/chapter/1.

Robinson, Douglas, editor. *Western Translation Theory: From Herodotus to Nietzsche.* 2nd ed., Routledge, 2002.

Rodríguez Monegal, Emir. *Jorge Luis Borges: A Literary Biography.* E. P. Dutton, 1978.

"The Roman Empire on the Death of Trajan." "The World of Rome (510 BC–AD 476)," by Andrew Drummond. Cotterell, *Penguin Encyclopedia of Classical Civilizations*, p. 100. Map.

"The Roman Empire under Augustus." *Wikipedia*, 8 Nov. 2023, en.wikipedia.org/wiki/Roman_province. Map.

Romero, Luis Alberto. *A History of Argentina in the Twentieth Century.* Translated by James P. Brennan, Penn State UP, 2002.

Rosa, Luis Othoniel. *Comienzos para una estética anarquista: Borges con Macedonio.* Cuarto Propio, 2016.

Rosato, Laura, and Germán Álvarez, editors. *Borges, libros y lecturas.* Biblioteca Nacional, 2010.

R. T. H. "*Ficciones* by Jorge Luis Borges." *Books Abroad*, vol. 20, no. 1, winter 1946, pp. 53–54.

Rubin, William S. *Frank Stella.* Museum of Modern Art, 1970, www.moma.org/documents/moma_catalogue_1945_300299009.pdf.

Ruffinelli, Jorge. "Borges y el ultraísmo: Un caso de estética y política." *Cuadernos Americanos*, year 2, vol. 3, May-June 1988, pp. 155–74.

Said, Edward. *Orientalism.* Vintage Books, 1994.

Said, Zahr K., and Jessica Silbey. "Narrative Topoi in the Digital Age." *Journal of Legal Education*, vol. 68, no. 1, autumn 2018, pp. 103–14.

Saítta, Sylvia. "'La fiesta del monstruo' de H. Bustos Domecq en tres tiempos: 1955, 1967, 1977." *Variaciones Borges*, no. 49, 2020, pp. 49–68.

Salinas, Alejandra. *Liberty, Individuality, and Democracy in Jorge Luis Borges.* Lexington Books, 2017.

Salmon, Russell O. "The Tango: Its Origins and Meaning." *Journal of Popular Culture*, vol. 10, no. 4, 1977, pp. 859–66.

Sarlo, Beatriz. *Jorge Luis Borges: A Writer on the Edge.* Verso, 1993.

———. *Jorge Luis Borges: A Writer on the Edge.* Verso, 2006.

———. *Una modernidad periférica: Buenos Aires, 1920 y 1930.* Siglo XXI, 2020.

Sartre, Jean-Paul. *Being and Nothingness: An Essay on Phenomenological Ontology.* Translated by Hazel E. Barnes, Philosophical Library, 1956.

"The Sassanid Empire." *Fsmitha.com*, www.fsmitha.com/h1/map20per.htm. Accessed 5 Jan. 2024.

Sasso, Eleonora. *The Pre-Raphaelites and Orientalism: Language and Cognition in Remediations of the East.* Edinburgh UP, 2018.

Schiffman, Lawrence H. *From Text to Tradition: A History of Second Temple Rabbinic Judaism*. Ktav, 1991.

Scholem, Gershom. *Major Trends in Jewish Mysticism*. 1941. Schocken Books, 1971.

Scobie, James. "The Paris of South America." Nouzeilles and Montaldo, pp. 170–81.

Shakespeare, William. *The Complete Works*. Edited by Stanley Wells et al., 2nd ed., Clarendon Press, 2005.

———. *The Merchant of Venice*. Edited by Harold Bloom, Bloom's Literary Criticism, 2007. Bloom's Shakespeare through the Ages.

Shaw, Donald L. *Borges:* Ficciones. Grant and Cutler, 1976.

———. Review of *Collected Fictions*, by Jorge Luis Borges, translated by Andrew Hurley. *Literature and Arts of the Americas*, vol. 32, no. 59, 1999, pp. 83–84.

Shellhorse, Adam. "The Avant-Garde: From *Creacionismo* to *Ultraísmo*, Brazilian *Modernismo*, *Antropofagia*, and Surrealism." S. Hart, pp. 36–62.

Shullenberger, Geoffrey. "Borges's Jewish Uncanny and the Psychoanalytic Other: Uses of Paranoia in 'La muerte y la brújula.'" *Chasqui*, vol. 42, no. 2, 2013, pp. 59–72.

Simon, Sherry. *Gender in Translation: Cultural Identity and the Politics of Transmission*. Routledge, 1996.

Simorangkir, Monica. *Borges in Hollywood: From Art House to Blockbuster Cinema*. 2017. Georgetown U, PhD dissertation, repository.library.georgetown.edu/bitstream/handle/10822/1047823/Simorangkir_georgetown_0076D_13820.pdf.

Slatta, Richard. *Gauchos and the Vanishing Frontier*. U of Nebraska P, 1983.

"Smyrna among the Cities of Ionia and Lydia (c. 50 AD)." *Wikipedia*, 30 Jan. 2024, en.wikipedia.org/wiki/Smirne. Map.

Sorá, Gustavo. *A History of Book Publishing in Contemporary Latin America*. Routledge, 2021.

Spiderweb. Directed by Paul Miller, 1976. *YouTube*, uploaded by Paul Miller, 30 Oct. 2013, www.youtube.com/watch?v=j_UfUxm9Xko.

Sprague, Rosamond Kent, editor. *The Older Sophists: A Complete Translation by Several Hands of the Fragments in* Die Fragmente der Vorsokratiker, *edited by Diels-Kranz: With a New Edition of* Antiphon *and of* Euthydemus. Hackett Publishing, 2001.

Stavans, Ilan. "Borges and the Jews." *The International Raoul Wallenberg Foundation*, www.raoulwallenberg.net/wp-content/files_mf/6173.pdf. Accessed 5 Jan. 2024.

———. *Quixote: The Novel and the World*. W. W. Norton, 2015.

Steiner, George. *After Babel: Aspects of Language and Translation*. 3rd ed., Oxford UP, 1998.

Stella, Frank. *Chocura IV*. 1966. *Whitney Museum of American Art*, whitney.org/exhibitions/frank-stella#exhibition-artworks.

———. *Moultonboro III*. 1966. *MOMA*, www.moma.org/documents/moma_catalogue_1945_300299009.pdf.

Sturrock, John. *Paper Tigers: The Ideal Fictions of Jorge Luis Borges*. Clarendon Press, 1977.

Sun, Haiqing. "China of Labyrinth: A Referential Reading of 'El jardín de senderos que se bifurcan.'" *Variaciones Borges*, no. 25, 2008, pp. 101–14.

"Teaching Principles." *Carnegie Mellon University*, 2023, cmu.edu/teaching/principles/teaching.html.

Todorov, Tzvetan. *The Fantastic: A Structural Approach to a Literary Genre*. Translated by Richard Howard, Cornell UP, 1975.

Toprak, Elif Leyla, and Gamze Almacioğlu. "Three Reading Phases and Their Applications in the Teaching of English as a Foreign Language in Reading Classes with Young Learners." *Journal of Language and Linguistic Studies*, vol. 5, no. 1, 2009, pp. 20–36.

Toury, Gideon. *Descriptive Translation Studies—and Beyond*. Revised ed., John Benjamins, 2012.

"The Translators to the Reader." 1611. *Why the King James Version*, edited by J. Reuben Clark, Jr., Deseret Book, 1956, pp. xxvii–lv.

Ubelaker Andrade, Max. *Borges beyond the Visible*. Pennsylvania State UP, 2019.

———. "Tennyson, Kipling, and 'El Zahir.'" *Variaciones Borges*, vol. 54, 2022, pp. 43–60.

Underworld. Directed by Josef von Sternberg, Paramount Pictures, 1927. *Internet Archive*, archive.org/details/underworld_202108.

Vacker, Barry. *Specter of the Monolith: Nihilism, the Sublime, and Human Destiny in Space: From Apollo and Hubble to* 2001, Star Trek, *and* Interstellar. Center for Media and Destiny, 2017.

Valdovinos, Mario. "Thomas de Quincey y los paraísos artificiales." *Literatura y Lingüística*, no. 12, 2000, pp. 197–203.

Vargas Llosa, Mario. "Fictions of Borges." *Third World Quarterly*, vol. 10, no. 3, July 1988, pp. 1325–33.

Venuti, Lawrence. "How to Read a Translation." *Words without Borders*, 1 July 2004, www.wordswithoutborders.org/article/how-to-read-a-translation.

———, editor. *The Translation Studies Reader*. 1st ed., Routledge, 2000.

———, editor. *The Translation Studies Reader*. 3rd ed., Routledge, 2012.

———, editor. *The Translation Studies Reader*. 4th ed., Routledge, 2021.

———. *The Translator's Invisibility: A History of Translation*. 2nd ed., Routledge, 2008.

Waisman, Sergio. *Borges and Translation: The Irreverence of the Periphery*. Bucknell UP, 2005.

Wallace, David Foster. "Borges on the Couch." *The New York Times*, 7 Nov. 2004, www.nytimes.com/2004/11/07/books/review/borges-on-the-couch.html.

Wardi, Eynel. "The Stories of Emma Zunz." *Narrative*, vol. 7, no. 3, 1999, pp. 335–56.

Watts, George Frederic. *The Minotaur*. 1885. *Tate Britain*, www.tate.org.uk/art/artworks/watts-the-minotaur-n01634.

Waugh, Patricia. "What Is Metafiction and Why Are They Saying Such Awful Things about It?" Currie, *Metafiction*, pp. 39–54.

Whelan, Estelle. "The Origins of the Mihrāb Mujawwaf: A Reinterpretation." *International Journal of Middle East Studies*, vol. 18, no. 2, 1986, pp. 205–23.

Whitehead, Colson. *The Underground Railroad*. Fleet, 2016.

Wilde, Oscar. *The Essays of Oscar Wilde*. Boni, 1935.

Williams, Mac. "Zoroastrian and Zurvanite Symbolism in 'Las ruinas circulares.'" *Variaciones Borges*, no. 25, 2008, pp. 115–35.

Williamson, Edwin. *Borges: A Life*. Viking, 2004.

———, editor. *The Cambridge Companion to Jorge Luis Borges*. Cambridge UP, 2013.

Wilson, Jason. *Jorge Luis Borges*. Reaktion, 2006.

Wimsatt, W. K., Jr., and M. C. Beardsley. "The Intentional Fallacy." *The Sewanee Review*, vol. 54, no. 3, 1946, pp. 468–88.

The Wizard of Oz. Directed by Victor Fleming, Metro-Goldwyn-Mayer, 1939.

Wolfe, Joanna. "A Method for Teaching Invention in the Gateway Literature Class." *Pedagogy: Critical Approaches to Teaching Literature, Language, Composition, and Culture*, vol. 3, no. 3, 2003, pp. 399–425. *EBSCOhost*, https://doi.org/10.1215/15314200-3-3-399.

Wood, Michael. "Borges and Theory." Williamson, *Cambridge Companion*, pp. 29–42.

———. "Productive Mischief." *London Review of Books*, vol. 21, no. 3, 4 Feb. 1999, www.lrb.co.uk/the-paper/v21/n03/michael-wood/productive-mischief.

———. "The Unreachable Real." *London Review of Books*, vol. 32, no. 13, 8 July 2010, www.lrb.co.uk/the-paper/v32/n13/michael-wood/the-unreachable-real.

Woodall, James. *Borges: A Life*. Basic Books, 1996.

Woodward, David, editor. *Cartography in the European Renaissance*. U of Chicago P, 2007. Vol. 3, part 1 of *The History of Cartography*.

Woscobinik, Julio. *The Secret of Borges: A Psychoanalytic Inquiry into His Work*. UP of America, 1998.

Yeats, William Butler. "Nineteen Hundred and Nineteen." *The Collected Poems of W. B. Yeats*, Macmillan, 1951, pp. 204–08.

Young, T. Cuyler. "The Achaemenids (559–330 BC)." Cotterell, *Penguin Encyclopedia of Classical Civilizations*, pp. 149–62.

Zavaleta Balarezo, Jorge. "Influencia y legado de Borges en el cine de Christopher Nolan." *Revista Laboratorio: Literatura y Experimentación*, no. 14, 2016, revistalaboratorio.udp.cl/index.php/laboratorio/article/view/72/6.